Praise for DEEP WATERS

"Mathews writes with poignant honesty about the challenges of marriage, family, and community in a moving story that highlights the strengths of human relationships. *Deep Waters* starts with a bang and just keeps going: lively, vivid, and personal."

—ROMAN DIAL,
author of *The Adventurer's Son: A Memoir*

"If books were birds, *Deep Waters* would be an arctic tern—powerful and graceful, beset by storms and learning to survive and more: to thrive. The writing is feather-light yet strong."

—KIM HEACOX, author of *Jimmy Bluefeather* and
The Only Kayak: A Journey into the Heart of Alaska

"*Deep Waters* is a survival story of the highest order, navigating the complex terrain of marriage, medical crisis, and a future reimagined. After the trauma of her husband's stroke, Mathews returns to a basic truth: through love, we discover who we are, and who we hope to become."

—CAROLINE VAN HEMERT, award-winning author
of *The Sun is a Compass*

"Mathews has penned a deeply personal love story with the careful rigor of the scientist she is, free of any giddy prose or rainbows. Instead, *Deep Waters* comes at the reader with the gloves off and goes a full twelve rounds, documenting in granular detail the fears and conflicts attending a life-altering event that can drive even a strong relationship onto the ropes, and the endurance, commitment, and deep love that can save it."

—LYNN SCHOOLER, author of *The Blue Bear*
and *Walking Home*

"Poignant, profound, and powerful."

> — MARV JENSEN, Superintendent
> of Glacier Bay National Park 1988-1994

"We felt like we were there with Beth, sharing her emotions, anguish and struggles through the stroke, hospital stay, and recovery. We felt like part of the family as we read, gasped, cried and hoped for recovery and for peace in her heart."

> —TBD BOOK CLUB, Seattle, WA

DEEP WATERS

A MEMOIR OF LOSS, ALASKA ADVENTURE, AND LOVE REKINDLED

BETH ANN MATHEWS

SHE WRITES PRESS

Published 2023

Printed in the United States of America

Print ISBN: 978-1-64742-466-4
E-ISBN: 978-1-64742-467-1
Library of Congress Control Number: 2022913054

For information, address:
She Writes Press
1569 Solano Ave #546
Berkeley, CA 94707

She Writes Press is a division of SparkPoint Studio, LLC.

All company and/or product names may be trade names, logos, trademarks, and/or registered trademarks and are the property of their respective owners.

Interior design and typeset by Katherine Lloyd, The DESK

To write this memoir, the author relied on journals and notes, boating logbooks, interviews, photographs, memories, and medical records. The names and identifying characteristics have been changed to protect the privacy of certain individuals. Some dialogue has been recreated from memory. Information in this book is not intended as a substitute for medical advice. Readers should consult a physician for all health matters and any symptoms that may require diagnosis or medical attention.

For Jim and Glen
and all who helped us move beyond.

CONTENTS

Part One:

HAYWIRE

Part Two:
SHIFTING GEARS

Part Three:
WHITE SNOW, DEEP WATER

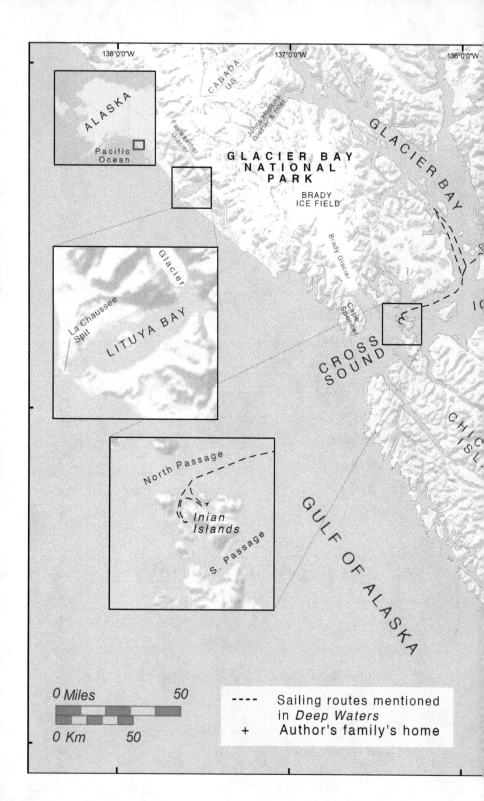

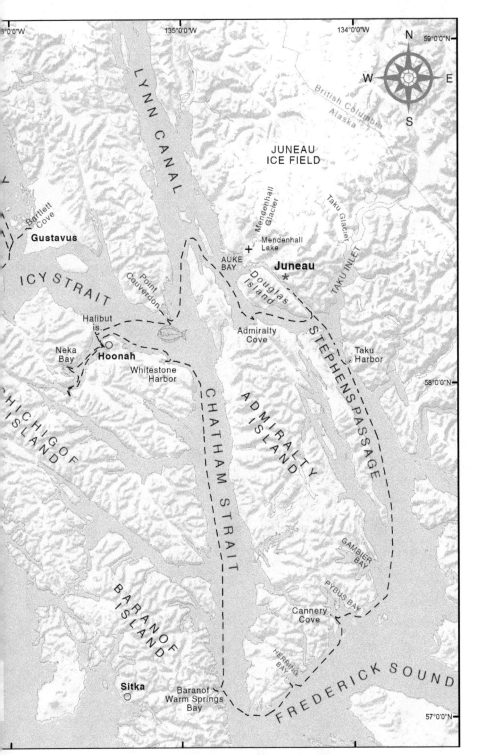

Expedition routes on sailing vessel *Ijsselmeer*

Part One:
HAYWIRE

We love life, not because we are used to living
but because we are used to loving.

~ Friedrich Nietzsche

1

FINAL TOUCH-UP

My husband folded the covers back, stood, hesitated, and walked out of our dark bedroom before our alarm rang. I thought about saying, *Everything okay, hon?*, but I'd stayed up late grading exams. If I had spoken—invited him back into bed—would that have kept him safe?

We lived in Juneau, Alaska, between the ocean and a retreating glacier, a dynamic landscape that challenged and nurtured us. A forty-two-foot sailboat—our Alaska home for seven years before our son was born—floated at the city dock, blanketed by a crust of snow but otherwise ready for action. The week before, nine-year-old Glen and I ran a mile in the annual Mendenhall Glacier race, while his father joined the pack of ten-kilometer trail runners. I'd stood with our son, cheering Jim's strong finish, aware of how I still found my husband attractive after twenty years.

Now, though, it wasn't his broad-shouldered presence, but the scent of coffee that pulled me from the stolen hour of sleep. Thin light bathed the second-floor room from a window above the bed. I plumped a pillow behind my back and thanked him as I reached for the mug. A marine biologist, I taught at the university and did research on harbor seals and Steller sea lions in Glacier Bay National Park. Raised in the Midwest, I came to

3

Alaska at twenty-seven to study humpback whales. My husband, a strong-willed field scientist from Utah, was hired at twenty-one to assist a grizzly bear biologist on the Alaska Peninsula. Chosen for his hunting and mountaineering experience, all that summer Jim carried and slept with a 12-gauge shotgun.

He stepped close and set his mug on the night table. Over jeans and a faded polo shirt, he wore twill coveralls. I recognized the look and stance that meant he wanted to make love. His proximity sent an enticing shiver up my spine, but I said I had a lot to do—finish a research proposal, give a lecture, and meet with advisees. "How about you?" I asked, thinking he should know work mornings were not good for sex. One early hour at my office equaled three in the afternoon.

He ran his hand through thick, chestnut-blond hair. Down-shifting clumsily from seduction to business, he settled in the chair. "I've got some final touch-ups on the skylight. Then I'm going to the harbor to check on the boat. Can you schedule the brokers' tour?"

We were putting our home up for sale to build a smaller, energy efficient house on a steep acre with an ocean view. I was reluctant to sell the home where we'd raised our son—I'd never lived anywhere I loved more—but I said, "Sure."

He stood and gave me a one-more-chance look.

I reached for my notebook, and he left.

As I made the bed, I heard Jim cough several times. I've got to get my work under control, I thought, tugging the sheet and quilt tight across the mattress. Lately, for me, no mornings were good for sex. Maybe I should start seeing that marriage counselor again?

His coughing turned harsh, like a dull ax splitting wood. I hurried to the living room. He lurched up the stairs, arms stuck out as if groping in the dark, even though golden light streamed in. "Honey. What's wrong?" His eyes jittered side to side. For a second, they locked on mine.

"I-I don't know," he gasped, staggering to the couch.

I grabbed the phone and punched 9-1-1.

"What's your emergency?" a woman said.

"My husband was fine a minute ago, but now he's coughing and can't walk."

"What's your name and location?"

"Beth Mathews. We're at home, thirty-eight, thirty-eight Killewich Drive. In the valley." She typed as I spoke. "We need an ambulance."

"Can he talk?"

"Yes. He's having a heart attack or a stroke. This has never happened before."

From across the connected rooms, Jim rasped, "G-get me some water."

I reached up into the cupboard, phone pressed between my ear and shoulder.

"What's your husband's name and age?"

"Jim Taggart. That's T as in Tango." I went to the faucet. "He's fifty-six." Heart ramming against my chest, I set the glass in the sink and twisted the cold-water tap.

"Does he have health issues—any recent problems?"

"No. No issues." Water tumbled into the glass. "He's very healthy."

"Does he have any numbness?"

I relayed the question. He shook his head. "No numbness," I said.

"Get me—Acchhh!—bring the water," he choked.

"The ambulance is on its way. Keep him calm. I'll stay with you."

"I've got to hang up." I needed to focus on Jim.

He sat, strong legs far apart, eyes wild like a cornered coyote. One arm braced on a cushion, he lifted the tumbler to his lips, tipped his head back. I waited for the water to douse the coughing—make everything okay. Instead, his body jolted, then buckled forward. Water spewed out across the floor.

Was it thirty chest compressions between breaths? I found the phone and jabbed 9-1-1. Same operator.

"My husband tried to drink water, but it all came out—like his throat was on fire."

"Get him to lie on the floor."

"If it's a stroke, shouldn't I give him a baby aspirin?"

"No, ma'am. No aspirin. And no more water. They should be there any minute."

I hung up and went to his side. "Sweetheart. You need to lie down." The couch and dining table were the only pieces of furniture in the room. The day before, he'd moved the rest onto the deck to prepare for the carpet cleaners. "The ambulance is coming." My voice sounded confident, but my body shook. I held his bicep as he rolled onto his back.

"I'm going to open the front door for them. I'll be right back." At the entry, a heavy drop cloth covered the floor beneath the skylight. I skidded the ladder to the far corner and shoved a paint can and metal tray out of the way. Chips of off-white paint were scattered like confetti. What on earth happened?

Back upstairs, his eyes found mine, asked for answers I didn't have. Inexplicably, he crawled toward the French doors to the deck. He opened one and collapsed onto his back. Spruce-filtered air spilled into the room. In our bedroom, I grabbed some clothes and returned. Watching him, I pulled off pajamas, jammed one leg and then the other into jeans. Questions crowded in. Was it a heart attack? A stroke? Every second mattered. Should I wake our son? Was this how it was going to end? Our last interaction a conflict over making love?

In the distance, I heard a siren—our siren.

While I buttoned my shirt, Jim tugged at the zipper tab of his paint-spattered coveralls, twisting his torso. "Help me with these." He struggled to take off his long-sleeved coveralls. I didn't want him to, but he was halfway out. I yanked each pant leg as if removing a child's snowsuit. Jagged throat-clearing interrupted his breathing.

Our son entered the room, snugging the belt of his sky-blue fleece robe. "What's going on?" As he drew the robe's hood onto his head, drowsiness flickered to concern.

"Your dad's having a serious problem. An ambulance is coming."

Jim craned his neck to see his son. Emotion twisted his face. "H-hey, Glen."

Glen knelt close and placed his hands on his father's forearm. "Dad, what's wrong?"

Jim shook his head, eyes brimming. He brought his other arm across his chest and took Glen's hand into his. "I-I'm sorry." He swallowed and lay back, eyes shut.

The sirens grew louder until the ambulance lurched into our driveway, and the wailing stopped.

2

BOOTS ON THE GROUND

Through the living room windows, I watched four paramedics stride to the front door. They wore tan vests edged with reflective tape. Two had black cases, and another carried a yellow stretcher under his arm, like a surfboard.

"This way." I led them up the steps. "My husband suddenly started choking and something's wrong with his balance." As we fanned out into the room, I realized the second medic was Brian, my fitness trainer from a previous winter. He nodded curtly, not remembering me. The firm sound of their boots on the stairs, their professional presence, and Brian's focus on the situation reassured me. Help had arrived. They would fix what was wrong.

The leader knelt beside Jim. "Stand back," he said when I stepped close. "We've got this." He shined a flashlight in Jim's eyes. "Any chest pain or discomfort?"

Jim shook his head, jaw clenched. Brian strapped a blood pressure cuff around his arm while the leader positioned a tear-drop-shaped mask over Jim's mustache and mouth. The oxygen tank hissed. "Do you have any history of heart trouble? Previous heart attacks? Any strokes?"

After each question, Jim shook his head.

Brian stripped off the Velcro cuff with a harsh rip, his mouth a tight line. "Pressure's way up," he said. "One-ninety over—" The equipment buzz obscured the diastolic reading.

When the leader asked if Jim was numb anywhere, he swept his right hand down his left side.

That's new, I thought. Could it be a stroke? My Jim is not someone who has a stroke. What is going on?

As they spoke in low voices, Glen watched from a corner, young face serious with worry. I went to him, knelt, and wrapped my arms around him.

"What's wrong with Dad?"

"They're not sure." I rocked onto my heels, holding his narrow shoulders. "Get dressed, okay? We're going to the hospital." He frowned, blinking, and went to his room.

The dark-haired medic stepped into the kitchen to make a call. Afterward, he announced to the others, "The doctor said give him nitroglycerin and bring him in."

I asked if it was a stroke or heart attack. He said the symptoms didn't fit either one. Once the tablet was under Jim's tongue, they set the stretcher beside him. He raised his head and rolled up onto an elbow, preparing to climb onto the stretcher.

"Hold it." Brian put a hand on his back. "We've got you."

I approached the cluster of men. "Can we go with him in the ambulance?"

"No, ma'am," the leader said. "Follow us to Bartlett in your car."

I locked eyes with Jim. "We'll be right behind you, hon." My hand twitched to reach between the medics and squeeze his shoulder, but they were already lifting him. The pressure behind my eyes hurt. My husband's body, strapped to the yellow plank, tilted as four men carried him down the steps. In the yard, a raven cocked his purple-black head at the procession, then flew off. Two mornings before, I'd waved to Jim from those steps as he rode off on his bike to buy groceries.

"Bring your fleece jacket," I said, as Glen and I dashed back inside. "And a book."

While the garage door rumbled up, my son and I jammed our feet into shoes. I yanked the keys off the hook and started for the car. "Don't forget your coat," Glen blurted.

Eyes on his, I pressed a palm to my heart while retrieving it.

At the end of our street, as the ambulance turned, the sirens began wailing again.

After long minutes waiting across from the nurses' station at Bartlett Regional Hospital, Glen and I stood to greet the ER physician. Beneath a white coat, he wore a blue Oxford cloth shirt with a burgundy tie. His clean-shaven face was solemn.

"Your husband's had a stroke—an unusual type of stroke."

I inhaled sharply. "What's the outlook?"

"His symptoms don't line up." The doctor hesitated. "Depends on where the damage is. We'll know more after the MRI."

"Where do you think it is?" I tightened my arm around Glen's shoulders, pressing him against my hip.

"We—" the doctor hesitated. "We think it's in his brainstem."

My chest felt as if it had been shoved. Brainstem? I knew the superficial anatomy and physiology of mammals enough to imagine any disruption to the part of our brain responsible for involuntary reflexes—breathing, heart rate, blood pressure—had to be bad. Very bad. This can't be happening. An image of a wheelchair intruded. I shoved it aside. "When can we see him?"

"Within the hour—after the MRI."

I slumped into a chair next to my son. He stared at me, eyebrows raised. "A stroke is where the blood flow to the brain gets blocked," I explained.

"What's MRI?"

"Magnetic resonance imaging. It's like an X-ray, but they use a huge magnet and a computer to take lots of pictures of the brain or other organs. It doesn't hurt, but you have to lie down inside a big tube that makes the magnetic field. From that, they create a bunch of pictures of your brain, like slices of the tissue."

"Slices?"

The word *slices* felt like too much, but he seemed to be following me. "Say you tossed three raisins into some dough and baked the loaf. The computer images could locate each raisin without cutting the bread. MRI lets you see inside someone's brain without surgery."

"Hmm." He nodded, but remained concerned.

I sat forward on the edge of my chair, elbows on knees, face in hands. "I'm going to call Dianne."

A glimmer of hope flashed into Glen's eyes. "Good idea."

Dianne was a wise and solid friend who led a more balanced life than anyone else I knew: long-distance kayaker, Buddhist, nurse, and more recently the hospital's education director.

From a pay phone, I dialed her office. "Dianne, Jim's had a stroke—in his brainstem. Glen and I are in the ER, here at Bartlett."

In minutes, she arrived, arms extended. "Oh, Beth, Glen. This is so out of the blue."

I caved in to her strong embrace but fought the impulse to cry. She squeezed my wrist. "What'd the doc say?" Dianne and I had grown close during the two decades we'd hiked, fished, and boated with our spouses in Glacier Bay National Park.

"What happened?" She put her arm around Glen. Nine years earlier, an hour after his birth, she'd held him tenderly in that same building.

I sketched out the morning's events. Partway through, a technician wheeled Jim in. The three of us rushed to him. Eyes still jittering side to side, percussive hiccups now jolted his body, and a kidney-shaped plastic pan sat near his head. "Di-Dianne. Glad you're here," he managed, then seemed to drop back onto the pillow even though he hadn't raised his head.

She clasped his shoulders and held his shaky gaze. "I'm so sorry."

The doctor returned and told us his MRI was inconclusive. "I've ordered an MRA of his cranial blood vessels—magnetic resonance angiograph—which should tell us what blood vessels are damaged."

"Have you given him—what's it called?—tissue plasminogen activator?" I asked. "Isn't there a three-hour window when it works?" This was taking too long. We were running out of time.

"We can't do that until we know what caused the stroke," he said. "TPA can help dissolve clots, but if there's hemorrhaging in his brain, it could cause more bleeding. We need a clear MRA before we start treatment. And I'm waiting to hear back from a neurologist in Seattle."

After he left, Dianne and I spoke softly, each with a hand on Jim who rested fitfully. Soon he was wheeled off for the imaging, and Dianne had to leave. I was at the nurses' station when a familiar man, about Jim's height—six feet—but thinner, turned the corner.

"Beth?" It was David Job. "I thought that was you," he said. "What's going on?" We knew David, an avid wilderness photographer and a respiratory technician at Bartlett, through an annual Easter brunch a mutual friend hosted.

"Jim's had a stroke."

He drew his head back in disbelief. "Jim?"

I described what had occurred.

"Have you reached his doctor?"

"He's on vacation. I left a message for the doctor covering for him. She's supposed to be here any minute."

David put his hand on my shoulder. "I have to check in at my office, but I'll come back."

Before entering the waiting room, I paused to gaze at our son. Bathed in light from a window as he read his book, he looked so much like his father in photos from that age—same blue eyes, blond hair, wiry build. A sharp vulnerability caught in my throat, a collision of love and fear.

We'd had our son late, when I was forty-three, Jim forty-seven. Jim and I had moved to Alaska after being together only a year. We first lived in a cabin, then on our sailboat. Teaching at the university in Juneau and research on marine mammals in Glacier Bay kept my schedule full as my love for Jim and Alaska deepened. I'd always wanted children, but fulfilling years flew by before I pried the topic open.

Jim had been married before. He and his wife spent half of each year in remote field camps in the Bering Sea studying red foxes and walruses. She did not want children. He'd had a vasectomy for her. Eight years flew by before I asked Jim to consider a vasectomy reversal. Through two more clock-ticking years—months of graphing my basal temperature and cycles of rising hope dashed—I tried to get pregnant. Then, one night, I waited in the upstairs bathroom for the test strip to change, the smell of Dial soap on my hands. I set the plastic wand on the counter out of view, touched my toes, up and down, up and down, no peeking until after the 180th second. One blue line, and the magic began.

I kissed our son on the top of his head and sat next to him. Parenting good-natured, curious Glen had exceeded my expectations.

"Who was that?" he asked.

"David Job. A friend." I draped my jacket across my neck and chest, like a backward cape. Eyes closed, I leaned against the chair, legs straight ahead, and worried over the doctor's words, the delays, and Jim's new symptoms.

"Beth. Glen." The soothing voice belonged to Kim—our neighbor, who was also a nurse. "Dianne told me what happened." The mother of our son's closest friend, dark-haired, petite Kim held us in her concerned gaze. Word travels fast in a small hospital. For that, I was grateful.

She sat beside Glen and took his hand. He seemed startled, about to cry. Her son, Tenzing, and Glen had bonded in preschool. They shared long summer days building forts in the green belt between our homes or messing with skateboards, and short winter days bundled up outdoors tromping in the snow and sledding down steep mounds Jim created with our snowblower.

I answered Kim's questions until they wheeled Jim into the room. He lifted his head. "Hey, Kim," he rasped as if she'd dropped by the house for a cup of tea.

We all rose, and she set a hand on him, holding Glen at her side. "How're you doing?"

He shook his head.

His left eyelid drooped. Had I missed that symptom earlier? I laced my fingers into his free hand. "Did they get what they need this time?"

"They-they"—a ragged cough interrupted—"didn't say."

Kim cranked the metal gurney to a better height.

"Ho-holy crap," he muttered.

She spoke soothingly to Jim and urged Glen and me to get breakfast in the cafeteria, but I didn't want to leave. What if the doctor came by with questions for me? Every minute mattered. Stroke outcomes are better with immediate treatment. Time was running out.

Jim cleared his throat. "G-go eat. I'll be okay."

I could skip a meal, but Glen needed to eat.

It was noon when we left for the cafeteria.

3

RISE TO THE OCCASION

"Hey, Beth." David got my attention from the hallway after we'd returned from lunch. Glen was with Kim. "I need to talk to you—in private." He gestured me away from the nurses' station. We stood face to face. His hazel eyes drew me in. "You know, Bartlett's a great hospital." He stroked his goatee. "I love my job. Everyone works hard. They're good at what they do." His face tensed. "But this situation is serious. We're a small county hospital. Jim needs experts, and he needs them now."

I took in each word, absorbing the weight of their truth.

"You've got to get him out of here—to Anchorage or Seattle. That'll only happen if you're firm with his doctor. When she gets here, you have to insist he's medevacked to a bigger hospital."

My breathing became labored as if I'd broken the surface after a long dive.

He continued, "There's this odd situation between the insurance and doctors. It costs a lot to evacuate someone out of Juneau. The docs are under pressure from insurance companies to keep patients here. Your nature is to be agreeable, but you need to do this. For Jim. You've got to insist he gets on that Learjet and taken to a larger center. You'll be doing your doctor a favor. If you don't push this, she'll be reluctant to order it. If you do, she'll have to try."

Juneau was surrounded by mountains, glaciers, and ocean with no roads out—no big medical centers nearby. Since we'd arrived at Bartlett, I'd passed the responsibility baton off to the medical team. I'd relinquished my decision-making role, expecting them to do what was best for my husband. But now our friend was telling me to step forward, take command, steer this crisis down a different path.

David glanced at his watch. "I've got to get back to my office. If you have any problems, call me." He placed his business card in my palm.

I hugged him hard. Taught to respect authority, politely follow the advice of professionals, my pulse quickened with dread.

"The other thing." He glanced over his shoulder. "There's one medevac jet for all of Alaska. It goes back and forth. You need to get on their list right away. If another, more critical, emergency comes up, they'll bump him. And I don't know if the plane is in Seattle or Anchorage or here."

Hand trembling, I dialed the clinic operator. "I need to see Dr. Reinhart in the ER right away. Call back if she can't be here in a half hour." She was already an hour late.

I returned to the curtained-off bay, purposeful strides masking frustration.

Kim said they'd taken Jim away for tests. "I should get back to my floor. Will you be okay?"

I said yes but I didn't want her to leave. I sat in a rigid chair next to Glen. My mind raced. What if Dr. Reinhart wouldn't listen to me? I wanted to consult with our family physician. For seventeen years, Lindy Jones had been our doctor. Throughout my pregnancy, he'd had long conversations with Jim about sailboats and coached us through Glen's last-minute C-section delivery. I folded my arms across my ribs, willing Lindy to appear and help me navigate this treacherous terrain. But he wasn't even in Alaska. I decided to push for Seattle, not Anchorage. My cousin and several friends lived in the area, and Seattle's medical centers and universities were top-notch.

Finally, a nurse summoned me. Jim's doctor stood beside the nurses' station. "Elizabeth," she said, "I'm so sorry."

We shook hands.

A compact professional I'd met once before at the clinic, she flipped through Jim's chart. "We're waiting for the results from the MRA."

I stood tall and said, "My husband needs to go to Seattle right away."

She looked at me but didn't respond.

"This is an unusual type of stroke and he needs to be medevacked to Virginia Mason today."

Although she had not been moving, Dr. Reinhart seemed to stop in her tracks. She stared at her clipboard and raised another page. "The consensus is," she said, words measured, "to keep him here twenty-four hours for more analysis."

I bristled. "I'm convinced the outcome from this stroke—if he stays here—will not be as good as if we get him to a medical center with more expertise."

Her eyes narrowed.

I met her gaze. "I want him medevacked to Seattle today."

She let the flap of pages drop. "I'll see what I can do."

Outside, lacy crusts of snow dripped and popped, fueling Salmon Creek as it gurgled down the mountain to the sea. Bald eagles, some perched in treetops, others in flight, peppered the landscape with high-pitched, thin calls, ill-suited for such handsome, steely-eyed birds of prey.

Inside the hospital, inside our stark fluorescent world, the afternoon droned on, air stale with antiseptic and human discomfort. Metal carts squealed along corridors, pushed by soft-soled technicians. Jim slept. Kim returned and took Glen outside to a nearby trail, then to the cafeteria. Steady in the face of what we'd experienced, Glen welcomed the distraction.

Jim woke, sweaty and confused. "It feels like the world is spinning."

I pressed a cool cloth to his forehead. "We'll get you through this, hon." I spoke as if I knew the way forward.

Kim was buzzed back to her floor. Doctors came and went. A nurse appeared and announced she was adding Phenergan to his IV to reduce vertigo and nausea. Technicians dropped by to check his monitors and adjust pillows. I went back and forth to the nurses' station, as much to ask about the status of the medevac jet as to burn energy. No news. I checked my watch. Nine hours since he'd staggered up the stairs.

It felt like we were slogging through heavy snow, trudging toward a whiteout horizon, getting nowhere. Meanwhile, in trauma bays next to us, other families dealt with crises and moved on as if we existed on two separate but layered tracks—ours slowed to a crawl as theirs sped up. I wanted to take my husband's and son's hands and lead them out of the numbing labyrinth, back to the light of day. What I'd give to return to our mundane Tuesday morning. Before.

Dianne arrived with coffees for us and a carton of milk for Glen. While she and I spoke in hushed tones, knee-to-knee, Jim remained groggy. Soon a woman approached. "Are you Elizabeth Mathews?"

"Yes."

"I'm Sharon with Airlift Northwest." She scanned her notes. "The request for your husband to be medevacked was denied—"

"What?" I stood, knocking my chair back. "But he's *got* to go!"

She pressed her lips together, then said, "I'm not finished."

Glen set his book down and came over to stand by me.

"Apparently," she continued, "your doctor called them back, and they finally approved."

"Oh, thank you." I rubbed my forehead. "I'm sorry I blew up."

"I understand," she said. "The initial refusal seems to be why it's taken so long. We now have him scheduled for the next evacuation to Seattle, and we need you to complete some paperwork." She handed me several documents.

A knot between my shoulders loosened, as I silently thanked Dr. Reinhart. "Can I fly with him?"

"It's not up to me." Her tone was flat. "Captain has the final say. There's not much room. For him to consider it, you'll need to complete this other form."

While I wrote, clipboard on my knees, Dianne moved to the seat next to Glen. "As soon as your mom's done with those, you should head home to pack. They never know exactly when the jet will take off. When they're set to go—when they have your father ready—they'll leave. They won't wait."

"Are we flying to Seattle with Dad?" Glen asked.

"Sweetheart, we don't even know if I'll be allowed to go. It's a special jet for emergencies." I turned to Dianne, "Would they let someone Glen's age come?"

She hesitated, then spoke. "They don't normally let kids on these flights. How old are you now?"

"Nine," he said. "And a half."

"Let me check on this." She stood. "I know one of the flight nurses. I'll talk to her while you get your stuff. Remember, essentials only." She left.

Glen and I sprinted to the car. Holding hands, we cut diagonal across a patch of grass to the parking lot. He slowed our pace and stared up at me. "Do you think I'll be able to go?"

We stopped walking. His earnest gaze made my chest tight. I did not want to leave him but had to prepare him. "Probably not."

His shoulders drooped and he spoke slowly. "But I want to be with you and Dad." His voice broke.

"If you can't come, you can stay with Tenzing and his family—go to school together." I thought being with his friend might change his mind.

He shook his head. "I don't know if I can do that." The corners of his mouth quivered down. "I just . . . wouldn't stop thinking about Dad."

I swallowed hard. "We'll pack your bag—in case. But we need you to be prepared to stay with Tenzing."

I drove toward our home in the valley, at the edge of too fast and not fast enough. We flew down the highway along Gastineau Channel, a shallow stretch of indigo ocean between the mainland and Douglas Island. To the east rose steep mountains. Jim had led us on hikes there, up rocky stream beds, down narrow, cobbled valleys.

As the snow receded, Arctic terns and humpback whales would soon return. New life erupted around us—pressing toward a full-throttled Alaskan spring.

Driving home, window down, my hair whipped about. What else should I be doing? It was all happening so fast. No time to fall apart. Ocean-tinged air tripped me back twelve years to another dangerous situation when I'd had to perform. No mistakes. Back then, Jim and I lived on our sailboat in Glacier Bay. We'd survived that storm, we could get through this one.

Late that October, prepping for a deer-hunting expedition, we discovered our sailboat's transmission wouldn't go into gear. I fetched tools while Jim disassembled, diagnosed, and repaired the gearshift.

A day late, beneath building clouds, we left Bartlett Cove and motored west to the Inian Islands, a deer-hunting, salmon-fishing, and marine-mammal viewing hotspot. The mountainous, wooded islands crop out where Cross Sound connects Icy Strait to the wide-open Pacific Ocean. Twice a day, the Gulf of Alaska floods into and out of the Strait's narrow channels. Known for severe rip tides, locals call South Inian Pass "the washing machine."

Once inside the cove, I took the helm. At the bow, Jim released the anchor, and a hundred feet of chain rumbled down after it. "Reverse," he called over his shoulder. I shifted into gear, inhaling the forest-scented breeze. Rubber boot on chain, he felt for tension to make sure the anchor grabbed.

Years earlier, in California, when he was offered the position leading the research division at the National Park, he invited me to move to Alaska with him. We'd met while teaching a month-long humpback whale ecology course together on a schooner. In Gustavus, the first home we'd shared was a log cabin heated by a wood stove. The next year, we purchased and moved onto our sailboat. He was the one with a passion for boating. I grew up in Indiana, climbing trees, roller-skating on bumpy asphalt, and scheming with my best friend to buy a pony. My youthful dream was to live on a farm, raise horses, a garden, and children.

That evening, as we inched backward setting anchor, ravens in the alder-tufted forest exchanged deep-throated, *klaa-whocks!* With a forecast for twenty-knot northerlies, we tucked in close to the steep, lee shore.

Boat secured, we embraced in a brisk ocean breeze, savoring our wilderness solitude.

The rain began as pinpricks.

"Jim D. sent us off with two moose steaks," he said. "I'll get those started."

In the warmth below, we shed fleece pants and jackets. The boat yanked against her anchor. He stopped chopping garlic to listen. After another *thud-clank!* he decided to add a snubber to the chain. While he attached the shock-absorbing line, I made rice and a salad.

"We're holding," he said, climbing down the companion-way, "but the wind's already up to twenty-five. These steep hills funnel it through the gaps between islands. Plus there's a back eddy from the current."

"I'll get the radar going." I felt more nervous than my voice let on.

"Good idea."

We ate beneath a patter of rain. As the boat swayed and shuddered, we took turns checking our radar position and scanning the shore.

Two hours later, I was brushing my teeth when he called down to me, "Get suited up!"

"What's happening?" Toothpaste foam spattered the sink.

"Wind's shifted one-eighty! We're dragging toward shore."

I shoved bare legs into thermal pants, pulled on rubber boots.

The diesel's low, start-up rumble was a reassuring addition to the storm's loud tantrum.

Up top, rain sliced through my fleece.

"We gotta get out of here," he said. "Keep her nose into the wind, while I take off the snubber and crank in the chain. As soon as the anchor's off the bottom, you gotta power up so she doesn't go aground. It shallows up fast."

I flashed an *Oh, Jesus* look.

The look he bounced back said, *We can do this.*

When we moved to Alaska, we explored building a house in Gustavus, a community of three hundred embedded in Glacier Bay National Park. I'd lobbied for a wooded five-acre lot next to a burbling river.

Instead of buying land, we drained our savings for a down payment and cosigned on a $100,000 loan to buy *IJsselmeer.* "Ice-uhl-meer," we'd practiced to get her Dutch name right. His rationale was we could either own five acres of land—or have Glacier Bay and Icy Strait as a million-acre ocean backyard.

He won me over.

The rigging wailed as I scanned the dark cove.

I wanted to be his all-in sailing partner, but my Midwestern core taunted, *You're an imposter.* My confidence in running our boat ebbed and flowed like Icy Strait's currents.

How could those boulders be so close? Another gust sent the depth sounder from fifteen to thirteen feet, then ten. My heart raced as I pictured our sailboat's keel scraping the seafloor. At the bow, Jim knelt to remove the snubber. With every plunge, seawater shot up around him.

What am I doing here? I should have held out for buying land.

He yelled something but the words hurtled past my ears.

"What?" I shouted.

"Drive into the wind. Up the chain!" He sliced his straight arm forward.

I pressed her into gear. What if the shift repair doesn't hold?

The bow blew off course. A shadowy image of *IJsselmeer* aground darted into my mind, hull at an ungainly tilt, like a beached whale.

Again, Jim hollered, "Into the wind!"

"I am!" I shouted. But I had to do more. *Focus.* I eased the helm to port, then sharp to starboard, fending off blows of wind like punches from one side, then the other. More throttle. Cut back. Ease the chain's tension.

Jim flashed an anchor's-off-bottom signal and leaned out to dislodge wads of kelp. Another blast shoved the untethered boat toward rocks. I revved to full throttle, helm hard to port. *IJsselmeer's* bow rose and, like a Clydesdale, she plowed ahead, consuming ground we'd lost. The depth sounder flashed nine, then ten.

Hold this heading. Eleven. Twelve.

Keep her in the middle. Jim's gear repair held. My body shook, but I was no longer cold. I was in the zone. *We*—the three of us—were in the zone. *IJsselmeer* was an extension of the two of us.

Hand over hand, Jim made his way to the cockpit, storm slapping his back. He nodded and took the helm. Gripping the rail, I scanned the horizon through shrouded night vision. The steep, forested shoreline ghosted closer, then receded. No, I thought. This is where I want to be—shoulder to shoulder with this man.

Beneath the howling sky, we powered out of the cove into the safety of deep water.

Jolted back to the present, I turned into our driveway. The memory sharpened my resolve. We had to get Jim to Seattle.

"Hurry!" Glen said, unbuckling his seat belt. "Let's pack."

4

EVACUATION

"What did they say about me coming?" Glen asked Dianne in the room where Jim dozed.

Elbows on thighs, she met his gaze. "The Airlift nurse said she'd pass my request to the captain. I told her I've known you since you were a baby. And that you're the most mature kid I've ever met. They won't have an answer, though, until right before they go."

He nodded but looked dejected.

"Are you packed?" she asked.

"We are," he said before I could.

Jim's hand shot to his left eye. I went to his side. "What's wrong with that eye?"

"I get these sharp pains." His face tensed. "Like it's being jabbed with a needle."

I took his free hand in mine.

A nurse wheeled in an IV bag. "Doctor's called for heparin to keep clots from forming."

Later, Dianne's partner, Sudie, a specialist with the Coast Guard, walked in. "Oh, Beth. This is so hard." Her dark eyes reassuring, she said, "But Jim will move beyond this. He's a fighter. We have to get him on that medevac to Seattle. He's got to go to Virginia Mason. They're the stroke experts."

I told Jim we'd been home to pack our things. His gravelly question, "Di-did you get the fur-furniture?" troubled me.

What was he talking about? He'd always had a slight start-up stutter, so that was not the issue. Was speaking gibberish a new stroke symptom?

A decade earlier, Jim and I had visited his uncle Glen, our son's namesake, after he'd suffered a stroke. At seventy-seven, Glen L. Taggart had led an active and productive life as president of Utah State University, beating graduate students decades younger at racquetball. In the assisted-care home, he appeared professional and fit, wire-thin, but far from frail. Jim's uncle Glen maneuvered a walker toward me. Exuding an affirmative glow, he shook my hand and smiled.

He spoke, gesturing toward a watercolor of a mountain brook flowing over smooth stones. Although his expression fit the situation, the words that rose and burbled out had nothing to do with the circumstances or the painting. It was as if hard wires linking Uncle Glen's mental dictionary to his mouth and tongue had been disconnected, then plugged back in with circuitry pins misaligned, causing him to say something like, "That box reminds me of stones with his father," instead of, "That painting reminds me of fly fishing with Jim's father."

If someone viewed a video of my conversation with Uncle Glen in the convalescent visitation room back then with the audio off, they would never have known his sentences made no sense. No sense at all.

Had my husband developed expressive aphasia like his Uncle Glen?

"The-the furniture," Jim repeated.

I shook my head, confused.

"D-did you bring it in?"

"Oh-h." Exhaling in relief, I understood Jim was referring

to the furniture he'd moved onto our deck in preparation for the carpet cleaners. "No. I completely forgot."

Sudie pulled out a notebook. "I'll take care of it."

Around seven o'clock, the Airlift Northwest coordinator returned while Jim slept. Dianne sat with us. "Your husband's on for the flight to Seattle tonight," the woman said. "How much do you weigh?"

"A hundred and twenty-eight pounds."

She told us the jet would leave within the hour. "Your carry-on can't be more than twenty pounds, total." She turned to leave.

Glen pressed his foot against mine.

"What about our son?"

"Oh, yeah." She turned to him. "The captain wants to meet you. He'll stop by in a few minutes."

Eyes wide, Glen tipped his head.

I gave Dianne the numbers of two friends, colleagues at the university, to notify: Brendan Kelly and Sherry Tamone.

Moments later, someone tapped on the door. A tall man in a white shirt with gold epaulets and a navy-blue tie walked in.

Together, Glen and I stood.

"You must be Beth," he said, voice deep. "I'm very sorry about your husband. We're going to get him to Seattle shortly here. I understand you have your son with you."

"Yes. This is Glen."

"Hello, young man."

Glen extended his hand.

The pilot reached down to shake it. "How much do you weigh?"

"Seventy-three pounds," Glen said as if he'd been waiting for the question.

The captain explained there would not be much room in the plane, that we would be in small seats at the back, and there would be no stewardess—and no snacks. "How do you feel about that?"

"I'm fine with all of it. I want to go."

My son's clarity caught me off guard. I blinked back proud tears.

"Well, Glen," the pilot said, "you can come with us, then."

His face lit up. "Thanks!"

"Let's go get your stuff," Dianne said. "Sudie, I'll walk them to the airlift van. Can you stay until they come for Jim?"

"You bet."

At Jim's gurney, I jiggled his arm. "Hon, we'll both be on the jet with you."

He pressed a hand against his temple. "Glen, too?"

"Yeah," Glen answered. "I get to come with you."

"Good." Jim set his hand on our son's arm.

"We'll meet you at the airport." I squeezed his shoulder and turned to leave.

"Wait," Jim said. "Don't-don't forget to make a r-reservation at a hotel near the hospital." Hiccups punctuated the sentence.

I cradled his head in my hands and kissed him. This is my man—even in the midst of a stroke, he's on top of our logistics. I held his unsteady gaze. "I love you."

Glen, Dianne, and I hustled down the back stairs. Our pounding feet generated a thundering echo up the metal stairwell. We emerged into the cold evening. It seemed so long ago since Glen and I had driven home, packed, and returned to the hospital.

The trunk of our Honda Civic popped up. "You packed too much," Glen said. "You can't take all that." My carry-on bag with laptop and course materials sat on top of a small duffel. Glen had snugged his belongings into his orange school pack.

"He's right," Dianne said. "Can you fit what's essential into your backpack?"

As I sorted items into two piles, Glen grew impatient. "Come *on*," he said. "We've gotta get going. They'll leave without us!"

My spine pressed the jump seat as the Learjet streaked up past snow-capped mountains. The canvas seat was low-slung, like a beach chair. A harness crossed my torso like a giant *H*. Knees bent, I wanted to wrap my arms around them, lower my forehead, and cry. Instead, I reached for our son's hand.

Ahead, the instrument panel glowed, silhouetting the pilot and copilot. In place of passenger seating between us, the left fuselage supported two inward-facing seats occupied by medics. The two women wore khaki jumpsuits and lace-up, thick-soled black boots. Across from them, inches from their knees, was a bench along the other fuselage. Buckled to it was my husband's stretcher. Fourteen hours had passed since he'd staggered up the stairs. During the gravity-defying climb into the night sky, he lifted his head and squinted at us. They'd said he would be sedated, but the medication hadn't yet pulled him to that internal twilight. I raised an open hand, eyes riveted on his. Did he know it was me?

At forty thousand feet, above the clouds—close to heaven if there was one—iridescent, emerald curtains shimmered, like in a dream. Momentarily swept out of the nightmare, I tapped the glass. "Look, hon! Northern lights," I said to Glen, as if we were camping—as if all my assumptions about the future were not shattering.

5

RARE EVENT

From the starlit troposphere, the Learjet descended toward Seattle. Colored dots and streaks of yellow light surrounded the ocean inlet below. Puget Sound snaked and branched across land like polished onyx. Glen slept, head propped on my arm.

Beneath a drizzle, we taxied across the glistening tarmac. A silent ambulance approached, lights pulsing red, yellow, red. The flight nurse leaned toward me. "Please stay in your seats until we move your husband. Someone else will take you and your son to the hospital."

"Can I talk to him?"

She shook her head. "He's sedated."

"I need a moment." I did not release her gaze.

"Once we've stopped you can check on him, but you'll have to be out of the way before they open the door."

The captain flipped levers and twisted dials. The roar of the first and then the second engine wound down, trailing off like loud turbo sighs. The Airlift medic flashed a thumbs up.

I slid Glen's head aside, unbuckled, and crouch-stepped beneath the ceiling to the bench. Oxygen tubes curled over Jim's ears and into his nostrils. His eyes were closed. I knelt, laid my head on his chest and wrapped my arms around his torso. A prayer formed, drawn from a faded childhood chapter.

Oh, Lord, dear Lord. Please be here for us. Please help Jim through this.

The medic touched my arm. I wasn't done.

I pressed my ear onto his heart. A blanket muffled the sound, but I heard it. So many times I'd rested my head on his naked chest, taking his steady *lub-dub, lub-dub* rhythm for granted. I squeezed his hand. What was that? Yes. Again. His grip tightened to meet mine.

The curved cabin doors lurched open, a pair of gaping jaws.

I backed into the low seat next to Glen.

Three men in orange helmets climbed aboard. Steam rose from their yellow slickers.

"Hey, honey." I smoothed Glen's hair back from his forehead. "We're in Seattle."

After the ambulance strobed away, a silver sedan arrived for us. In two and a half hours, the sleek jet had whisked us nine hundred miles south at 82 percent of the speed of sound. The fifteen-mile, stop-and-go drive into the city center consumed an agonizing half hour.

It was after midnight when Glen and I thanked the driver, snatched our packs, and ran toward the emergency entry. We burst in like we'd finished a hundred-yard dash. A woman wearing what looked like a policeman's cap slouched on a stool behind a tall counter.

"Where did they take my husband?" I asked. "He came ahead of us—in the ambulance."

"Ma'am, slow down. I need some information. This is a secure area. We got lots of ambulances bringing folks in. Y'all have to get a pass to go inside."

For many minutes I answered questions, filled out forms. Glen elbowed me as if to say, *Let's go. Do we have to do this?*

The attendant peered at her monitor, tapping more keys than my brief answers seemed to warrant.

"Your husband's in intensive care. Please wait over there." She pointed down the hall.

Seated side by side in the empty room, I shuffled through a stack of magazines and chose a *National Geographic.* My attention refused to be diverted, even by an article about two border collies with hundred-word vocabularies. I set the magazine down, leaned back, and rubbed my eyes. Wake up. Make this not real.

"Mrs. Taggart?" A technician in scrubs had arrived.

"Yes." I sat forward.

"The doctor asked for your help getting some history."

I stood.

"Can I come?" Glen asked her.

"No," the woman said. "He'll have to stay here."

I saw my son grimace, tears imminent.

I set my hand on his shoulder. "You'll be okay, hon." I didn't care for how she'd addressed me and not Glen. I followed her through swinging doors along a tiled hall that smelled of Lysol and iodine.

Three doctors in white coats clustered around a metal bed. Jim was awake but groggy. "Hello, sweetheart." I leaned down to hug him.

He jolted through a hiccup, but his firm embrace reassured me.

One of the physicians reached across him to shake my hand. "I'm Dr. Laura Neilsen." Everything about the woman exuded confidence: firm grip, dancer's posture, eye contact. "The first thing we need is a usable MRA—images of his cranial blood vessels. Neither of the two from Juneau is usable because he couldn't lie still with those hiccups. We'll give him a sedative to control those. Plus, our scanner is more sophisticated."

"What's the diagnosis?"

"We're working that out. It'll depend on what specific part of his brainstem is damaged. Does he have a history of high blood pressure?"

"A year ago, he started having issues with cholesterol and blood pressure after his job got more stressful. His doctor put him on Simvastatin."

Her pen scrawling against paper put me at ease.

"Yes, we got that. And his general fitness?"

Jim's hiccups continued, but he seemed engaged.

"It's excellent. He rides his bike a lot, even in snow, and runs—less recently since we've been preparing our house to sell. Sometimes he lifts weights."

"What happened leading up to the stroke?"

I took Jim's hand and described the morning: the coughing fit on the ladder, loss of balance, the expulsion when he drank water. I left out his request to make love.

Dr. Cortez, one of the neurologists, asked me if Jim had done anything unusual or had symptoms before the stroke. The young doctor had black hair and a crew cut like my father's when I was a child, but longer on the top. Everything before seemed long ago. "Two days ago, on Sunday, we painted the living room and stairwell walls. We worked all day. Yesterday he scraped, repaired, and painted a skylight."

We'd been terse with each other that Sunday. There'd been so much to do to get the house ready. And wrapping up my semester required an extra push. Always a hard worker, Jim had bought the supplies and a gallon of the shade of white I'd chosen. He was there on the ladder above me wearing those coveralls. I put on some dance music to make the job more fun. But he hadn't lightened up. God, if I'd known this was going to happen, I thought, I would have been nicer. Because I'd resented his sour mood, I'd ignored it. Only as images flashed in my head in front of concerned professionals did I appreciate that his gruffness might not have been because we had to paint the walls, but because it was our weekend together. My work demands were an ongoing issue. Why hadn't *I* switched gears? Stopped to ask him what was wrong? Treated him better?

"Also last night, during dinner," I continued, "I'm not sure if this is relevant, but he took a bite of spicy rice and choked so hard he had to leave the room."

"Has that happened before?"

"Never. My son and I were worried. I thought I might have to do the Heimlich maneuver. But he came back and told us he was okay."

The doctor's eyebrows rose. "One of his vocal cords may be paralyzed. It's not uncommon with medullary strokes."

"What does that mean?" I hadn't heard that term.

"Medullary refers to the medulla oblongata—the central region of the brainstem. That's the likely site of damage. It's like your brain's motherboard."

I squeezed Jim's hand. The comparison to a computer's motherboard troubled me.

Dr. Neilsen peered at his face. "The way your eyes are jittering involuntarily is called nystagmus. It's no wonder you feel dizzy—yours is the speeding rotational type. That, with the facial and eyelid droop," she gestured to the left side of his face, "are signs of what's called Horner's syndrome. Your specific symptoms help us diagnose which nerve pathways have been compromised."

"What caused this?" I asked.

She told us they'd know more after reviewing the new MRA. "It's late. You and your son should get some sleep."

"I don't think Jim will sleep with these hiccups," I said.

"We'll give him something to help."

He looked at me with gratitude—or was it fear?

"You okay being alone tonight, hon?"

He nodded but his expression didn't change.

"Glen and I'll be here first thing." I loosened my grip, but his fingers lingered in mine until I hugged him, bent awkwardly across a rail. I inhaled him deep into my lungs.

It didn't feel right to leave, but we all needed to sleep.

, , ,

Glen and I walked hand in hand down an illuminated street to the hotel I'd reserved adjacent to the medical center.

In bed, my body felt like a flattened plank. In an altered state of exhaustion and denial, I watched car lights scroll across the ceiling. Glen's rhythmic breathing finally nudged me away from the day's events like waves against a shore.

I woke before six, showered, and tiptoed out to get coffee in the lobby. Back in the room, I settled at the small table and made a list: Buy spiral notebook, ask about hiccups, email Alex — to check on our boat, call Jim's sister.

At six thirty, I jiggled Glen's foot. "Hey, sleepyhead." A smile blossomed across his dreamy face. He stretched and slowly emerged from the tangled bedsheet cocoon. His expression darkened. "How's Dad?"

"I don't know, but we'll head right over."

Glen led the way across a glass-enclosed overpass connecting the inn and the hospital to the intensive care unit, all part of the Virginia Mason Medical Center, a thriving teaching hospital in the heart of Seattle. In the bright hall, we passed orderlies, two doctors deep in conversation, and other visitors. The tasteful artwork on display, sounds of doors sliding open and closed, and murmurs of people in motion exuded a professional sense of purpose and action that failed to quiet the urgent voices in my head.

We found Jim sleeping, half a dozen cords attached to his chest. Waveforms of green, amber, and blue pulsed across a monitor. A saline bag hung from a stand and fed the needle taped to his forearm. Even in a relaxed state, the left side of his face appeared different—more asleep than the right.

"Let's let him rest," I whispered, "while we get breakfast."

Glen mimed writing on a pad of paper.

We left a note.

When we returned, his bed was surrounded by another swarm of white-coated physicians, three from the night before plus two others. Glen and I hung back, in the doorway. The head of his bed was raised, but Jim couldn't see us. His torso was tilted to one side.

"Mr. Taggart's experienced an acute neurological event," Dr. Neilsen said to the group. "Jim, Dr. Cortez is going to give you some simple tests."

The doctor from the night before, the one with the crew-cut, stepped in close to Jim and said the tests would help them localize which cranial nerves were involved. "Follow my hand with your eyes, not your head."

Jim's *okay* hand signal was interrupted by a hiccup, but compared to the day before, he was alert.

The doctor held a pencil up and traced a large plus sign. "See how the nystagmus is more pronounced when he looks to the left," he said to his colleagues.

"What's that tell you?" Jim asked.

"Your stroke was on the left side of your brainstem. Push your right hand against my fist. Now press down." The neurologist repeated the test on the other side. "Not much difference," he told the note taker. "Can you shrug?"

Raising his shoulders made him slump farther to the left against the pillows. I suppressed an urge to enter the room and help him sit up straight.

"Okay. Close your eyes, and touch your nose with your right index finger."

Glen and I leaned in to watch. Jim's arm swooped up, and he touched his nose.

"Now same thing, left side."

Jim, eyes shut, raised that hand, but his fingertip landed on his forehead. "Well." He smiled. "I-I guess I failed *that* part of the test."

The neurologists chuckled.

Glen and I smiled at each other.

As the doctors filed out, Dr. Neilsen saw us and stopped. "Hello. This must be your son. Those tests we did with your father help us figure out how the stroke's affected his nervous system. Your dad's got a lot in his favor. He's a strong and active person."

Glen listened attentively.

"Brainstem strokes are rare, though, so there's not much research. But he's come to the right place. We have top-notch neurology and rehab departments. We think he'll pull through."

What did she mean by *pull through*? I wondered. Survive? Spend the rest of his life in a wheelchair? Return to normal? What I'd give to return to our lives as biologists in Juneau, raising our son. Before I could formulate a question, the doctor patted Glen on the shoulder, said goodbye, and walked briskly down the hall.

Glen and Jim hugged through a round of hiccups. "How's your hotel?" he asked, voice gritty.

"It has an elevator," he said, like it was an amusement park ride.

I told Glen I needed time alone with his father. "How about you read in the waiting room?"

He made a sour face.

I flashed my no-debate face. "The chairs out there look comfortable."

"Ohh-kay." He slung his pack onto a shoulder and moped out.

I took Jim's hand in mine and asked how he was doing.

"You-you don't want to know. I'm so thirsty—didn't sleep much. They woke me up to take my blood pressure every hour. I swear. And these damn hiccups are about to drive me nuts. One minute I'm on top of a ladder painting." He shook his head. "Now I'm here." He scowled. "How's Glen holding up?"

"Pretty well. I'm glad he's with us."

"Hmm." He adjusted a pillow. "I don't like him seeing me like this."

I smoothed the hairs on his arm. "Brendan called. Dianne contacted him. He's flying through Seattle this afternoon, on his way to Juneau from DC."

Brendan was Jim's closest friend. He'd recently moved from Alaska to Washington DC, but his son and ex-wife still lived in Juneau. The two men had met in their late twenties on a US Coast Guard icebreaker during a two-month survey of bowhead whales in the Arctic. Among the scientific crew of eight, they hit it off right away. As the massive *Polar Sea* sliced its way through ten- to fifteen-foot-thick winter ice, or rose and fell through huge waves, they often stood watch, binoculars and clipboards in hand. Along with the other biologists, they also surveyed the expansive landscape in Sikorsky helicopters manned by two pilots. Day after day, they scanned endless stretches of pack ice buckled by pressure ridges and dotted with ringed and bearded seals and an occasional group of walruses. Thousands of birds, hundreds of belugas, and sometimes a handful of bowhead whales aggregated in narrow, open-water leads. During those intense months in the barren, frozen landscape the two men had forged a tight friendship.

"He's arranged a layover here to see you."

"That's awfully nice."

You'd do the same for him, I thought. Before entering the room, I hadn't made up my mind whether to share what else Brendan had said, but something pushed the words out. "He's offered to take Glen back to Juneau."

Jim pondered the option as if it was a math puzzle.

Brendan's son, Corwin, was like an older cousin to Glen, Brendan like an uncle. Touched by his offer, I didn't know how I'd hold up without our son's stabilizing presence—moments of normalcy I needed. We'd always operated as a tight triangle. Could I shoulder the added strain of being split up?

A nurse entered and set a large Styrofoam cup heaped with chipped ice on Jim's tray. She peered into the other cup. "Where're you puttin' all that ice?" she teased. Taped above his bed, a sign read: *Diet—Nothing by Mouth except ice chips. Meds—crushed in purée.*

"When can I have water?" Jim cleared his throat.

"Not until your choking risk goes down." She slid her hands into the pockets of her smock. "We all take swallowing for granted. We use about twenty-five muscles to swallow a piece of bread."

After she left, I lifted spoons full of flaked ice to Jim's mouth until he grew too tired to suck on them. I lowered the head of his bed, and he dozed fitfully. We did not return to the conversation she'd interrupted.

6

SLOW BOAT TO SIBERIA

When Brendan strode into Jim's room, Glen and I leaped up as the three of us chimed out his name. I hugged him hard. "It's so good to see you."

"You, too." With an Irishman's rugged looks, thick hair, and bushy mustache, he was the only person I knew with an adventurous drive larger than my husband's.

Like a German Shepherd crossed with a friendly retriever, Brendan could be appropriately fierce and commanding in a wilderness—or academic—situation, but he was also one of the most thoughtful, engaging, and fun adults we knew. A natural leader, Jim's friend was a pivotal mentor to me at the university.

He squatted to take Glen's shoulders in his hands. The gesture brought back my memory of the first time he'd scooped one-week-old Glen from my arms with care and confidence. He'd cradled our son, his gaze a beam of light, large strong hands coaxing coos from our tiny boy. Seeing our nine-year-old now held by those weathered hands made me feel as if I were the one being shored up. "How're you doing?" Brendan asked Glen.

"Okay. How're you?"

"I'm all right. Thanks. You've all been through a lot. Good thing your dad's so darn tough." Brendan held our son's gaze until he nodded, then stood and went to Jim, who lay on his back.

"Hey, man. What the hell's up? I thought I told you not to be painting any damn skylights."

The two friends embraced.

"D-damn is right," Jim bunched a pillow under his head.

Brendan scooted a metal-legged chair in close. "Seriously. You've thrown us all for a loop. You're the one who runs up glacier trails and rides a bike to work in winter."

Interrupted by hiccups, Jim described what had happened. To give them time alone, I invited Glen for a walk.

Shortly after we returned with coffee for Brendan, a physical therapist pushed a walker into the room. "Mr. Taggart, today's your day to get out of that bed."

Brendan stepped aside to give her room.

She helped Jim ease up and slide his legs over the mattress edge.

"What about all this?" he gestured to the IV bag stand and tubes attached to his arm.

"It'll be okay."

He scowled, putting a hand on the walker. "I-I don't need this."

"It has to be parked in front of you. Your fall risk is too high." She held his arm. "One, two, three!"

He rose, body tilted and wobbly.

"Way to go, hon!" I said, but I felt queasy.

Brendan motioned me out to the hall. He rubbed his jaw. "What's his prognosis?"

I told him we still didn't know, and that they'd only recently gotten usable images. "We should have a better idea soon."

"If anyone can get beyond this, it's Jim." He clasped his hands, and his thumbs circled each other as he thought. "How about you? How're you holding up?"

"I'm doing okay." What I didn't say was how I would have liked to hold those strong hands or fall apart in his arms—in someone's arms.

"Have you thought about my offer?" he asked. "To scoop up Glen? He could stay in Juneau with me and Corwin until I head back to DC, then with Tenzing's family. I can take him to school."

Jim and I had not returned to this topic, but the option had pestered me. Brendan was like family. I valued his opinion. He believed removing Glen from the Virginia Mason equation was best, but I disagreed. I needed to be a strong advocate for my husband, and Glen stabilized and recharged me. Although, I worried there could be some harm to our son witnessing his father in this damaged state, Jim perked up whenever they interacted. My decision to stay together as a family was because I believed it maximized Jim's odds for a better recovery, and that was best for all of us, especially Glen.

"We sure appreciate your offer, but I've decided to have him stay for now. His teacher emailed work. Plus, school's almost over." A splinter of angst penetrated my logic. Normally, Jim and I consulted on decisions like this.

The corners of Brendan's mouth tucked down, but he said, "It's your call."

This man who cared about my husband—who had known him two decades longer than I—was deferring. He did not agree.

When we returned, Jim was on his back again. He looked worn out.

Soon a woman in floral scrubs entered. Brendan and I stood across from each other at the foot of the low bed. Glen was reading in a chair against the wall.

"I need to ask you and your wife some questions," she said. "Are you comfortable with him being in the room?" Her elbow poked out at Brendan like a bird's wing.

"Yeah," Jim said.

"Do you have an advance directive?" she asked.

Jim struggled onto an elbow, confused. His jittery gaze relayed the task of answering to me.

"We do."

"Does your wife know what you would want if something were to happen? If you could not speak for yourself?"

Jim stared at me, that caged-animal alarm returning.

"Have you both signed a medical power of attorney?" she asked.

My pulse quickened as I understood her job was to prepare us for worst-case scenarios: paralysis, a coma, death. "We have."

Glen set his book aside and came to the bed. "What's this about?" His question was left hanging, unanswered.

I looked at our friend for guidance. Alike in many ways— he and Jim sought challenges that pushed them physically and mentally. Their remote research in the Arctic had taken them to the edge before. What would Brendan want if he were in Jim's situation and things went downhill?

Brendan registered my attention, then put his hand on our son's shoulder. "Hey, Glen. How about if you show me where the cafeteria is? I could use some lunch." His expression relayed this was my call—only I could judge my husband's preferences.

What exactly was she asking anyway? What would I do if Jim fell into a coma? If we learned the stroke would turn him into a paraplegic? My head swirled. Please no. I can't go there.

Her questions unearthed a conversation from six years earlier.

While living in California before I knew him, Jim had met a brain trauma doctor who counseled victims of motorcycle accidents. Before the mandatory helmet law, she told him, most people in serious motorcycle crashes died on the scene. Afterward, there was a huge increase in survivors, but many were basically a brain surrounded by a nonfunctional body.

After Jim told me the neurologist's story back in Juneau, he adamantly stated, "If I'm ever paralyzed—you pull the cord. No way I want to live if I can't walk."

I challenged his assertion: "What if there were new treatments on the horizon? Or if you retained all your cognitive abilities?" He didn't back down.

Through our connected gaze across the hospital bed, I believed we were recalling the same conversation. Back in Alaska, when we debated the hypothetical question, I tacitly agreed to follow his request. Faced with the actual possibility head-on, I discovered how much I wanted my husband in my life, no matter how incapacitated.

I turned to the woman with the clipboard. "Yes. We've talked about this. He has an advance directive. I'll have a friend fax it." I acted confident that the piece of paper would guide us forward. But I didn't know if I could honor my husband's declaration from the long-ago day in our living room, when he'd asserted his wishes from the vantage of his robust body.

To give the two friends time together, I set Glen up to read in the waiting room and took a walk outside. Seeing Brendan reminded me of all the adventures the two men had shared—and survived—which steered my thoughts back to a spring afternoon before Glen was born. Brendan and I were walking across campus to our offices after teaching marine mammalogy together. I had expressed my trepidations about a trip Jim was planning to Lituya Bay. We'd never taken our boat offshore into the Gulf of Alaska, and our destination was an eight-hour run beyond protected inside waters. Lituya Bay was known as much for its natural beauty as ships wrecked and lives lost in treacherous tidal currents while entering or exiting the fjord's narrow and shallow entrance.

"You two navigate the Inside Passage all the time," Brendan said. "You'll do fine offshore. If Taggart didn't believe you or the boat were up for it, he wouldn't go."

I hadn't spent much time in big seas on our boat, and I told Brendan getting into Lituya scared me.

"You'll figure out how to cross that bar safely, and he'll make sure you and the boat are prepared. He's one of the best expedition planners I've run into. Has he told you about the time a ball of string saved his life?"

"Mmm . . . no."

"This was twenty-some years ago, when he and I met during that research to figure out where bowheads spend the winter. We were flying a whale survey over the Bering Sea when we spotted this large concentration of walruses on the ice. Jim and I were keen to observe them since there was so little known about their winter mating season.

"The next day, the helicopter dropped us off on the ice, twenty-five miles from the icebreaker and about two from the walruses, far enough so the landing wouldn't spook them. There were three of us: a young Yupik ice guide named Ray, Taggart, and me.

"We took a compass bearing and headed toward them. We were on this gigantic plate of solid ice covered with snow." He gazed across the campus and spread his arms as if he could see the white expanse to the horizon. "We'd totally misjudged the height of the pressure ridges between floes. Imagine the wind moving all these slabs around, like plate tectonics, but sped up and on a smaller scale. They're smashing together, subducting and buckling over each other, creating these giant creaking ridges. When you're crossing the ice—the snow squeaking—you don't get a sense they're moving unless you're near an edge."

I asked what the weather was like, and he said, "Bluebird skies with twenty-knot winds coming down the Bering Strait— mid-February. But we were dressed for it. Big parkas, insulated bunny boots. It was tough going, but hiking like that, we were plenty warm. Eventually, we came to a place where the slab we were on and the one we needed to get to were separated by a hundred feet of water. Farther down, there was a section with a jumble of car-sized ice chunks between the two slabs that formed

45

a sort of bridge. Ray, who's a small guy, scrambled across. When he leaped to the other side, the ice chunks rocked a bit. He signaled for me to follow. It was an up-and-down climb, hands and feet. Near the top, I handed my pack down to Ray and told Jim to give me his. Taggart heaved it to me. Once I made it to the other side, Jim started climbing hand over hand. Halfway across, we heard a loud *crack!* Ray and I watched the whole smashed-up bridge break free. All of a sudden, Taggart was drifting away, not connected to either pan. He was headed down this black-water space between the two plates."

"Did he jump?"

"No way. The open water was V-shaped with the bigger space downwind. He was headed toward Russia. I remember thinking," Brendan said, "What the hell do we do now? The helicopter wasn't due for four hours, and the days were short. That's when Taggart shouts, 'Top right pocket of my pack! Open the zippered pouch.' I fumbled for the pack, tugged at the zipper. Inside, there's this grapefruit-sized ball of parachute cord, tightly wound. Taggart directs me to secure an end and throw him the other." Brendan mimicked an overhand toss. "Meanwhile, the gap's grown. Taggart catches the ball, wraps the cord around this stump of ice."

"Ray and I pulled, but the cord cut into our hands, so we attached it to the middle of this six-foot metal ice probe I had, then pulled like a couple of yoked-up oxen. It was hard and slow. The line got all stretchy, humming. We pulled and pulled, coaxing the floe against the wind. Finally, he jumped across—after freeing his precious cord."

"What a story. What did you do then?"

"Boy, I don't remember. Maybe some back-thumping." Brendan smiled. "I'm pretty sure I didn't kiss him."

We laughed, but I felt shaky.

"Taggart and I were intent on finding those walruses, so we

kept moving that direction. At the time it didn't seem lik[ ] deal. It wasn't until much later the full impact hit. That scene's risen up in more than one sleepless night. Damn, we were five hundred miles from the US, a hundred from Russia. No way to reach the pilots or the ship. Taggart was on a slow boat to Siberia." He shook his head. "He'll make sure you're prepared. Who the hell else would've had two hundred feet of parachute cord stashed in their pack?"

As I turned up the tree-lined block back toward Virginia Mason, I found it hard to align the quick-thinking, agile Jim in Brendan's Arctic story with the man trapped in the hospital bed.

Later, Brendan hugged each of us and left to catch his plane. Jim, Glen, and I sat in silence as his absence reverberated in the dim room. I reached over to smooth Jim's hair as he stared at the ceiling. I reassured myself he would again be that competent, ambitious explorer who plans for unimagined contingencies. "You're going to make it, hon," I said, confused by the clash between my words and an impulse to cry.

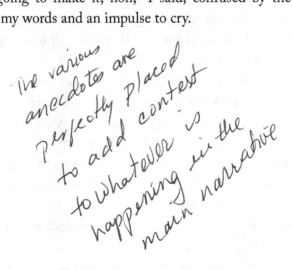

The various anecdotes are perfectly placed to add context to whatever is happening in the main narrative

7

PERFECT STORM

The speech therapist offered Jim a bowl of purée the color of manila file folders. He gave it a quirky look, then raised a spoonful. When he choked on it, I jumped up, alarmed.

Glen looked up from his reading.

Jim cleared his throat as she patted his back. "You okay?"

He nodded, face red.

She told us his difficulty swallowing—dysphagia—was most likely due to damage of the vagus nerve controlling one side of his vocal cord. "Your barium swallow test will tell us what specific therapy you need."

On the way back from dinner, Glen and I took the steps two by two. Making my heart pound from physical exertion felt good.

I skidded the curtain aside, and Jim's eyes flickered open. "Hey, welcome back. What did you have?"

"Chicken fajitas." Glen tapped his hands on the blanket by his dad's thigh in a syncopated rhythm. "Spicy—the way you like."

He squinted with envy. "Sounds good."

Soon doctors, Neilsen and Cortez, entered, and Dr. Neilsen announced they had a diagnosis.

I stood and rested a hand on Jim's arm. Glen came to my side.

"Your situation's so rare, we reached out to other neurologists and combed the literature." She ran her fingers through cropped hair. Although her eyes looked tired, she was energized. "You've experienced a dissection of your vertebral artery."

"No kidding?" Jim said, alert.

"Dissection?" I asked. I associated the term with biology labs and the strong smell of formalin. Had something cut his artery?

She told us the word in this case referred to a blood vessel delaminating on the inside. Our two vertebral arteries transport about 20 percent of the blood to the brain. Hand on the back of her neck, she added, "Where they exit that bony channel at the top of the spinal cord, they make an S-turn into the skull."

"So his stroke wasn't from a clot?" I was confused.

"That's right. The inner wall of Jim's left artery peeled away from the outer layers—imagine the layers of an onion. This created a pouch of tissue that filled with blood and blocked the flow."

Jim shook his head slowly.

"But why?" I asked.

"The combination of sanding and painting the skylight with his neck hyperextended"— she tilted her head back and moved her chin up and down, demonstrating—"most likely triggered the dissection. The vertebral arteries are a bit larger than the diameter of a pencil lead, and they're not designed for repetitive bending."

Her words transfixed me.

The doctors thought perhaps the severe coughing fit at dinner was related and speculated that bending his neck again when he was on the ladder the next morning might have triggered the ultimate blockage.

Jim listened, beads of sweat on his forehead.

"I've never heard of a stroke being caused like that." I squeezed Glen's shoulder.

"Brainstem strokes like this are rare," Dr. Cortez said, "but they're the most common type in young people—usually under forty. We had a patient here a couple of months ago hit with a lateral medullary stroke—a plumber working in a cupboard under a sink." The doctor bent to the side and moved his hand and head like he was tugging on a big wrench in a tight space. "Blood pools up behind the delaminated section, blocking the flow, which deprives brain tissue downstream of oxygen."

"Geez Louise," Jim said.

"But what other factors are there?" I asked. "Not all plumbers get a brainstem stroke."

"That's true. There's not much published, so we don't know what makes certain people susceptible."

The news made me dizzy.

"I-I assumed I'd had a clot," Jim muttered.

"The most common cause of lateral medullary syndrome is painting ceilings." Dr. Neilsen acted as if she were holding a long handle, leaning her head back as her arms rolled paint onto a high surface. She described how a younger man at a meeting around a table triggered a vertebral dissection when he turned his head abruptly to yell at a colleague.

"No kidding?" A spark of Jim's usual curiosity returned.

"I read about a young woman," Dr. Cortez added, "with long hair who had one while getting her hair permed."

"How in the world would that happen?" I asked.

"As the beautician unwound the rollers, the upward tugging and releasing bent her client's neck up and down, triggering a dissection of the artery wall."

I shook my head. "Unbelievable."

"The good news," Dr. Neilsen said, "is you don't have any inherent susceptibility to stroke or blood clots. Our biggest concern now is swallowing. You're fit, and your cognitive skills weren't impaired. Plus, you've got the right attitude to get the most out of rehab. This was a freak accident—a perfect storm of circumstances."

"Adelle," I whispered. "It's Beth."

I sat on the bathroom floor of our hotel room, knees bent,

back supported by the white porcelain tub. It was eleven p.m., thirty-nine hours since the stroke. Even through a folded bath mat, the floor tiles were cold. At once wired and exhausted, I'd finally called Jim's sister. Glen was asleep. The coiled cord from the bedside phone was stretched under the closed door. Receiver held tight, I imagined the telephone in Idaho ringing on her nightstand. I hugged my knees.

"Oh, hi. How are you?" Cheerful and warm, she was a night owl. I'd never called this late.

"Adelle. It's Jim—" My voice cracked.

"What is it?"

Even though he was the family black sheep, his three sisters adored him. After his first year in college, he let his parents know he was not a Mormon. The rift had rattled the close-knit family, but they never disowned him as some do.

I met Adelle the summer Jim and I were getting back together a year after we'd met. Adelle and her husband, Jay Dee, had rented an RV and were driving it down California's Highway One with three of their five children. The evening before he was to join them, Jim called his sister and said, "Oh, by the way, is it okay if I bring a friend?"

"So . . . is this a male or female friend?" Adelle asked.

A year earlier, Jim and his wife of thirteen years had separated. Both accomplished scientists, I had known them in grad school but didn't instigate their breakup.

Before Jim and I met up with his sister's family—active Mormons—in San Francisco, I worried she'd be critical of her recently divorced brother's new girlfriend, a Midwestern biologist with marginal religious roots.

Instead, Adelle and Jay Dee welcomed me aboard. Within minutes, I bonded with their two teenage daughters and eleven-year-old son. We laughed and played cards, as good-natured Jay Dee piloted the ship-like RV along the two-lane coastal road.

At Point Reyes National Seashore we hiked down a steep dune and watched Jim's nephew dart in and out of ice-cold, pounding waves. Jim, an energetic and engaged uncle, rolled his pant legs up and stood by, dashing in to rescue his nephew whenever he tumbled. That day, watching him interact with family, I fell another notch in love with Jim Taggart.

I pressed the phone hard against my ear. "He-he's had a stroke—"

"Oh my goodness," Adelle said. "How is that possible?"

"It's a rare type of stroke. We're here in Seattle, at Virginia Mason hospital."

"I can't believe it. Not Jim."

Trembling, I pulled a large white towel off the rack and wrapped it around my shoulders.

At one in the morning, I finished telling Adelle what had happened. She agreed to call his two other sisters.

"You have to get some sleep," she said. "Take care of yourself and Glen. We love you."

That day, I'd read that 12 percent of lateral medullary stroke patients died within a few days. I did not mention this.

8

TAMP THE FLAMES

I splashed cold water on my face and dressed. Before leaving, I scrawled a note for Glen, envious of his full-bore sleep.

In the lobby, I twisted a spigot and watched feeble coffee drizzle into a paper cup. I sat in a wingback chair by the hotel phone and called Brendan. "Thank you for offering to send some of our things from home."

"No problem. A bunch of us up here would like to help." His confident, deep voice made me feel as if he were right there again with me. "Just give the word, and we're on it."

I sat tall and read my list, acting like the composed person I needed to be. "Jim's new cell phone and laptop—on the kitchen counter; red rain jacket in the front closet; a couple of—"

"Hold on," Brendan said.

I paused, visualizing his slanted print on a yellow memo pad. "Five shirts from our closet—those short-sleeved, button-down, cotton ones."

"Got it."

"Three pairs of those cargo shorts he always wears. They're in the bedroom dresser, third drawer. Seven boxers and pairs of socks, bottom drawer."

I read off the list for Glen.

"We really appreciate this." I filled in the silence as he wrote. "What about you?" he asked.

"Oh, yeah." I'd left myself off the list. I thought a moment. "Five shirts and three pairs of pants from the closet would be great." My mind stalled, then slipped into autopilot, as if speaking faster might make the rest of my answer less embarrassing. "And . . . some underwear. Top left drawer. Same dresser as Jim's."

On no, I thought after hanging up. I had just asked my former boss to grab a handful of my bikini underwear and shove them into a duffel. Did I throw away that worn-out pair? Please let those not be on the top.

Spiral notebook held like a hymnal, I paged to the next list: respond to emails, find a library, check voicemail, add money to AT&T calling card. Using the lobby phone, I retrieved messages from our landline in Juneau. Word was spreading. Jim's other two sisters, my six siblings, a cousin from Portland, and several colleagues had called. Dianne, Kim, and Brendan had also checked in. Our real estate agent left a message: Why weren't we answering her calls?

The next recording hit me hardest. "Hey, Beth, it's Bill." Bill Brown was my friend, an economist whose office was next to mine at the university. Over the years he'd become part of my family—close friends with Jim and like an uncle to Glen. "I hope everything's going as well as possible." His voice sounded shaky like I felt. "If you could call me, I'd really appreciate it. Love you guys."

I'd never heard Bill say that. I blinked away the urge to crumble into his telephonic embrace.

Back in our room, Glen dozed as if it were a sport and he the champion: head back, one arm flung out. I composed an email to let family and friends know what had happened. I copied ninety addresses from a spreadsheet, reformatted them in a Word document, pasted them into the email recipient box, and pressed SEND. The outgoing message stalled and churned. Fifteen minutes later, the taskbar nudged to 70 percent. Each glance at my watch increased my frustration. Moments later, the hotel's wireless connection broke. *No!*

While Glen showered, I divided the addresses into three batches.

Ready to go, our nine-year-old stood next to me. "What're you doing?"

"I've got to get this last batch out. The internet's not cooperating."

"Let's *go*."

"Give me *one* minute." Hating my irritable tone, I gave up waiting and left the computer grinding. In the elevator, I remembered a website my student Rusty had mentioned—CaringBridge. It had been established to help people in a medical crisis.

On the walk to the hospital, Glen decided we should skip. "Wow. This feels good," I said, once my arms and legs remembered the rhythm. The hopping stride seemed to knock pockets of stress out of my body.

Our antics reminded me of a study that found that even faking a smile reduced stress.

"We skipped here," Glen told Jim when we burst into his room.

Confused, Jim tilted his head.

Glen pumped out two more high-stepping strides.

"Oh. N-nice." His hiccups had returned. While the two of them talked, I timed the involuntary spasms: one every four seconds, more frequent than the day before.

Glen left to do homework, and I brought Jim a big cup of ice. He lifted a scoop of the slivers to his mouth. "Geez. I could use a drink of water." He took a third spoonful. Then, he was choking—that same ragged cough. I pounded his back.

He raised a hand, fingers splayed, signaling *I'm okay*. But no air was going into his lungs; it was only coming out. I turned and ran down the hall. Not this. Not again.

I found the nurse on duty. "My husband's choking. He can't breathe!" I ran back.

Hunched over, he coughed, face red.

She strode in, saying, "You're okay." She touched his shoulder. "Swallow, then inhale through your nose. Good. Let it out slowly through your mouth."

The choking subsided.

My hands shook. I turned away to tamp the flames of fear, so quick to ignite. I'd overreacted.

Soon Rebecca, a perky young woman with auburn hair, stopped by to do his physical therapy intake test. She helped him pivot to the edge of the bed, then, facing him, placed his hands on her shoulders. He stood slowly.

"How's that feel?"

"Strange," he said. "Like the floor is moving."

"Well, you've got strength. That'll make a big difference." She locked her eyes on his. "Take three steps—with me."

If not for Jim's flimsy hospital garb and awkward tilt, Rebecca could have been his dance instructor. His foot rose with a lurch. Alarm swept across his face.

Glen pulled on my sleeve. I leaned down. "Why's it so hard for Dad to walk?" he whispered.

"I'll explain later."

After a few steps, Rebecca guided Jim back to the bed.

He looked dejected.

"Don't worry. Once you're in rehab, we'll work you. We'll have you walking soon." Rebecca wrote on his chart and smiled at him. "High-intensity training starts tomorrow."

After she left, I went to his side. "She's good. I liked her."

He gazed out the window. "Yeah." His voice was flat. I'd expected working with her to cheer him up.

"What's this?" I pointed to a ten-inch blotch of sweat on his gown. "You're all wet under this armpit, but barely damp on the left." I tickled his dry side.

He raised his head to look. "Asymmetric sweating's another symptom," he muttered. Despite my playful attempt he remained glum.

"You okay?"

He huffed. "I-I don't want to talk about it."

I rubbed his shin. Please don't shut me out, I thought.

Midafternoon, a woman from the pharmacy arrived with a booklet on Coumadin, the oral anticoagulant ordered to replace the heparin in his IV fluid.

I asked if Coumadin was the same as warfarin, the rat poison.

"It is. At low doses, it's an effective blood thinner. But of course, the relative doses and desired outcomes in rats versus our patients are . . . well . . . very different."

She and I smiled.

Jim didn't catch her puff of humor.

She explained they would test his blood daily until they got the dose right. "Be careful to not get injured, since your bleeding risk is high. Also, no aspirin, ibuprofen, or green tea. They also reduce clotting."

He asked her how long he'd be on the drug.

"Your doctor will decide that." She set a brochure on the bedside table. "Be sure to read this. And also no more than two glasses of alcohol a day."

"Hmm." His eyes glimmered. "Can I start those tonight?"

Finally, a hint of humor.

Glen and I were camped in Jim's room as usual, backpacks, playing cards, and papers scattered around. I'd avoided conversation, afraid of being pulled down further by Jim's bleak mood. Late in the afternoon, a voice boomed through the curtain.

"Hey, Tag!" Mike Sharp, a career law enforcement ranger we knew from Glacier Bay, swung the curtain aside.

Glen hopped off the bed.

"Look at you, Mr. Tall." Mike grinned at our son and raised a fist. Glen punched up at it, prancing, and they both said, "Up high!" and "Down low!"

"I got you!" Glen shouted and jumped.

Mike grabbed him around the waist and flipped him upside down. "You're gettin' too big to tickle." Glen laughed and squirmed, face red. Mike set him back down, then noticed the papers taped to the wall. "Aw, man. They got you eatin' baby food."

"Barely enough at that." Jim pressed his fists down, lifting his back up against the headboard.

"So. What're they tellin' you?"

I was trying to decide if Glen and I should stay or go.

"Everyone keeps saying I'll be fine," Jim said. "They're moving me to rehab tomorrow. Th-they say I'm going to pull through." Jim shook his head. "I'm no fool." He pressed his hands on his thighs. "Man, I can't fuckin' walk."

I shot Jim a raised eyebrow reminder of our unspoken agreement to not use that word in front of our son. My maternal telegraph bounced back—unanswered. But his mood had shifted from despair to anger—an improvement.

"Hey, hon. Glen and I are going to do those errands. Mike, I'm so glad you came."

"You couldn't 'a kept me away."

As Glen and I gathered jackets and packs, Jim said to Mike, "They're talking about walkers and canes. What-what I want to know is if I'll be able to go deer hunting again. Ride my bike. Snorkel for Dungies."

"Jesus, Jim." Mike's face turned serious. "I'm still tryin' to make sense out of how this could happen to you."

❟ ❟ ❟

After saying goodnight to Jim, Glen and I stood in the entry to a small restaurant on the ground floor of the Inn at Virginia Mason. Hungry and tired, I couldn't face another meal on a lime-green plastic tray in the fluorescent din of the hospital cafeteria.

The tables were dressed in white linen, burgundy napkins, and gleaming stemware. A man in a suit led us to a corner. He held my chair and handed us leather menus. While the busboy poured water, the waiter described the evening's special: grilled chicken with fresh green beans and herb-roasted potatoes. At two other tables, couples spoke quietly, beneath the soothing acoustic guitar soundtrack, as if we'd traveled back decades to a candlelit microcosm of genteel calm.

"I'll have a glass of the Pinot Grigio." Did I sound too eager? This was our first unrushed meal since the stroke.

The waiter delivered a basket of rolls with my wine. Glen folded back the red cloth, chose one, and tore it apart. I brought the cool wine to my lips. The next day, Jim would be transferred from critical care to rehab. We'd finally made it beyond the tidal wave that had slammed and engulfed us.

"How're you doing?" I asked.

Glen finished chewing and swallowed. "Good. I'm about done with my book, though. Can we go to a library tomorrow?"

"Sure."

"You said you'd tell me why Dad can't walk." He loaded butter onto another golden roll.

"One reason is because his inner ear was messed up by the stroke. Not his hearing, but these special fluid-filled tubes that detect gravity and movement. The stroke screwed up the wiring connected to those organs. His brain can't quite tell which way is up. That's why he leans to the left and feels dizzy."

"Will he be normal again?"

I took a long drink of water. "His brain has to rewire itself. They say he'll be able to stand up straight—eventually."

"And walk?"

I nodded, swallowing hard to suppress my doubts.

"How about if you write a letter to Tenzing while we wait for dinner?" I handed him a notepad and pencil.

My son craned over the paper, his handwriting like his father's—almost illegible. They are so alike, I thought: curious and driven to learn, solve, and explore.

I pulled out a Hewlett Packard pocket PC from my purse and plugged it into the trifold keyboard Jim had bought months earlier. He'd been excited to discover the cutting-edge portable technology. I'd been too busy to take much advantage of his progressive purchase. As I added to my list, the feel of the keyboard—or was it the alcohol?—triggered an unexpected urge. I took another sip of wine, appreciating the subdued lighting and anonymity. A spare sequence of words flowed onto the tiny screen, like a poem.

Brush Strokes Skylight

Neck bent, brush strokes skylight.
Blood flow diverted.
He coughs, staggers, drops.
Please. No.
Sirens wail.

Artery dissected.
Brain denied, eyes jitter.
Muscled legs disobey.
Please. No.
Learjet races emerald night.

Assumptions implode.
Smooth love, abraded,

Those words, my last?
Please. No.
Recent discord echoes.

Trapped within
Step, stop, step.
He questions living.
Wheelchair ménage à trois?
Please. No.
Neuroplasticity alluded.

Neck bent over paper, our child writes.
Father's blood flows with mine.
Abandon him?
Please. No.
His dreams, our daylight.

What makes a poem? I wondered. The bare-bones outpouring on the keyboard cooled my seared soul, like rain on flowing lava.

The waiter arrived with our salads, his polite presence a welcome interruption to my mind's ricochet between hope and fear.

9

PRIME CANDIDATE

I groped for the blaring alarm. Five o'clock already? I shoved dirty clothes into a pillowcase and carried the bundle down to the hotel's coin laundry.

Back in the room, I poured water into the coffeemaker, thankful Glen was a sound sleeper. Outside, starlings squabbled over a morsel of garbage. A hazy dawn loomed beyond the downtown skyline.

Transcribing messages of concern and support from our answering machine in Juneau, I felt deep appreciation but also overwhelmed. How could I possibly respond to everyone? Hearing Sherry Tamone's supportive voice reminded me of work I'd left dangling, although she didn't mention work. I had a final exam to create and grade for Behavioral Ecology, a stack of papers to review for another course, emails from students to answer. At least I'd already submitted grades for my field research course.

Thoughts of wrapping up the semester made my head cramp. That life was so distant. The tables had flipped—work usually came before Jim. I wanted to lower my teaching responsibilities into the deep freeze, come back to them later. Yet, I couldn't leave students in limbo. I shut my eyes. The words "cleansing breath" came to mind. Dianne had used the phrase. Three cycles in and out. Let it go.

I opened my laptop and typed in keywords. A site called Car-ingBridge surfaced. The first page spoke to me. "A health crisis throws everything into chaos. Because your family and friends care, questions and phone calls won't stop. . . ." The site said I could create a "centralized, private place to share health updates and request help." Whoever created this website understood what I needed. In the title box, I typed *Jim's Story* and froze. What to say? How to say it?

I had to get word out about the situation. Pulled from frag-mented memories and notes, I wrote a letter to family and friends. I took a break to wake Glen so he could shower. Back at the table, second mug of coffee at hand, I reviewed my message, realiz-ing it would also reach colleagues, the university's chancellor and dean of my department, Jim's state and federal collaborators, as well as friends and family. I hesitated. What I'd written was too personal. I needed to create a second professional version of my letter. I must have whimpered at the prospect.

Glen appeared at my side and tugged my sleeve. "Mom, let's go!"

I rubbed my neck, bit a nail, and pressed submit.

The morning at the hospital unfolded with more tests and med-ications, another session with the speech therapist, more cups of shaved ice for Jim, coffee for me. Glen and I left before noon to buy pajamas for ourselves and shoelaces for Jim. Ironic, I thought, he'd asked for those, given he can't walk. Is it because his feet are what he stares at all day?

Glen and I found a bookstore where he bought the next *Warriors* book, part of a fantasy series about four clans of wild cats. I chose the year's *Best American Short Stories*, a comfort-food-for-the-brain habit I'd adopted from my mother. At a café, we ordered lunch and read our new treasures until sandwiches and soup arrived. Before leaving the Wi-Fi bubble, I purchased a subscription to Audible.com and downloaded *The Audacity of Hope* by Barack Obama, which Jim had requested.

While we were gone, Jim had gotten help bathing. He wore a fish-print shirt and cargo shorts. I loved seeing him in regular clothes instead of a flimsy, neutering gown.

Soon after Glen left to read in the waiting room, Dr. Cortez arrived and confirmed Jim would be discharged from critical care to rehab that afternoon. "You're a prime candidate for physical and speech therapy."

We both perked up.

"Dr. Zenkel runs an excellent program. Before the discharge, though, I need to review your neurological issues with you and your wife."

I retrieved my notebook and stepped closer.

Cortez described how Jim's lateral medullary stroke had been caused by an acute dissection of his left vertebral artery which damaged neurons that control muscles used to speak, swallow, walk, and move his eyes. "Your nystagmus is better, but you're still at risk for choking."

"One thing that seems odd," Jim said, "is the asymmetric sweating." He raised both arms. His right armpit was soaked, the left side dry.

Dr. Cortez smiled. "You're a classic case."

"But why are my eye and vocal cord symptoms on the left?"

"Good question." The doctor pulled a pen out of his shirt pocket and used it to help explain how the cranial nerves to the face don't cross over, but the tracts associated below the site of the stroke, which control the body, cross from the left to the right side.

"Oh, right. Now that makes sense. So," Jim stiffened his arms to reposition himself, "will I be able to walk again?"

I moved my hand to his thigh.

"Your walking's been compromised on multiple fronts," the doctor said, "balance and vertigo, proprioception—your spatial awareness—and coordination of your leg muscles."

Jim's mustache twitched.

Dr. Cortez described how pressure receptors in our feet trigger motor impulses from the brain to specific muscles, and all those neurons have to be precisely coordinated by the cerebellum. He placed his palm against the back of his head. "And they all pass through the brain stem. Once we've learned to walk, we don't think about it. For several weeks, you'll have to concentrate to walk—like a toddler. That's how you'll stimulate new connections from your legs to your brain. You're building a new highway system."

"How long will that take?"

"Mmm . . . I'd guess you'll be out on a walker within the week."

"And on my own?"

"Hard to say. More like a couple of months—there's some chance you'll need a cane after that."

Jim worked his jaw. "Will I ever get back to normal?"

The doctor said most progress happened in the first two to three months, with a plateau at three. "We usually see what we call functional recovery in six months to a year, ninety to ninety-five percent of what you'd consider normal. Some symptoms may linger, like sweating more on one side and issues with your eye, swallowing, and balance. With rehab, your prognosis is good."

I'd expected him to say "excellent."

"The harder you work now, the better." He slid his pen back into his pocket.

"What about these friggin' hiccups?"

Dr. Cortez thumbed to a page on the clipboard. "Let's see. We've tried Reglan and chlorpromazine. We don't see enough cases like yours with hiccups to put a probability on when they'll stop. Could be days or weeks—rarely, months."

"Jah-ee-sus." Jim shook his head.

A cheerful orderly pushed a cart into the room. "Good afternoon." She stopped in front of the small porcelain sink and opened the mirrored cabinet. "I'll be taking these." She pulled out a plastic-wrapped razor and a miniature can of shaving cream. "They don't want you shaving with a blade."

"Why not?" Jim asked.

"With Coumadin, even a nick could cause a bleed." She turned to me. "You'll need to buy him an electric razor."

I opened my notebook.

"Could I have that?" Glen pointed to the red-and-white striped canister.

She read the label. "I don't see why not."

He looked as happy as if she'd given him a remote-controlled airplane.

When she asked Jim if there was anything he needed, he quipped, "How about a grilled steak?"

Rolling the squeaky cart out the door, she saluted. "I'll see what I can do, sir."

In the mirror, we watched Glen squirt a frothy mound of shaving cream into a cupped hand. He blew on it, spattering white dots onto the sink and mirror. Nozzle aimed at his index finger, he traced the length of it and dabbed a foamy strip above his lip.

Gazing at our reflections, he spoke in a lowered voice, "Hey look. I'm Dad."

His antics made me laugh until my cheeks hurt. Jim's lopsided smile lit the room like a sunrise.

At the hotel, I showered and crawled into bed earlier than any other night. "How's your book?" I asked Glen.

Two pillows supported his head. "Great. Thanks for letting me get it. This part's pretty scary, though. Graypaw's about to be attacked by Shadowclan."

I wrote in my journal and within minutes clicked off my light. "Your dad seemed pretty good today," I said.

"Yeah. Better. How long d'you think we'll be here?"

"I'm not sure." I felt drained, weighted down as if the blanket had turned to lead. "A while though."

"Hmm." He looked at the ceiling, brow furrowed, then returned to his book.

"Good night, hon." I rolled away from his light. "Love you."

"Love you."

"Don't stay up too late."

"Okay. Love you."

"Love you."

The next morning, on our way to the rehabilitation unit instead of intensive care, we waited for an elevator. After several minutes, Glen suggested we take the stairs instead, declaring, "We never have to wait for them to be free." He lugged open the heavy door. "Let's race! Ready. Set. Go!"

We pounded up the steps, foot slams echoing through the concrete tower. We zigged and zagged, startling a medic on her way down. I gained a few paces, but he soon stole back the lead. When we pushed through onto Jim's floor, we shifted gears, dialing down through giddy energy, like rowdy teenagers entering a church.

After that, we often raced up the stairwell. Those bursts of playful competition let off tension, creating a brief respite from the unending questions: What will Jim's mood be today? What will his therapists tell us? Will the neurologist check in?

As we hustled along the hall to his new room, I thought about Chuck's call the night before asking if Jim would be up for a visit from a few friends. We'd known Chuck and Fawn sixteen years, since our first days at Glacier Bay. They'd recently moved from Alaska to Washington with their two children. Chuck was the chief ranger at Mount Rainier National Park. Fawn, an outdoor education teacher, worked as a park naturalist.

Behind the curtain, Jim sat tall in bed, dressed in his own shirt and shorts. He drew us in for a three-way hug. "Can you believe it? There's even a window." The natural light made the corner room feel bigger.

"You look good." I traced my knuckles across his stubbly cheek, then nibbled his neck. "Smell good, too."

He snugged an arm around my waist.

"And how do you feel?" I asked.

"B-better. I have a quiz for you two. What's different?"

We looked around. His muscular legs were on top of the blanket, crossed at the ankles, feet in the same turquoise booties with nonskid dots on the bottoms.

"You're wearing real clothes?" I asked.

"That was new yesterday. Glen, what's different?" Jim raised his arms, wrists cocked up like he was about to take flight.

Glen studied Jim, then blurted, "No tubes!"

"You got it. No more tethers. They finally took me off the drip bag."

Hips against the bed rail, I smoothed Jim's hair. From his mother, he'd inherited thick hair that only required ten seconds of fingertip attention to look like he'd shaped it with a blow-dryer. "Chuck called."

In Alaska, we'd shared Friday happy hours with Chuck and Fawn, as well as lively dinners, overnight boating and fishing adventures, and countless hikes along burbling streams with their two children.

I relayed Chuck's proposed visit with their daughter, Kiana, and another mutual friend and his son from Alaska. "Mike Sharp might drive out, too. It'd be a Glacier Bay mini-reunion. What do you think?"

Jim tapped his fingertips against the bedding. "I'm not so sure."

"We can keep it short."

He gazed out the window. "It's not that." His jaw worked as he searched for words. "I-I'm not ready for people to see me like this." He looked at his body with distaste in a manner I'd never witnessed.

"Oh, honey." I took his hand. "You're doing great. It's Saturday. That's why they can visit. We could delay, but with the kids in school, it'd be next week, and no guarantee they could all come then."

"I'd like to see them. It's just. . . ." His mouth squirmed as he thought.

"They really want to see you."

A minute passed.

"Okay. You can say yes."

"There's another thing." I lowered my voice so Glen wouldn't hear. "I need your advice. Chuck and Fawn offered to have Glen come back with them to Eatonville—spend a few days there."

"No kidding. How nice," Jim rasped.

My first reaction to Chuck's offer had been positive. If I had more time in the morning, I could take care of university work and finish setting up the CaringBridge website. But a secondary jab of insecurity had followed: Glen's positive outlook made every day better. Still, Forrest, Kiana, and Skylar, another friend's son, had been my buddies in Glacier Bay through the tick-tocking decade when I ached for a child of my own. I wanted our son to know them. I could deal with a few days of separation.

"How long?" Jim asked.

"What's that?" Glen looked up from the floor where he was reading.

"Chuck and Fawn invited you to spend a couple of nights with them. They have two dogs now, and Kiana recently got a horse. It's a sweet place—five acres in the country. Do you remember their dog, Kitka?"

He shook his head.

"We took care of him one weekend in Juneau when he was a puppy."

"Oh yeah." He smiled. "I remember. Black and white—*sooo* cute." He cradled his arms as if holding him.

"You could hang out with Forrest and Kiana. And Skylar lives close by. What do you think?"

"Well." Glen gazed down the corridor, considering the prospect. "I'm not so sure."

His reluctance caught me off guard. "You'd have a great time. They have a trampoline."

"Hmm." His expression relaxed, then tensed as he gazed at his father. "I'd rather stay here."

Jim glanced at me, also surprised.

I wondered whether our son had somehow detected my conflict about having him leave. I visualized him running and playing outdoors, thriving in Fawn's creative light, immersed in their rural haven.

"Let's wait and see how you feel after they're here," Jim said.

Around midday, our friends arrived carrying boxes, one with books on tape for Jim, another filled with games. A boisterous exchange of hugs and greetings enlivened the room.

Jim perked up, amusing everyone with his husky, ex-smoker-like voice. "Thanks so much for driving out." The glint in his eyes returned.

The kids headed down the hall with the Legos and game boxes, leaving the adults gathered around Jim's bed.

Later, as the visit was breaking up, I pulled Glen aside. "What do you think about going with them?" Across the room,

Jim was engaged in a lively discussion with the three men. "Your dad's doing well. It's okay if you leave."

He twisted his mouth. "I guess . . . I would like to go."

We hurried back to the hotel and packed his bag.

At the hospital, after we'd hugged goodbye, I watched our son trot down the hall, the smallest in the animated pack of friends. So much gratitude filled me, it spilled down my cheeks.

10

ABOUT THAT MORNING

Crouched in front of a display of electric shavers in the neighborhood pharmacy—Gillette, Norelco, Panasonic—I could not decide which brand or type to buy. With Glen gone, the morning felt bleak. "What's the difference between a floating and a rotary head?" I muttered to no one in particular. Jim had always used a basic two-blade razor. Rechargeable or corded? I wanted to get out of the fluorescent drugstore and be with him.

"May I help you?" A man with a clip-on name tag loomed next to me.

Startled, I stood too fast. I put my hand on a shelf and said, "Too many choices. All I need is an electric razor for my husband. Nothing fancy."

"How about this one." He rested chubby fingers on a mid-priced brand. "We sell a lot of these."

"Perfect. Thank you."

Choosing an umbrella was as frustrating. Compact pop-out or old style, stiletto-tipped? Automatic or manual release? Solid fabric or splashed with perky tulips? I rubbed my forehead, aware my impatience exceeded the situation's complexity.

I draped my wet jacket over Jim's door. When we kissed, his sandpaper stubble triggered a shiver of desire and sadness.

"I-I was hoping you'd be here sooner."

"I stopped to buy you an electric razor." I gave him the p

"Oh, thanks." He massaged his jaw. "I suppose I cou. shave."

I touched his cheek. "I like it like this, but another day or two . . ." I shook my head. I sat on the bed and massaged his foot. "There's something I've been meaning to ask."

"What's that?"

"About that morning. When you were lying on the floor"

His upper lip twitched—nearly a snarl.

"Why did you take off your coveralls? You were having a hard time breathing. Do you remember?"

He stared out the window, mouth tense. "Yeah." He paused. "I remember."

"What was going on?"

"Well. I-uh. This will sound crazy. It-it's not logical, but what was going through my mind was I didn't want to be in an ambulance wearing those dirty coveralls. I didn't want to die a slob."

"Oh, honey." I tightened my grip around his ankle.

"It's weird how a thought like that pops up. I had to get them off."

I nodded once and waited for a hailstorm of emotion to recede. "Another question. When Glen was there with you. What crossed your mind?"

He looked away.

The wheels of a delivery cart rumbled down the hallway.

"You shut your eyes. What was that about?"

Seconds churned by.

"I . . ." he rubbed the back of his neck, "I didn't want him in the room. I thought I was going out. That it was all over." His eyes narrowed. "I wasn't afraid. But I was very sad. I thought. I . . . I thought." He swallowed. "I assumed I had a lot more time." A muscle in his jaw tensed. "I did not want him in the room. I did not want my son's last memory of me to be of my death."

73

, , ,

Midmorning, a dark-haired young woman entered on a buoyant step, pulling a walker. "Hi. I'm Annika." She set a canvas bag beside the bed. "I'll be one of your physical therapists." A glance over five-foot-two, she was compact and muscled. She tucked a strand of shoulder-length hair behind an ear. "So, Jim. You've had a stroke and haven't walked now for five days."

"Six," he said. "Too long."

"Let's get you belted up and moving." She pulled a long, three-inch wide strap from her bag. The fabric layers were stitched in long rows like a karate belt. "This gait belt will help us keep you from falling."

Annika sat beside him and looped the belt twice around his waist. He took the ends from her and tied a safety half-hitch.

"Looks like you know knots," she said.

"I-I've done some climbing."

That's an understatement, I thought.

"Cool." Annika pulled the metal walker to him and grasped the belt above his hip. "I'll keep you from leaning too far. The walker will keep you from falling forward. On the count of three, let's stand."

Seeing Jim's hands on a walker felt wrong. My husband was a runner and an avid hiker, someone who initiated ten-day back-country skiing expeditions into Alaska's Chugach mountains.

The two rose together, his feet planted wide.

"Get your bearings. We'll go out the door and back."

"I better be able to go farther than that," he grumbled.

Even with Annika stabilizing and a walker, he leaned to the left.

"I'm ready."

"Start with your weaker side."

His right foot jittered up and forward, then landed with a lurch.

"Careful." Annika tugged hard on the belt. "Small steps." They continued out the door into the hallway. She counterbalanced his six-foot frame, leveraging him against her hip, generating more control than a woman her size should have had, like an ant carrying a leaf across the forest floor.

With each pulse forward, the walker squealed. "Look ahead to the end of the hall."

He lifted the next foot, paused to rebalance, then continued step-sway-step.

"Great. You're doing great." Annika's confidence emanated like sunshine.

This man who had run cross-country track like a gazelle, climbed Grand Teton mountain in winter, now moved as if he had robot legs. Even from behind, I felt his concentration like a vibration. The fundamental flow of walking without thinking had been erased—rubbed out.

Arms tight across my waist, I fought the urge to sidle in and help.

The next morning, I set my purse and coffee on the table and kissed Jim's forehead. He was awake and alert.

"Can you believe it?" He was agitated. "They woke me up before dawn to put in a goddamned urinary catheter."

"Why do you need one?"

"I don't," he snapped. "It's absurd. They ordered it because I'm not peeing enough."

"And why's a catheter such a big deal?"

"Jesus!" He was riled. "If I can't piss in a toilet—or under a tree—I might as well throw in the towel. You pull the plug when that happens. As soon as they get one in, there's no going back."

"Scooch over." I pressed in close along the narrow edge and leaned back onto the pillows. The heat from his body and contact from bicep to thigh calmed me. It was odd, but I found his angry energy amusing—a relief compared to his earlier steaming silence. We held hands and talked. Then he rolled on top of me. We kissed like illicit lovers—finally alone—no longer a stroke patient and his advocate wife. I turned my head, laughter and guilt jumbled into one heap as if we were high schoolers necking in his parents' basement. I liked having his full weight on top of me. He nuzzled my neck, sending a shiver to my pelvis.

When a nurse walked in, we were making out.

I scrambled off the bed, smoothing my clothes. Suddenly, we were those two teens caught by his mother.

Not amused, the woman said, "Mr. Taggart. I understand you don't want a urinary catheter."

"That's right." He scrunched up taller, raking his fingers through his tousled hair.

"We're not getting the evacuation levels we need. If you don't want a catheter, you've got to increase the volume going into that cup in the bathroom. If you can do that by this afternoon, we'll skip the catheter—for now. If you can't, we have to put one in. Doctor's orders."

After she left, we looked at each other wide-eyed.

"How-how about if you load up *two* big cups of ice?"

We choked on our stifled laughter.

On the sixth morning since "the accident" as Jim called it, I entered his room, winded from taking stairs two at a time. He sat tall with earbuds in, deep in thought.

"Hey, sweetie," I said.

He pulled his earbuds out.

I stood back, eyebrows raised.

"What?"

I pointed at the board. "That." In confident blue marker, someone had written, Release Date: May 7th. "We get to go home in nine days." We slapped palms together in a high-five.

After he woke from a nap, we sat side by side on the hospital bed.

"I called Glen."

"How's he?"

"Good. He told me he got to feed the chickens and pet Kiana's new horse. He's played computer games with Forrest and jumped on their trampoline. I'm glad he's there."

"You should go, too. Spend a night with Chuck and Fawn."

"Maybe." Fingers laced with three of his, I couldn't imagine leaving.

Moments later, a question popped out. "What else do you remember about that morning?" I asked. "Before the stroke?"

He stared ahead at the wall. "I-I woke up early. I . . ." He bit his lip. "I wanted to make love. I thought about waking you, but decided to let you sleep." He gazed out the window. "It was still dark. I went into the kitchen. Made espresso, then sat in the living room and updated my lists for selling the house and getting the boat ready for the Sitka trip. At six thirty I brought you coffee. I still wanted you. I was hoping you'd be up for it."

Hearing his version of that morning was strange, like seeing myself through the other side of a mirror. I'd relived those hours over and over: during the two-hour Learjet flight, the first night in Seattle, and nights alone in the narrow hotel bed. What could I have done differently?

"But you were so distracted about work," he continued. "I could feel it the way you held your coffee." His version of the morning had the same number of puzzle pieces, but their shapes were different from those in my worn-out, replayed account.

"It was my last week of teaching. I had a lot to do—"

"You always do," he interrupted.

Now, sitting beside him, his chest rising and falling, voice made raspy by the stroke, those work demands felt trivial. "That's one time it was good I wasn't in the mood," I said, voice low, even though we were alone. I'd imagined how awful it would have been if Jim had had the stroke during intercourse. I would have blamed our shared intimacy, convinced it had caused the blood vessel dissection.

He sat forward and turned to face me. "Is that what you think?" He stared as if I'd told him I didn't believe in evolution. "If we *had* made love, I wouldn't have done the touch-up job on the skylight, and I-I wouldn't have had the stroke."

I pulled my hand from his. "What?" Could he possibly believe his stroke was my fault? I stared back, pressure building as I suppressed a defensive outburst. How could our views be so different?

That night, alone in the hotel room, I lay awake. I could not accept that my saying no to Jim's invitation had caused his stroke. The doctors had said the scraping and painting—the coughing fit during dinner the night before—most likely contributed. Even so, I could not ignore the strands of truth in his interpretation. My broader failure to embrace our life together, to cherish it as a fragile entity, rather than scratching it in at the bottom of a to-do list, had nudged us toward diverging tracks. If I'd been more available, as a partner and a lover, perhaps he would have managed those difficult months leading up to the stroke with less strain on his mental and physical state.

For two decades he'd been inspired and invigorated as a marine ecologist studying the effects of marine reserves in Glacier Bay. Starting from scratch—without a research vessel—he brought together a team of top scientists, staff, and grad students to study how no-fishing zones might help stabilize or enhance commercially harvested populations of fish and crabs. In year three, he and sea otter biologist Jim Bodkin negotiated an unprecedented time-share solution with fellow scientists to purchase and convert a used, fifty-foot commercial salmon seiner into a research vessel. A champion of the park's international value as a marine reserve, he and his team published papers on the effectiveness of high-latitude ecological reserves. His work provided a meaningful and stable base to our lives.

But the transition from Clinton's progressive conservation policies to the George W. Bush administration, which beat back existing environmental regulations, had been rough for his agency. Under Bush II, functional gag orders descended on some federal scientists, constraining research on climate change and marine reserves. Those high-level edicts—and some missteps on Jim's part—coupled with having an inspiring, broad-thinking boss replaced by a micromanaging one, drained his spirit and corroded his health. The situation became bad enough that he formulated a plan to retire early and continue working as an independent contractor.

I hadn't wanted him to leave his federal job, afraid it might not be good for him and that doing so could put our family at financial risk. For months, I witnessed the toll the new regime extracted—he didn't sleep well, and his weight and cholesterol levels rose. Finally, I agreed to his exit strategy.

He wrapped up key projects and helped his staff transition to reasonable alternatives and then retired at fifty-six and a half, the exact day he could do so with health benefits for our family. His plan was to morph from agency scientist into the subcontractor for building us an energy-efficient house north of town and become an independent research biologist.

A problem with the plan was that I loved our neighborhood and the home where we were raising our son. I worried even a small house would take longer than we expected to design and build, cost more than budgeted, and that all the little choices—from light fixtures and appliances to doorknobs and toilets—would wear us down, burn through our life energy. I knew a couple who had spent three years planning and managing construction, then divorced three months after moving into their sparkling house. Neither of us had a smoldering desire to build a home. Would the

n eliminate other dreams, like his desire to sail our boat
m ocean? Who would we blame for lost opportunities?

His departure from the federal government backed us into a
negative feedback loop. He didn't like how much I worked, but
without his income, I needed to work more to earn more.

When the city opened a lottery for parcels of land, we bought
a spruce-covered acre on the outskirts of Juneau. We hiked the
densely forested slope at Lena Point with our son, climbing over
fallen trees through canopy-filtered rays of light. New spears of
skunk cabbage melted their way up through lingering patches
of snow. Glen balance-walked across the trunk of a fallen,
four-foot-diameter spruce. Its splayed roots clenched blue sky,
like giant grieving fingers. Devil's club leaves the size of an ele-
phant's ears caught light like ancient umbrellas on spiny stalks.
Squirrels chittered at us from above. We peered up through binoculars at a bald eagle nest on the adjacent property. Jim adjusted
the house plan to include a higher deck platform where we could
watch gangly eagle chicks hatch and fledge.

We hired a contractor to excavate a steep driveway, haul in
boulders and rocks, and scrape out a small foundation. Money
poured out of our account into the rustic hillside.

And then his vertebral artery delaminated.

A door slammed, bringing me back to the hotel room. How
could I have assumed his health was a given? Had my buried
resentment over his leaving a secure job contributed to the stroke
by pushing us apart? Alone in the dark room, my mind zeroed
in on our conflicts before the stroke. The harsh echo of Jim's
blameful words that morning stirred doubt into my view of us as
a strong couple.

The fact that they were slipping
away isn't set up early enough.
When he blames her, it
seems cruel because the
sense to this point is of
mutual devotion
sans major problems.

11

SLIPPING

Like a travel-weary couple in an airport terminal, Jim listened to a podcast while I flipped through a magazine. We were still simmering from hot to warm over our alternate views of what caused his stroke. The phone rang.

"Hey, Beth." It was our friend Lesley, a veterinarian from Juneau we knew through Bill Brown. "I'm in Seattle for a doctor's appointment. I'd like to drop by to see Jim."

I covered the receiver and relayed her offer.

He shook his head, mouthing, "Not today."

I stared back until he nodded.

Lesley arrived, dark shiny hair worn down, rather than bundled in a tight knot. She glanced around the room and said, "This is the shits."

Interest ignited Jim's expression. While he scooted to a more upright position, I hugged our friend.

Whenever she visited us in Juneau, her stories of dog and cat surgeries, and her interesting travels, peppered with unfiltered language, made me check to make sure Glen was beyond earshot. She set a woven basket on the bed. "I smuggled in some contraband—real food. You gotta have a break from the crap they serve. Here's some guacamole and a round of Brie."

"Wow. Thank you. What brings you to Seattle?" Jim rasped.

going to give you two time to talk." I gathered up my jacket and left.

Grateful for a break, I walked to the hotel. Raindrops spattering my hood made me feel closed in, alone. Seeing Lesley, I found it hard to believe that a week earlier we'd been in Juneau, caught up in the demands of my job, prepping the house to sell, and parenting. What I'd give to go back to that—do things differently to change the future.

For months, I'd been pulling away from Jim. Had I been afraid to face what wasn't working between us? He wanted me to put more energy into our personal lives, less into my job. I hadn't wanted to. I'd avoided the topic, holding my emotional breath to make it to summer.

At the inn, I returned a few calls and then shoved dirty clothes into the duffel Brendan had used to ship items to us. In the basement, I started a load of laundry. Back in the room, I finished a CaringBridge entry. While moving clothes to the dryer, I argued myself into a run. The spitting rain, Jim's uncertain prognosis, our recent clash—and a craving for Glen's steadying exuberance—made me ache for home. I was stumbling too close to the emotional equivalent of a steep, muddy slope. I pulled on jogging tights and jacket and got out the door before a mudslide of despair engulfed me.

Afterward, I went to the basement to retrieve the laundry. The duffel had been moved. Odd, I thought. Folding and stacking warm, clean clothes into the bag, I savored the simple satisfaction of accomplishing something.

I showered, dressed, and remembered Jim wanted me to bring his cell phone. I unzipped the outside pouch of Brendan's duffel where it had been. No phone. I ran my hand through the other compartments. Where could it be? Had I removed it? *No.* Did it fall out? I hurried back to the basement and searched the table and both washers and each dryer. As before, there was no one else in the room. Ear to the floor, I checked under the machines. Not there. Dust motes only.

"No, ma'am. Nothing turned in today," was the answer to my question at the front desk.

Could someone have stolen it? The thought alone hurt. Not possible. Life is not like that. People here aren't like that.

On the rehab floor, Rebecca waved hello from down the hall. I rounded the curtain to Jim's space, dreading his mood. "Hey, hon. How was your visit?"

"Good. Lesley was right on."

Those were the most positive words I'd heard in days.

"She seemed to get what it's like to be trapped here. Stuck in this body. I-I didn't expect it, but she hit the mark. We had a good conversation. She's scheduled for a lumpectomy tomorrow, to find out if her cancer's spread."

"I forgot she was dealing with breast cancer. She's a tough cookie. So kind of her to stop by."

"Yeah." He reached out and patted the bed for me to lie down.

Head on his pillow, I snuggled in, an arm and leg draped over him. Her visit had broken our logjam.

"Did you remember the cell phone?" We were among the last of our Juneau friends to buy our first cellular phone. His fingers were too big to finesse a normal keypad, so he'd bought a special AT&T model with a slide-out keyboard. We'd owned the novel device one month.

"Bad news. It was stolen."

"What?"

"I forgot it was in a pocket on Brendan's duffel, which I used to carry the laundry. Someone took it while our clothes were drying."

"Damn." Jaw tense, his eyes narrowed.

I climbed onto him, chest to chest. "I'm so sorry."

haled hard. "It's no big deal. Thanks for all you're doing."

I fought back tears. The theft on top of everything else felt like a bad omen.

He rubbed my back. "Really. It's okay."

Soon Dr. Zenkel, head of the Rehab Department, arrived. His salt-and-pepper hair and beard were neatly trimmed as if he'd visited his barber instead of going to lunch. I liked how Zenkel engaged us both. Already fully aware of Jim's history, he asked about his motor skills and led him through the visual test every new doctor had given.

"I see you're still leaning. How's walking?"

"Better. They're letting me go short distances without holding the belt."

"With or without a walker?"

"With."

The doctor was trim and fit, a reassuring attribute for someone leading the physical therapy team.

Jim said he'd recently heard that ideas about the brain's inability to rewire as we age had been challenged. "What do you know about that?"

Zenkel switched gears from doctor-doing-rounds to animated professor. "You're right. There's exciting research coming out. A book was published last year, *The Brain that Changes Itself.* It's a collection of remarkable stories of the brain's plasticity and cutting-edge research."

Jim perked up. "A couple of months ago, I listened to an interview with the author, Norman Doige."

I grabbed my notebook and wrote down the title.

Zenkel told us about a physician who'd had a stroke in the 1950s. Back then, the dogma was human brains were hardwired after about eighteen years. The man lost his ability to walk, but decided to try to retrain himself from the same stage as a baby—crawling. At first, he dragged his body around the house, scraping his knees raw. He pushed himself through the next stages, like a toddler. He became frustrated at his slow progress but eventually, he walked again. "Before that," Zenkel said, "stroke survivors were assumed to be permanently impaired. Patients were sent home with a wheelchair and that was about it."

"No kidding," Jim said.

"Years later an autopsy revealed the section of the man's brain involved in walking and mobility had, as expected, been damaged by the stroke. But cells nearby had been recruited to take over their roles. The doctor's work went unrecognized for decades. New studies reinforce these ideas."

"Fascinating," Jim said.

Zenkel told us about mounting evidence that our brains benefit from hard workouts, just like our muscles. "Every minute a stroke isn't treated, we lose about two million neurons and fourteen billion neural connections. That's about the size of a pea every twelve minutes a stroke goes untreated. If you have more neurons and connections before a stroke, as you probably did," Zenkel gestured to Jim, "recovery tends to be better, because you've lost proportionally fewer. By pushing ourselves to acquire new skills, rather than doing only what's familiar—or what we're already good at—we can keep our brains healthier. The more you challenge yourself—by taking up tennis, say, or a new language or instrument—the more neurons you'll have."

"I'd like to learn more about this," Jim said.

Zenkel shook our hands and said he'd get him a copy of a recent research paper.

After the doctor left, Jim sat taller, engaged and alert in a way that gave me hope we'd turned a corner.

When Chuck returned with Glen, I scooped our boy up. "Sweetheart, how are you?"

He grinned and squirmed as I planted kisses on his rosy cheek. "I've only been gone a couple days." I set him down, tousling his hair.

"We loved having him," Chuck said. "Every chance he got he was out throwing the ball for Kitka and Yukon. We'd have kept him longer, but with the kids in school and us at work, we couldn't."

Glen leaned against Jim. "Dad. You have to see their place. Oh, yeah." He reached in his backpack. "We made this for you." He unfolded a red heart with *Get well soon, Jim!* on it and signed by everyone.

Chuck placed a hand on Jim's shoulder. "I'm sorry I have to make this a tight turnaround."

We thanked him and waved goodbye.

"Hey, Glen," Jim said. "You can help me get better. I'm supposed to play catch to improve hand-eye coordination." He pulled a green ball out from the bedside drawer and tossed it.

Glen caught it and stepped back against the wall. He threw the ball and Jim snatched it with a quick swipe. On the third toss, Jim missed. The ball ricocheted off the sink. Glen slid on his belly under the bed, scooped it up, scrambled out, and threw it back.

Watching them, my shoulder muscles loosened.

"Tonight you get lasagna," said an orderly as he set a tray in front of Jim.

Jim had graduated from a liquid-only diet to nectar-thick purées by the teaspoon. For a man who loved to fish and scheduled fall deer-hunting expeditions to fill our freezer, this diet was a severe step down.

Glen peered at the tray. "Which is the lasagna?"

The orderly hesitated, then pointed to a pinkish purée. "I assume this one."

We exchanged skeptical looks.

Glen's eyebrows rose. "Can I taste it?"

"Uh, sure."

He leaned over the bed and scooped a spoonful of the yogurt-like substance. He made a face before swallowing. "Hmm." The corners of his mouth turned down. "Not as bad as I expected."

Jim took a spoonful. "Edible, perhaps." He squinted at Glen. "But not even the same species as your mom's lasagna."

On our way back to the hotel after saying goodnight, we agreed Jim was doing better.

Glen suggested pizza for dinner. While he showered, I dozed off. When the food arrived, I spread a towel on my bed and opened the warm, cardboard box.

Refreshed and clean in underwear only, Glen pranced impatiently. He lifted the largest pepperoni-dotted triangle above his head with both hands and slid the narrow drooping tip into his mouth. "This is great," he mumbled.

I set a slice on a paper plate and sawed at it using a plastic knife and fork.

He stood, savoring big bites. Between chewing, he sang, "Pizza, pizza, pizza pie." His skinny body danced to the made-up ditty, ending with, "I'm so hungry I could eat the sky."

Watching him made me smile. It had been a long, difficult week with all meals in restaurants or hospital cafeterias. Being there together in the small room put me at ease. I snapped open the Caesar salad we'd ordered to share, stripped cellophane off a plastic fork, and gave it to him.

He set his half-eaten slice on the oil-blotched lid and lifted a wedge of dressed lettuce with his fingers.

"*Hon*-ey." I heard my whiny voice. "*Don't* use your hands to eat salad."

He swallowed, then leaned back onto the other bed, elbows jutted back on the mattress, gears working. Lifting a knobby-kneed leg, he guided a bare foot toward the salad container. His expression expanded to an eye-crinkling smile. His first two toes scissored against each other, hovering over the tray until they snagged a piece of lettuce.

"What are you doing?" Then it hit me: He was obeying.

He raised the foot with the pale green rag of lettuce dangling from it and cocked his leg to deliver the morsel to his mouth. His gyrations made me buckle over with laughter. The harder I laughed, the more absurd his antics became. Without warning, laughter twisted into uncontrollable crying.

Glen stepped in close and asked if I was okay.

Gulping air, I repeated, "It's okay. I'm okay." I held his hand tight. The collision of joy and sorrow was the release I needed.

As I fell asleep, stomach muscles aching, I vowed to never take the sweet taste of normalcy for granted.

12

BEAR TRAP

I woke before first light and reached for Jim. How could I forget? I stared at Glen's smooth face circled by splayed-out too-long hair. Day eight, I thought. Today, we'll find a barber. He slept with one leg sprawled on top of the covers. Half the sheet was twisted out from the side of the narrow bed and wadded over the blanket. I marveled that one sleeping boy could generate so much turmoil. Remembering his salad antics made me smile. Where did he get that sense of humor?

One morning when he was three and a half, we were in the kitchen. He'd dumped out his bucket of magnetic letters, so I joined him on the floor. I arranged five from the colorful medley and asked him what they spelled. He was learning the alphabet.

His lips moved and then he called out, "Donut!"

I removed two and waited.

"Nut."

I added three new letters and he said, "Peanut!"

We were connected in a learning volley, as exhilarating as a sustained tennis rally.

"What would 'peanut' be if we add an *s*?" I asked, sliding the red letter into place.

With an elfish smile, he said, "Dinner!"

Six years later, and my son still made me laugh more than anyone.

While coffee percolated, I looked out the window at the four-story stone building next door. We'd spent all our time at the hospital, venturing outdoors only to eat or buy supplies. With Jim healing, I decided this was the day we could also visit the Seattle Aquarium.

I opened my laptop and navigated to the CaringBridge website. In the electronic guestbook sat forty-three entries. A pulse of gratitude rose so steeply it hurt.

For a quiet hour, I read replies and composed my second entry, invigorated by Jim's improved outlook.

At six thirty I typed, *Thank you all for your support,* and pressed submit. I was standing at the window when the phone rang. Who would call so early? I belly-flopped onto my bed and snatched the receiver off the night table. Glen rolled toward me, eyes closed.

"Hello?" My voice came out hushed like I was involved in a drug deal.

"This is Dr. Royal. I'm calling for Mrs. Taggart."

I didn't recognize the man's voice or name.

"I'm calling about your husband."

"What's wrong?"

"Last night I was the on-call doctor in ICU."

"What's wrong?" I sat up.

"I'm about to leave but wanted to talk to you first." Each sentence sucked air from the room.

"What is it? What's happened?" I clutched the bedsheet.

Glen bolted up and moved to the edge of his bed. He grabbed my free wrist and stared into my eyes.

Dr. Royal continued. "Around three this morning, your husband reported a sudden headache. His blood pressure shot way up—diastolic at or above three hundred, difficult to measure."

No, no! I thought. *This can't be.*

"We're not sure about that reading. He was rushed back to ICU, where I first saw him. We've been trying to stabilize him since, but his pressure keeps spiking. I wanted to tell you before I left. I'm sorry I can't stay. I've been on the floor since yesterday morning. There's a good team working on this. I wanted to tell you, since you'd expect to find him in rehab, and you might want to get here—to intensive care—soon."

Breathing shallow and fast, I thanked him. "We'll be right there." I hung up.

"What's wrong?" Glen asked.

"Your dad's back in ICU. We've got to get to him."

We ran along the carpeted hall, crossed the glassed-in overpass, turned at familiar corners, and sprinted up the stairwell. We pushed through doors into the ICU, a wing we thought we'd left for good. I went to the stall Jim had been in before. Not there. I wanted to shout his name as if he'd gone missing in a dark forest. I veered toward the nurses' station.

"We're here for my husband, Jim Taggart." The attendant sat behind a half wall of glass. "He came in last night—middle of the night."

Her eyebrows rose. Did she know something she couldn't share?

"Bay five, over there," she motioned to the far corner.

We charged in the direction she pointed. Woven blue-gray curtains delineated rectangles of so-called private space. I yanked the curtains apart. Shades were drawn across a high row of windows. A monitor's sharp *Blip! Blip! Blip!* triggered unwanted memories. A nurse stood next to a man lying on a bed. Was this my husband? His face was contorted, as if he'd been seized by a massive bear trap.

"Jim!" I grabbed him. "Oh, sweetheart, sweetheart. What is it?"

"H-head." He clamped his eyes shut. "Hor-horrible head-ache." He exhaled slowly. Speaking seemed to make things worse. "Started last night. Off . . . the char-chart."

"What's in the drip?" I asked the woman.

"Meds to control his blood pressure plus morphine. He's set up to self-administer above baseline. We're having a hard time staying ahead of his pain."

"What happened? Why is he like this?"

"Last night around three o'clock, he developed an acute headache with hypertension." She looked at his chart. "Over the next two hours, his blood pressure kept going up. It says, they had a difficult time measuring it."

"Why?" I interrupted.

"Well, let's see here. Because it was so high—suspected at or above three hundred over one-twenty. It's down now, but still high. Rehab had him moved back to acute care. Systolic pressures—that's the first number when the heart contracts—above one-forty are classified as high." She raised an eyebrow. "Above one-eighty is a hypertensive crisis."

I sensed the next wave coming. My gut tightened as his shoulders hunched, lines in his forehead deepened, and his mouth turned to barbed wire.

"Ho-*ho*-ly shit," he groaned through tight lips. He shook his head in minute increments as if the slightest movement made the excruciating pain worse. I squeezed his hand hard, willing my grip to siphon off some of the pain from whatever was stabbing his brain.

The nurse pressed a button. "I'm giving him more." Her posture tensed, suggesting she was also gripped by the wave.

"*Aahh-ahg!*"

I had never heard Jim cry out in such agony. He'd suffered traumas, flown off his bike going downhill at thirty miles an hour, shoulder rubbed raw from skidding across gravel—never a sound like that. I clenched his hand, my other hand tight on the bed rail.

"Please give him more," I begged, desperate to stop the torture.

"Jim. How would you rate your pain now?" she asked.

No answer, as he sucked air in through his nostrils.

"Using the same scale—zero to ten."

We waited.

"Jim?" she repeated. "Can you give me a rating?"

"S-s-seven," his answer came slow and jagged.

That meant it had been three or more notches worse during the night. What the hell's gone wrong? Stay present. Focus on breathing. Then I remembered our son. He stood in a corner of the curtain, skin pale, arms dangling. For those moments, I'd forgotten him. A thundercloud in my head erupted, threatening to obliterate my ability to think. "Oh, Glen. Sweetheart." I fell to my knees and reached for him, pulling him close.

Words crawled out of Jim's mouth. "Ge-get. Glen. Ou-out. Of. Here." He spoke as if his jaw were wired shut. "Ca-call J-Janey."

"Okay." The room swirled. My feet were concrete blocks. I didn't want to leave him. But he was right. I had to take care of our son.

In the hallway, I leaned my forehead onto the metal payphone, fumbling for quarters. Goddamn whoever stole our cell phone. Glen stood close.

"What's happening to Dad?" he asked, voice shaky. In his plaid, button-down shirt, he looked so grown up. "Why can't they get his blood pressure down?"

"I don't know."

"Why does it hurt so much?"

"I don't know, honey." I rubbed my forehead. "They don't know." I felt hollow. "They're going to help him, though. They'll get it under control." My body trembled and I didn't trust my words. A coin flew out of my hand, clanking onto the floor. "I'm going to ask Janey to come and take you to their house."

He blinked, considering the alternative. "Okay."

I bent to pick up the coin, then dropped four quarters into the slot. I dialed Brian and Janey's house, north of Seattle.

Janey's cheerful "Hello?" threw me off, then became a lifeline. We'd first met as grad students years earlier at UC Santa Cruz.

"Jim's taken a turn for the worse. He's back in ICU. Can you come and get Glen for the day?"

"I'll be there as fast as I can."

An hour later, I left Jim's side to meet Janey in the hallway, where Glen was waiting. She hugged him, then held me and asked what happened.

She listened, arm around Glen, as I briefed her.

"I'm so sorry. Do you want my sweater?" she asked. "You're shivering."

"No, but thank you."

"Can I see him?"

I waved her in and waited in a hall chair with Glen, seated in my lap. I crossed my arms around him and held him tight as we stared ahead in numb silence.

Years earlier, Janey's family had lived with us in Juneau for three weeks while their house was being treated for lead paint. During that time, she and Jim became close. She told me she loved how he asked important, challenging questions—nudging her to examine choices or prompting a new way to tackle a problem.

When Janey emerged, her expression carried the weight of the visit. "I'm sorry I can't stay longer. My friend Rebecca's in the car with Sara." Janey's daughter, our goddaughter, was a year younger than Glen.

"Don't worry about Glen." Hands firm on my forearms, she gazed into my eyes. "Take care of Jim. Take care of yourself. He needs you."

They started down the long hall. As she took his hand, I heard her say, "Your dad's got the best doctors here."

The nurse and I stayed with Jim as he rode surge after surge. In my blue notebook, I penciled two columns.

Time	Systolic/Diastolic
8:25	174/74
8:43	196/68
8:59	183/81
9:14	180/65
9:28	161/63
9:44	140/71
10:14	170/67

Time crawled. I held his hand, massaged his forehead, rubbed his thighs, laid my head on his chest. Recording data was a relief valve for my imploding sanity.

At 10:25 a man with kind eyes parted the curtains and entered. "Hello, Jim. I'm Dr. Hanson." He spoke softly from the foot of the bed.

Jim glanced and nodded, then lay back, eyes clamped shut.

"As I think you know, your situation's highly unusual. How're you feeling now?" This doctor had an unrushed manner as if Jim were his only patient.

"Not-not so great." Hiccups fragmented his sentences. "Now it-it's worse again."

The doctor took the clipboard from the attendant's cart. "I see your systolic pressure's stayed between one-forty and one-seventy this past hour—an improvement since we started the medications, but still high. Last night's CT scan did not show new bleeding—that's good. Another bleed's been a big concern."

The attending nurse mentioned a rash on Jim's left hand and bruising on his right thigh.

Dr. Hanson stepped around and lifted the sheet to examine his thigh. Next, he reached across and took Jim's hand into his. He turned it over and ran his thumb gently across the palm, which was puffy and purple. "Have you ever had a rash like this?"

Jim craned his neck to look. "No." His legs and arms jerked.

"What do you think caused all this?" I asked. "He was doing so well."

The doctor hesitated. Even though I'd asked the question, he spoke to Jim, voice low and measured. "My best guess, at this point, is you reacted to the anti-nausea medication."

A reaction to medication, I thought, surprised he was telling us this and not trying to obscure what might have been a mistake.

"But I'm waiting to get the history on when you first received it. I've ordered another MRI, and we've discontinued that drug. It's a rare type of reaction." He rubbed his neck, watching Jim with concern. "There's not much known, but it's the only thing that lines up."

Throughout the morning, Jim drifted in and out of debilitating pain. Whenever his systolic pressure rose above 140, his body twisted against the assault. I held his hand, massaged his shoulders and temples. At the peaks—some still above 170—I blotted sweat from his forehead with a cool cloth. Each time he was dragged up the agony index, I shut my eyes, one hand on him, the other on the rail. We were strapped in a runaway roller coaster.

Another wave pushed him onto his elbow. "I-I'm going to throw up." He convulsed but nothing came out.

During a pressure lull, an orderly entered. "Are you Beth?" she asked. "There's a call for you."

It must be Janey, I thought. The woman led me past the nurses' station to a long table with three computer monitors and a telephone. She lifted the receiver and punched a blinking button.

"I've got Mrs. Taggart for you."

I took the phone.

"Hey, Beth. It's Brendan. I'm calling from DC. How's Jim?"

"Oh. Brendan. Do you know?"

"Know what?"

"Did you know?" I swallowed hard. "What's going on?"

"Well, Jim's had a stroke. But. No. What do you mean?"

"Oh, Jesus." Lightheaded, I began to cry. "He's back in ICU." Though I'd navigated the previous week with almost no tears, now this moment—with Brendan miraculously appearing to shoulder the burden with me from the other side of the continent—they fell.

I became my nine-year-old self running home to my mother, the taste of salt and iron on my tongue. In a neighborhood dirt-clod fight, I'd been hit with half a brick. Blood oozed from my lip down my chin. I ran down the street, up two steps—dry-eyed—screen door banging behind, down the tiled hall, into her arms. Once enveloped by her kneeling body, my cheek against her chest, her hand smoothing my tangled hair, only then did the floodgate open.

No matter that I was now a grown woman, seated in a hospital workspace, green-suited medical staff shuffling by in paper booties, others tapping keyboards, Brendan's, "Hey, Beth," was that reassuring beacon in the storm—permission to fall apart.

He listened and consoled as I described the latest turn of events.

Later, in the bathroom, I ran my fingers through unbrushed hair and splashed handfuls of water on my blotched face. I returned to Jim and told him about Brendan's fortuitous call. "I thought he knew you were in trouble again," I said. "He didn't. He just happened to call." Tears welled again. I pushed them back.

A flick of appreciation broke Jim's grim expression.

Before midday, I remembered Dianne had rescheduled her flight from Denver back to Juneau to include a long layover in Seattle, so Glen and I could meet her for lunch.

After her plane landed, I called to let her know Jim's condition. "I'll take the bus to the hospital instead."

At noon, the curtains parted and she entered the dark inner sanctum. Jim did not turn his head to greet her, but his eyes found her. "Di-Dianne," was all he said. He sounded confused but the cord of tension across his forehead eased.

As she embraced him, I released his hand. Dianne and I held each other tight. Jim pressed his palms onto his eyes. Photophobic was the term the attendant had used for his extreme sensitivity to light.

Dianne and I moved into the hall. Through tears and nose blowing, I described what had happened, what we knew so far. Dianne listened hard. Emotionally connected, adventurous, and unassuming, she made people feel better simply by entering a room. One afternoon in Juneau, after she'd visited us at home, four-year-old Glen said, "She is lovely." Back then, I was recording our son's expanding vocabulary in my journal. He'd never used that word before.

She'd been there to help us navigate Jim's evacuation from Juneau the week before, and now she was here on this torrential day, the second God-sent break in the hurricane.

When we returned to Jim's bay, I introduced her to the ICU nurse as our friend from Alaska. We'd agreed to not mention she was a nurse.

Dianne scanned the room, registering the EKG's panel of information and what meds dripped into Jim's bloodstream. She knew this medical habitat like a marine ecologist knows tide pools.

Standing on either side of his bed, we held his hands in silence. Jim began to wince, his body writhing, knees bending, as the pressure built. He turned his head toward me, burying his cheek in the pillow.

"Can you increase his morphine baseline?" Dianne asked the nurse, only a hint of impatience in her soft voice.

The nurse startled as if caught off guard. "Let me check his levels." A minute passed. "Maybe we should increase it." She turned a valve and wrote something down.

Later, Dianne escorted me to the door and urged me to take a break—get something to eat.

When I returned, she was at his bedside, hands cupping his forearm. He was resting.

At three o'clock she signaled she had to leave. In the hall, we held onto each other. I did not want to let go. "You can't know how much I needed you today."

For another hour and a half, his moaning and writhing episodes came less and less often. Face muscles, one by one, loosened. His systolic readings continued to undulate but no longer careened out of control.

In the evening, Dr. Neilsen, the lead neurologist, arrived. We had not seen her since the first team briefing the day after the stroke. "This has been quite an ordeal," she said. "It's taken a lot longer than usual to get your blood pressure and heart rate under control, but I have an important update. I have your latest MRI and MRA results."

Jim squinted at the doctor.

She explained they first thought he'd had a bad reaction to the anti-nausea medication, but after consulting other experts, determined he'd experienced an unusual case of reperfusion syndrome.

"What is that?" I asked, alarmed.

Through the opiate haze, Jim appeared to follow her. He looked upset.

She told us this could be a good sign. "After a stroke, tissues adjacent to the blockage can be further damaged due to low blood flow. The typical treatment is to regulate a patient's pressure at higher than normal levels—to make sure blood reaches as much brain tissue as possible—without causing additional hemorrhaging. Apparently, the vessels in Jim's brain were so healthy, the pressures recommended for older patients were too high."

Animated about solving Jim's medical mystery, Dr. Neilsen spoke directly to him. "The MRA you had this afternoon looked *perfect.* We saw no signs of additional damage. No additional bleeding. We were concerned about that. Also, your left vertebral artery appears to be healing."

I asked what caused his horrible headaches, and she said they suspected they were triggered as he regained flow to the damaged artery.

Her news spun my brain like a roulette wheel. Yes, it seemed encouraging. But we'd almost lost him again—in the hospital.

"I've brought some images I'd like to show you since you're a biologist. I can do that right here." She gestured to the central area where I'd taken Brendan's call.

After checking in with Jim, I followed her. She sat in front of a large monitor and pressed a CD into the slot. "We've never seen this reaction in a vertebral artery dissection."

Standing beside her, I leaned on straight arms supported by the table. I was curious, but light-headed.

Her fingers flew over the keyboard, tapping in a password and other codes. "These are 3-D views of his first, and most recent, MRIs." She rotated the side-by-side views of illuminated blood vessels. "*Look* at these vessels. First, there's no atherosclerosis. Now see how they're open here, but not in this earlier view."

I saw a difference but was having a hard time concentrating with him lying debilitated nearby.

"This is the circle of Willis." She traced her pen around what looked like a necklace of blood vessels below Jim's brain. "Do you know about it?"

"I don't."

"It's an arterial ring at the base of the brain that joins the carotid arteries with the left and right vertebral arteries. The circle of Willis is remarkable because even if one of the vessels supplying it gets blocked, blood flow still continues to all parts of the brain beyond the blockage. This redundancy in the vascular system is a remarkable adaptation that protects the brain from oxygen deprivation."

"Oh, okay. Wow." I was impressed with what she'd shown me, but my mouth was dry. Crossing the wide gully between wife and biologist made me queasy.

"I know this has been a hard day," she said. "But these images are encouraging. Your husband's good condition before the stroke is really helping."

Twenty hours after Jim's blood pressure shot up in the middle of the night, pulsing the elastic walls of his arteries to their limits, it finally stabilized. Sustaining high pressures that long could have triggered aortic dissection, heart failure, or another stroke.

I held his hand between both of mine. "I have to leave soon to get some sleep."

Voice faint, he muttered, "I-I thought we-we were through the woods," as if apologizing to me. I kissed his forehead then pressed his hand to my lips.

Thankful he was on a twenty-four-hour, one-to-one surveillance, I walked back to my hotel room. Slumped in a chair, I stared between my knees at the carpet. Tomorrow, he will be better, I thought. Outside, cars rolled by. The heater fan clicked on. I sensed empty spaces where I yearned to hear Glen's voice, escape with his energetic abandon as he jumped back and forth from one rumpled bed to the other.

13

FIGHTER'S FIRE

I skipped breakfast and went to Jim's private room in ICU. Once again, he wore a faded hospital gown and was connected to monitors and an IV drip.

"Hey, sweetheart." I leaned down and hugged him. "How was your night?"

He gazed somewhere beyond the ceiling. His lack of expression sank my already foundering spirit. I waited for him to speak.

"I-I'm not sure I can do it all over again."

In the twenty-two years I'd known this man, I could not recall a time when he'd appeared this deflated. "Do you mean the rehab?"

"Yeah. That. But it's worse. I was getting better. I've lost even more ground. They were saying I could go home in a week—May seventh." He gestured to the whiteboard. "Now it's two weeks later."

I blinked fast, searching for words to make it better. "Let's keep moving forward. You're the king of moving forward." I ran my fingertips across his forehead and around his ear. "You'll catch up to where you were, then go beyond. We'll get past this." I hoped he didn't notice the forced conviction in my voice.

He stared ahead as if I hadn't spoken. I stroked his hair, letting the silence hang. A deadweight panic knotted my stomach.

Without Glen to distract us, we were sinking into a pit of despair. How will we get beyond this if Jim loses his will to fight? I could not think of anything else to say.

Minutes passed before I remembered I had printed pages from the CaringBridge website. "Hey, hon," I said, using my best gear-shifting voice, "I brought some messages from family and friends."

An eyebrow twitched.

I dug out the folded papers. "These were posted before yesterday, while you were still in rehab."

No detectable change in expression.

Pages smoothed across my lap, I read notes from our siblings and one telling us Brendan and his son Corwin had switched our car's studded tires back to regular treads, a legally required April ritual in Alaska.

There were supportive messages from Dianne and Sudie and other friends. We learned the crocuses were up in Juneau. Several people mentioned Jim's positive outlook. When I glanced up, his eyes were shut. I touched his arm. "Are you listening?"

"Yes. I am." He pressed a palm against his eye.

My voice broke as I read a note from Jim's niece. "Beth, your strength is amazing. Jim, you've always been an example of how to live life fully. I feel like a little girl again writing my really cool uncle. I have faith in your recovery because that's what cool uncles do!"

Other friends expressed shock at the news and acknowledged this as a reminder to reassess what's important. Jim's colleague Jennifer wrote that he'd soon be back in his wetsuit catching Dungies. J.J., a long-distance runner, said she looked forward to trying to keep up with him on the trails again soon.

I drank some water. His eyes remained closed, though he wasn't asleep. I read on, counting on the voices of friends and family to remind him there was much to live for. Gustavus resident and former student Rusty Yerxa and another male friend playfully thanked Jim for getting them off the hook for all future painting and plumbing jobs.

A note from Lesley mentioned her visit and, in line with her wry sense of humor, that Jim had been eager to check out the stickers the oncologist had applied to her right breast. "Promising progress!" she'd written.

I had a hard time matching the alert Jim she'd witnessed three days earlier with the man lying blankly on the bed. Normally, he'd chuckle or smile at messages like Rusty's and Lesley's. I stopped reading.

A new expression flickered across his face. No big transition—a slight shift from that of resigned prisoner. Had Lesley's playful words—a reminder of how much ground he'd lost—made him feel worse?

No, I thought. That's not the Jim I know. My Jim does not give up. I convinced myself the expression contained an ounce of hope because that was what I needed to believe.

On the way to the hotel, my mind jumped to a time I'd witnessed Jim in full fight and defend mode, though no punches were thrown. The contrast of him back then—physically taking charge and mentally alert—to the husk of a man I'd left in the hospital pulled me back to a situation we faced together the winter Glen was six.

The three of us had flown from Alaska to Costa Rica in search of tropical heat and adventure. If I'd known the long-awaited vacation would end in a confrontation that could have gotten Jim thrown into jail, I might not have boarded the southbound jet.

During our first week, we woke to howler monkeys whooping, hiked jungle trails, and watched a tarantula hawk wasp stalk its eight-legged prey. On a river safari, our guide showed us a harem of thirty long-nosed bats clinging to a tree trunk. As I filmed them, Glen tugged my pant leg. "I hear them, Mom. Do you?"

I didn't.

Our last days were scheduled in the Monteverde Cloud Forest Reserve. We dug out buried jackets and long pants to hike in the mountain rainforest. Enchanted by bromeliads, orchids, tree frogs, and coatimundis, we nonetheless decided to cut the mist-shrouded visit short in exchange for a last dose of sunshine and warm ocean swimming. Tropical beaches, two hours away, beckoned. It was January, and we would soon return to a Juneau winter—blanketed in snow and sixty degrees colder than the Puntarenas coast below.

We drove down the mystical mountain and stopped at the first beachside hotel. After checking in, we rolled luggage past a large pool where guests relaxed on chaise lounges. Some read paperbacks while others sipped tropical drinks. A dozen young men in their twenties cavorted around the pool, diving and cannonballing into the water like a bunch of juvenile sea lions. I wondered if they might be some international sports team celebrating a hard-earned victory.

Wearing bathing suits, we wove our way through the crowded, chlorine-infused courtyard, past the bar-restaurant, and out to an expansive beach. We swam and floated in the ocean. Then Jim taught Glen how to ride low waves belly down on a boogie board. I filmed them, our son's glee contagious, until the sun blazed orange and the sky turned peacock blue.

After dinner, we returned to the hotel. The young men had grown rowdier. Our room faced the noisy courtyard. They kept me awake despite the blanketing hum of an air conditioner and a pillow over my head. There was no phone in our room, or I would have called the manager to have him make the drunk boys shut up and go to bed.

A sharp rapping at the door woke me. I reached for Jim, but

he wasn't there. Glen was gone too. I sat up, groggy. With the next round of knocking, I heard Glen shout, "Mom, wake up! Get up!"

Surely Jim knows I'd rather sleep than eat breakfast after a god-awful night like that, I thought. Why had he sent Glen to wake me? I opened the door.

"Hurry!"

"What is it, honey?"

"Come quick! Dad needs you. Right now." I'd never seen our six-year-old so alarmed.

"Is he okay?"

"This lady," Glen caught his breath. "She drowned."

"What are you talking about?"

"Get dressed, quick. Come on!"

I stepped into shorts, buckled on sandals, and chased him down the stairs.

A handful of people were gathered at the edge of the pool around Jim. He knelt next to a brown-skinned woman with long, wet hair. She wasn't moving. Oh my God, I thought. He was bent over the girl, head inches from her face—listening or talking—I couldn't tell. I made my way to him. "Is she okay?"

He shook his head, lips tight. "When Glen and I got back from birding, she was face down in the pool. Carlos pulled her out. He works here." Jim gestured to the dark-haired man at her other side. "No one, except Carlos, did anything."

"Has someone called an ambulance?"

"Carlos did. They're on the way."

"Did you do CPR?"

"I was ready to start, then she coughed up a lot of water." His eyes locked on mine. "I'm going to stay here and make sure she's okay. I need you to figure out what happened. Those boys were involved. But nobody's talking. Go find out."

"What do you mean?"

"A couple of them seemed upset. They might talk. Find them. Ask questions. Figure it out. They're all shit-faced."

I squeezed his shoulder.

"Take Glen." He turned back to the girl.

My heart pounded. This was the last full day of our vacation. Part of me did not want to do what he asked. At the bar-restaurant alcove, I found two of the young men—bare-chested, sunburned, wearing swimsuits. One stood with hands on the back of a chair shaking his head and muttering, "*Scheisse. Scheisse.*" Shit. Shit.

Other guests were in the breezeway, including a bleached blond in her late forties. The day before, she and I had exchanged pleasantries. In a whisper, I asked if she knew what had happened. She stepped close. "It's a bit sketchy, but I think one of those boys threw the girl in."

"Oh geez."

"I don't think it was these two," she said. "We've been putting up with this group all week. They're a bunch of rich kids on vacation from Switzerland. We were having breakfast. Heard a commotion. The rest of the pack scattered. Your son and husband came along and helped pull her out. Got her breathing." She gestured to the guy behind the chair. "This kid's the only one talking." Another one sat with elbows on knees like he was about to throw up. "They were up all night drinking."

"I heard them. Can our son stay with you? I need to figure out what happened."

"Of course." We shook hands. "I'm Gail."

Glen looked at me, mouth in a tight line.

"Stay with Gail while we deal with this." I gave him my no-discussion face.

I went to the guy gripping the chair and made eye contact. "What happened?"

He swayed side to side, mouth downturned. "Scheisse."

I signaled for him to sit with me at the foot of two lounge chairs, facing each other. "Do you speak English?"

"A little."

"Is she someone's girlfriend?"

"No girlfriend." He shook his head, mouth the shape of an O. "Ve vere swimming, messing around." He paused, face blotchy. "She come to clean the pool. They talk to her. Messing around."

I nodded, coaxing. "What next?" He reeked of stale beer.

"One of them picked her up. Playing. She said she could not swim. He threw her in." He grimaced, body rocking. "She could not swim."

I gripped my thighs.

He glanced at the pool. "Scheisse. She could not swim."

While we finished talking, an ambulance arrived, and medics took the woman away on a stretcher. I found Jim and told him what I'd learned.

He glared. "Fucking assholes."

Such aggressive language between us was rare. When I met my husband in graduate school, I'd categorized him as a curious, reserved scientist. I'd since learned he was so much more, including he had a protective overdrive gear.

We joined Gail's table, checked in with Glen, and ordered two coffees. It was nine o'clock. Jim stared across the courtyard. Guests throughout the hotel were aware of the ongoing incident. Gail asked Jim what he'd learned about the young woman.

"She's a local. Works here. About twenty." He rubbed his chin. "Thank God Carlos happened by. She was unconscious several minutes before she coughed up a lot of water."

Gail leaned in. "Thank goodness you and your son were up early."

Jim looked around. "Where are those boys? They nearly drowned a woman and didn't try to save her," he hissed. "We gotta do something."

"I support you on that," Gail said. "In my experience here, people with money get away with almost anything."

Jim stood, scraping back his chair. "I'm going to talk to the manager."

The couple having breakfast next to us nodded at him, as if in approval.

"Hey, I could use some help," he said to the stocky, athletic-looking man at that table. The man glanced at his wife.

"Would you be willing to talk to the manager with me?" Jim asked.

"Sure."

Both hands on my mug, I watched the two walk around the pool to the front of the hotel. A slim Costa Rican man in a crisp white shirt and black pants stood behind a wide desk, filing papers as if nothing were amiss. Jim spoke, and the manager responded. I couldn't tell what was said but heard Jim raise his voice. "Glen, you stay here," I said. "Gail, I'll be up front."

As I approached, the manager said, "There's no problem here, sir. Everything's under control."

"What do you mean?" Jim leaned in, jaw muscles working. "You need to call the police. Those Swiss boys—your guests—almost killed one of your employees." Jim was pumped up, stance wide.

"Sir, everything's under control. No need for police. We have no problem here."

Jim grabbed a corner of the steel desk and banged it. "Yes, you fucking do!" he shouted. "I'm your fucking problem."

People in the courtyard grew silent, eyes on Jim. Even the palm trees seemed to stop shimmering. The desk clerk stepped back, and the backup guy startled. I stood behind Jim, close enough to smell his signature sweat.

"And I'm not going anywhere until you call the police."

"Uh, sir, I can't do that without talking to the owner, and he's asleep."

"Well, wake up the lazy bastard." My husband's indignation was like a laser beam.

The thin man backed into an office and closed the door. He returned. "The owner will be here momentarily."

I brought Jim a plate of food, and he ate standing at the counter. I spotted the disheveled Swiss guys carrying their designer luggage around the building and elbowed Jim. They were making their way toward the parking lot. He set his plate down and strode over to the troublemakers. "Stop right there."

"Hey," one of the Swiss men said, lifting his chin at Jim. "We've got a plane to catch. We gotta go."

Jim stepped toward him. "That's tough. None of you are going anywhere."

The spokesman scowled but didn't move. His friends stared at the gravel. Jim returned to the lobby counter and kept an eye on them. Finally, the owner arrived from an adjacent building. He acted bored but looked irritated. The man in the white shirt updated his boss. I couldn't tell if he relayed the full story. My Spanish was limited.

"Tell him," Jim said, "I am not leaving this spot until the police come and interrogate these guys. And they are not going anywhere."

Eventually, an armed policeman arrived. Hands on his holster, he questioned the Swiss boys. He singled out two and walked them down the compound, beyond earshot. After several minutes, they returned. The officer's inquiry seemed to rattle some of them, but he let them all go. As the pack of Swiss men walked toward two taxi-vans, a jeer of good riddance erupted across the pool courtyard.

Later Jim and I stood at the front desk. Exhausted and infuriated, while packing we'd agreed on a plan to visit the girl before we left the country. In the lobby behind us, Glen sat with our bags. I told the manager we wanted to check out. He tapped at the keyboard as if he didn't recognize Jim. "And we want a full refund for both nights."

"No refund less than twenty-four hours." He glanced at the clock. "But I give you tonight."

"That's not good enough," Jim countered. "We're here on vacation. No one slept last night because you didn't break up that party of drunks. Then those assholes almost drowned your employee." Jim tossed up a hand. "And you're all fine with letting them get away with it." His voice got loud. "*Now* we're supposed to pay you to stay here?"

The manager stared at the computer, jaw slack. He rubbed the back of his neck. "One moment." He entered the office and returned with a key. Without speaking, he opened a drawer and counted out a stack of bills, the cost of both nights.

The next morning, after a sound sleep at a different hotel, Jim drove us along a dusty back road, while I scrutinized a map. Jim had gotten directions to where the girl lived from Carlos. I consulted Carlos's handwritten note as we bumped past small homes constructed of corrugated metal and wood. A horse stood tethered to a post, one leg bent.

Jim parked and we walked past agitated chickens and roosters. We entered a tidy yard and stepped onto a porch. I knocked, glancing at notes I'd written earlier.

A man with a weathered face opened the door. "*Si?*"

"*Hola,*" I said. "*Estamos aqui para ver Marianela.*" We are here to see Marianela.

He appeared frightened, about to close the door.

I read in Spanish from my script, "Two days ago my husband helped save her from drowning."

The man's expression eased. He asked us to wait. A woman with black hair combed into a thick braid gestured for us to follow her into the bedroom where the young woman was resting. When Marianela was introduced to Jim, she teared up and said, "*Gracias.*"

He reached a hand to hers and held it.

Her parents insisted on giving us the only chairs in the small room, one at the foot of the bed for Jim, the other next to her for me. Our son leaned against his father's thigh. In the next half hour, with the help of our Spanish travel dictionary, we learned Marianela was the oldest of three children and she'd worked at the hotel five years. She'd been held at the hospital only a few hours before coming home with instructions to rest.

Because she'd inhaled so much water, Jim asked if she was being treated to prevent a lung infection. Perhaps we didn't understand their answer or they hadn't understood his question, but we were left with doubts about her medical care. Her father asked where we lived. When we said Alaska, they asked Glen to tell them about snow. During the visit, Marianela coughed several times and seemed to grow weaker.

Jim explained our flight back to the United States was that evening. As he spoke, I wrote in simple Spanish on a piece of paper: *Let us know how your daughter is doing a month from now.* I handed the note and a self-addressed envelope to Marianela's mother. I took her hands in mine and looked into her eyes. "Please let us know."

Jim cleared his throat. "We also want you to have this." He stood, reached into his pocket, and pulled out the folded stack of bills we'd extracted from the hotel. He handed three hundred dollars to the young woman.

On the jet back to Alaska, I sat in the middle. After Glen fell asleep against my arm, I said to Jim, "What if we hadn't stopped at that hotel?"

"It wouldn't have made a damn difference," he muttered, fuming about the lack of consequence for the Swiss boys. "For all we know, they might have thrown *me* in jail." He shook his head.

I leaned onto him. "She survived because of you and Carlos.

And those rich kids felt some heat." I squeezed his hand. "You did the right thing."

Back in Juneau, we never received an update from Marianela or her parents.

I unlocked the door to our hotel room in downtown Seattle and sat in the chair. The recollection of the disturbingly unresolved ordeal in Costa Rica left me shaky, yet oddly reassured. The vision of Jim from three years earlier was the beacon of hope I needed. I leaned forward, head in hands. He is a fighter. My man does not give up.

14

SOLVING RIDDLES

April rolled into May, and I thought of the many springs we'd spent in Alaska when wild blueberries blossomed, and fields dappled with Indian paintbrush and lupine beckoned: yellow, crimson, purple. We were missing the migration of sandhill cranes, their quavering calls and six-foot wingspans unmistakable.

Inside a five-story brick building, brightened by a plum-colored awning, a gaunt man with a cowboy mustache stood behind the front desk. With Jim's delayed release, I decided to move to the Baroness Hotel. My geologist friend at the university had mentioned they catered to families of out-of-town patients. Some units were small apartments.

"All I got left with a kitchen is a one-bedroom with two twins. Third floor. You're welcome to take a look." He extended the key.

The elevator groaned as it rose, generating a vision of a greasy gear and frayed pulleys. There was a sitting room and a tiny kitchen. Glen and I could eat meals there, I thought. I could roast a chicken, make lentil soup. We'd save money and time. The dated furnishings and worn carpet were drab, but the scent of Pine-Sol reassured me. The two beds almost filled the room. White-and-black ceramic tiles on the bathroom floor sparkled. The tub enamel had been rubbed thin, but it, too, was clean.

Back in the main room, a narrow secretary desk in a corner caught my eye. Bonus. A place to write in my journal, stay on top of email, and grade papers. I twisted a key and lowered the hinged walnut desktop. My professional life back in Juneau felt as if it existed on another planet. This desk, like some primitive time machine, would help me stay connected to that alien place.

Back in the lobby, eager to secure the suite, I asked to rent it for three weeks starting the next day. I noticed the cowboy was weathered like the room—and also clean.

He glanced at a wall calendar. "Sure."

The prospect of moving to the modest apartment let me duck out from under the gloom of Jim's situation. Transferring our stuff, buying groceries, and setting up the space for Glen's return would be welcome diversions.

"What if we need to stay longer?" I asked.

"Just ask, ma'am," the desk clerk said. "One lady checked in for a week and she's been here three months."

His words did not reassure me. I handed him a credit card.

The next two days in the ICU inched by with continuous monitoring and repeated tests.

On the third morning, Jim was still wrung out when I arrived. I leaned over the chrome rail to kiss him.

"I only slept two hours," he muttered.

"Why?"

"Round-the-clock monitoring. You'd think helping sick people sleep at night would be a higher priority in a hospital."

I rolled my eyes.

"All the goddamned noise."

I decided to ignore his negativity and read a magazine. After ten minutes of silence, I said, "Hey. You're not hiccuping as much."

He gruffed a terse, "Maybe."

The morning wore on. He napped fitfully. On my laptop,

I sent an email thanking a friend's daughter for caring for our cockatiel. Next, I cut two essay questions from my Behavioral Ecology exam. I wouldn't have much focused time for grading. I checked my watch. Janey was due to arrive with Glen in an hour.

Soon Dr. Cortez stopped by. He stood close to Jim, his tone more like a friend than a doctor on rounds. "One of the nurses mentioned you seemed really low."

Jim shrugged and frowned.

He could at least thank him for coming by, I thought.

"I understand this must feel like you're in a hole that's gotten deeper."

I wanted to jiggle Jim's foot—provoke a response. His glum expression did not waver.

"We've been impressed with how you tackled your physical therapy—before. I know you can fight yourself out of this."

Jim stared at a wall.

"What's on your mind?"

He took a long breath. "Before this, the rehab staff told me I was headed for a full recovery." He paused, lips pressed together. "Even then, I didn't believe them. All around—on that floor— people were disabled. Some were dying. Down the hall was that elderly couple. The husband had to have his leg removed. Man. That looked tough."

"The rehab team helps a lot of people," the doctor said.

"I was the youngest on the floor. I'm not saying the therapists were lying, but they told me things to keep my spirits up. I get it. And their interpretation of recovery is different than mine. But now?" He shook his head. "I'm screwed."

"I'm here to tell you you're not screwed. Your scans look pretty good. Your vitals have stabilized. You'll be moved back to rehab tomorrow. It *will* take longer. I understand two more weeks feels like an eternity. But it's not. You've got it in you."

Jim considered his words.

The doctor asked where our son was.

"H-he'll be home this afternoon."

It was the first time since the stroke I'd heard Jim use the word *home* to mean *here*. It seemed like a bad sign. Was he resigned to being in the hospital for such a long time? I rolled his reply over in my mind, a riddle to solve. But something in his expression loosened when he said the word, leading me to conclude that *home* meant together—the three of us together.

I met Janey in the parking garage. "We had a wonderful time. He and Sara have been inseparable."

I briefed her on Jim's status. "He's lost a lot of steam."

"I wish I could see him," she said, "but Sara's got an appointment. Give him my love."

When we walked in, Jim reached out from the bed to clasp Glen's hand. "How'd it go?"

"Great. We went canoeing with Sara's friend, Britta, and her mom. The moms were in a different boat. We went under a bridge and the three of us got stuck in the mud. I paddled us out." Glen used both arms to show his dad how he'd maneuvered the canoe from the bow.

"Good job," Jim said, voice thick.

"Zoey, their dog, was in our boat, too. It was fun."

As our son described his visit, Jim remained on his back with the head of his bed low, but the impenetrable gloom that had encapsulated him was dissolving.

"Oh yeah!" Glen said. "We also went to Britta's mom's birthday party. She's nice." His eyes lit up. "Britta, I mean."

He's got a crush on her, I thought, smiling. That's a first.

Glen grew quiet leaning against the bed. He smoothed the hairs on his father's forearm. "I missed you."

"I missed you, too," Jim said, eyes gleaming.

When Jim's meal tray arrived, Glen and I left for lunch at a restaurant but I wasn't hungry. After he ate the other half of my sandwich, I paid and we stepped out onto the sidewalk. "Hey, do you want to see the apartment I moved us into? You can visit your dad or come with me, but I need a nap." I didn't understand why I was so tired.

"I'll go with you."

At the Baroness, Glen ran ahead to unlock the door. We were met by the smell of coffee grounds I'd left in the filter cone.

"Cool!" He sat and bounced up and down, first on the couch, then the armchair. "Much better!"

On the fourth morning since the setback, we found Jim back on the rehab floor. We took turns maneuvering around his breakfast tray to hug him. He sat tall against the bed rail, legs out straight, on top of the covers. "Here's an interesting story." His expression became playful. "For a week now, twice a day, several different technicians have drawn my blood. They even wake me up in the middle of the night to suck my blood. Sometimes it hurts; other times it doesn't."

Glen listened, chin in hands, elbows on the mattress.

"I asked one woman who'd done it well several times how long she'd been a nurse. Twelve years. Then this new intern showed up. When she inserted the needle, I felt the poke. I tried to see what she was doing wrong."

"Did she miss your vein?" I asked.

"No. I couldn't see why it hurt. Later, this male nurse with twenty years here did a good job. I thought I'd connected the dots. With more experience, it didn't hurt; with interns it did. "Yesterday, the twelve-year nurse came back. I watched her do everything the same. But that time it hurt. At two this morning, the intern's blood draw *did not* hurt." He shook his head. "It has nothing to do with skill."

"What is it then?" asked Glen.

"They all draw blood pretty much the same way. It's *me*. Each time, they alternate arms. When they poke me on the left, I feel it every friggin' time. When they draw from my right side, I don't feel a thing. Those pain receptors don't work anymore. It so happened the experience theory at first correlated to when it hurt." His face bloomed into a lopsided grin I loved. "It was just my screwed-up body."

His laughter pulled us in. For months—even before the stroke—he'd been so serious. Having him make fun of his scientist self and damaged nervous system was a new kind of progress.

Midafternoon, a couple we knew dropped in to check on Jim. After the visit, Glen stayed in the room while I walked them to the elevator. The husband, a physiologist, scoffed at the reperfusion explanation for Jim's blood pressure setback. He speculated the story was a cover-up for some mistake hospital staff made. He believed the first explanation—a severe reaction to nausea medication that they shouldn't have administered.

Moved by our friend's protective stance, I wasn't sure what to do with his interpretation. I lay awake trying to make sense of it. All of our interactions with the Virginia Mason medical team pointed toward the blood pressure blowout most likely being an anomaly of Jim's physiology, and yes, probably aggravated by some medication. But in no version of multiple scenarios could I make the puzzle pieces fit if I had to invoke medical malpractice by any of the doctors who had fought from day one for Jim's recovery or those who worked tirelessly to retrieve him from the dark vortex. Challenging the integrity of the medical staff would divert energy I needed to get my husband back on track. As far as I could tell, there were no bad actors. Honest mistakes, perhaps. I had to let it go.

Rain spattered windows as I pushed Jim's chair down the hallway.

"It sounds like the apartment's working a lot better than the inn," he said. We'd left Glen in Jim's room absorbed in a computer game with an Alaskan friend.

"Definitely. Having a kitchen is a big improvement. Mornings, I can work without waking Glen."

He cleared his throat. "I-I'd like to figure out a time when we can make love there."

I stopped walking. "What?"

He glanced over a shoulder. "Have sex."

"Shh. Not so loud."

This topic had not crossed my mind. Like a lot of couples, our physical relationship ebbed and flowed. Before the stroke, with the strain of getting the house on the market and the end of my semester, it had been ebbing.

"It's way too soon for that," I whispered.

"It's not too early to try. I'm feeling better. I need to know if things work."

"Four days ago, you were in intensive care."

"It's important. If those neurons were damaged, early stimulation is more likely to build new pathways."

"What if we trigger another stroke? Or make your blood pressure go crazy again?"

"I don't think that's an issue."

I let out an exasperated sigh. He spoke with more authority than I thought he could possibly possess.

"Let's talk to Zenkel," he said. "He'll tell us if there's a risk."

I let go of the chair handles and stepped around to face him. "We can't ask your rehab doctor if it's okay to make love."

"Why not?"

"It's too personal. It's like . . . like asking our parents."

"It won't be the first time the subject's come up."

I pushed his chair faster. Why was I blushing? Part of me wanted to smile. This was a good sign. But still, his request was way too soon. "People don't ask about this while they're still in the hospital," I muttered. "We'll figure it out once you're released."

He twisted around to look at me. "Do you have any idea how long that's going to be?"

I stared back.

"Three damn weeks." He reached across his chest to cover my hand with his. His tone dropped from assertive to tender. "I want to make love with you. I need to know."

15

TWO FLIGHTS

"Since I got here, you've been edgy." I was seated next to Jim's bed. Glen was down the hall solving math problems. Was he holding a grudge over our unresolved conversation about sex? That didn't seem like him, but we were both irritable. I hadn't slept well.

"Sorry. I'm just tired of being in this room," he said. "In this bed. And it's too hot in here," he muttered. "I can't stand not having fresh air." He slid his legs away from me and stood, bracing himself in the six-inch space between the bed and wall with its sash window.

"What're you doing?" I almost didn't recognize my pissy voice.

"Let's get this damn thing open." Taking a weightlifter's stance, he yanked up on the wooden frame. His frustration hissed like steam from a pressure cooker. "Geez! It's painted shut."

Hernia flashed across my mind. "Be careful, hon."

He strained harder to release the sealed window.

"Let me get a knife to score the edge." I hurried to the nurses' station where they stored a few sets of flatware. Back in the room, I ran the dull serrations back and forth through years of chalky paint.

He hoisted and the window lurched open. "Whoa! That's better."

Spring air wafted in, delivering the familiar smell of cotton-wood buds. He sat back on the bed, forearms crossed. The sweet, musky scent and his let's-fix-this attitude snapped the lid off my cranky mood and tripped a memory from our first months in Alaska.

Seventeen years earlier in California, the superintendent of Glacier Bay National Park called to offer Jim the position of fisheries researcher. I'd spent the night at his apartment south of San Francisco. He wanted that job. With our relationship in its infancy, it would have been reasonable for him to snatch the rare opportunity and tell me he needed to pack up and head north on his own, saying, *Let's check back in six months. Maybe you can join me then.*

Instead, he hung up and did that thing with his jaw that I'd learned meant he needed time to think. He stared out the window, elbows on the table. Fingers laced, he rubbed a thumb against the other palm and asked, "Would you like to move to Glacier Bay with me?"

I sat tall, startled. In three heartbeats I said yes.

That autumn, Jim moved to Alaska. I finished teaching at the University of California in Santa Cruz and joined him that winter in Gustavus, the three-hundred-member community at the mouth of Glacier Bay. The log cabin we rented seemed idyllic in all the ways my Midwestern-city self could imagine. In the triangular loft beneath the roof's apex, we made love and slept beneath wool blankets and a down comforter. But this was no turnkey home with central heat. To stave off chilling drafts, our quaint home demanded a continuous supply of fuel.

From the dense forest nearby, he chain-sawed standing dead trees into six-foot lengths we dragged across crusty snow back to the cabin. There, he cut them into one-foot sections, which we stacked into satisfying pyramids.

In January, I began teaching at the University of Alaska's

Juneau campus. With no roads between Glacier Bay and the state capital, I rented a room in Juneau. Most weekends, I'd board a single-engine plane for the half-hour commute over mountains and inland waters to Gustavus. One Friday, the stressors dissipated as I pressed my nose against the vibrating window and gazed down on Lynn Canal, a deep fjord notorious for divergent moods from raging, white-capped seas to her lake-calm deceptive self.

All week, I looked forward to Friday. On the tarmac in Gustavus, Jim and I collided in a twirling embrace, then raced to the cabin in the old red truck. The cool spring air was laced with black cottonwood musk, my first exposure to the tree's distinct, earthy smell.

The next morning, while splitting kindling to stoke the stove, I whacked a half-inch slit into my knuckle with the hatchet. Faced with losing the weekend to fly back to the ER in Juneau, Jim offered to stitch the bleeding flap of skin.

Clenching my severed knuckle, I stared at him sideways. "You're kidding, right?"

"Uh . . . no. I have a sterile thread and needle kit from my Bering Sea walrus research days."

"Do you know how?"

He told me when he was in fifth grade he'd wanted to be a surgeon. He'd studied a manual from the library and practiced suturing sedated mice while his dad administered ether.

"But your father's not a doctor."

"Not even close. He held the sedation cone over their noses. Your cut's minor, but it's deep and needs to be taken care of. Choices are you fly back to Juneau, or I stitch it."

When I wavered, he told me about a field situation on a remote island when he'd set a red fox's broken femur and stitched up the injury. "The fox lived and was still a key breeder for several more years."

Edgy about his offer, I asked if he had Novocain.

"No. But the nerves in that flap are already severed. You won't feel the needle going in."

Unwilling to lose our weekend, I washed up.

We sat at a small table, knees touching. "Hold still," he'd said, tenderly placing the first stitch. I braced while he pushed the pre-threaded, curved needle through throbbing flesh. After he tied off the first suture, I shifted my gaze outside to a cluster of conifers. The fire crackled. Stove smoke and cottonwood essence mingled with the intoxicating scent of his concentration.

Three more stitches, and I never flinched.

I looked at my husband, penned in the hospital room like a wolf in a trapper's forgotten snare. Breaking our silence, I said, "That is better." Fresh spring air washing the room, the rustle of leaves now audible, and the memories of Gustavus dissolved my irritability with him. I rubbed the skin at the base of the long-ago sutured knuckle with my thumb: no scar. If I were in his place, I'd want the window open, too.

"How about I read another chapter from *The Brain that Changes Itself*?"

"Sure." He unfolded his arms.

I opened to our bookmark and read, "Chapter Three, Redesigning the Brain." A mockingbird chattered and sang from a nearby tree. Jim closed his eyes, and I read about Michael Merzenich, a leading but controversial neuroscientist.

Using a microelectrode he'd invented while in grad school, the budding scientist diagrammed the brains of primates to show exactly where sensations from each fingertip, and other sensory-rich zones like lips, were transmitted, building more detailed mental maps than previously possible. His team severed bundles of neurons in primates and reattached them with their point-to-point alignments shuffled. Eventually, the neurons unshuffled *within* the brain, challenging neuroscience dogma. At first, even

Michael's professors questioned his revolutionary hypothesis that adult brains were not hardwired. The reconfiguration of a person's mental map in response to stimulation—or removal of a stimulus—is now known as brain plasticity.

"I had no idea he was behind all that," Jim said.

I paused. "Should I keep going?"

"Yes. Please." He adjusted a pillow and folded his arms behind his head.

I read about Dr. Edward Taub's pivotal experiments. Encouraged by early research on monkeys, he later studied stroke victims who had lost most of the function in one arm. During intense rehabilitation sessions, participants agreed to have their healthy limb constrained, forcing them to use their paralyzed arm. At first, it was frustrating. They could not make their arms do what was being asked. Bit by bit, however, through behavioral shaping exercises repeated several hours a day in what is now called constraint-induced movement therapy, some people regained use of their damaged limbs.

"No kidding," Jim said.

Functional MRIs revealed that their brains had recruited new areas of the cortex to take on the responsibilities of damaged tissue. I finished the chapter.

"That's an important book. Thank you." Jim stared out the window, his earlier brusqueness gone. "Hey. Zenkel's scheduled to come by around two. I want to bring up the topic we talked about yesterday. After hearing that chapter, it's even more relevant."

I made a face.

"It can't hurt to talk to him."

"Bringing up sex with your rehab doctor doesn't seem right."

"I need to know what I'm facing here—what I've got to work with." He squeezed my hand. "Do you want me to ask Zenkel when you're not here?"

"No." I had to hear the doctor's answer—to be sure there weren't details Jim might miss or forget to tell me, especially if Zenkel gave the green light. "You can ask. But, please. Do it when no one else is around."

He gave me a don't-treat-me-like-an-idiot look.

"Let's get out of here." Jim sounded like he intended to leave the hospital for good, but I interpreted the assertion to mean he needed a change of scenery.

"Sure." I reached for the karate belt.

"I don't need that," he snapped.

His gruff response hurt, but I said nothing. Why did I need him to act chipper—say please and thank you—as if things were fine? I understood how much was on the line. My husband was polite and gracious with the staff—not always so with me. What mattered was his willingness to work hard at recovery, and he was the star pupil on the rehab floor. Why couldn't I be that ever-forgiving overflow valve, the spouse who gracefully absorbed all of her husband's complaints and pissy moods?

I helped him get into the chair and flipped down the foot supports. He was regaining lost ground. My bigger self knew I was the only person with whom he could openly express his frustrations. Back home, he'd certainly listened many times when I ranted about some incident at work in a manner I'd never share with a colleague. We were normally adept at providing each other a safe place to vent and sort out injustices—find solutions. What was wrong with me?

Before leaving his room, I smoothed the pillow-mussed hair at his crown with my fingertips and kissed him on his neck. I liked the way his red T-shirt revealed toned muscles. The twelve pounds he'd lost in the hospital, rather than making him appear frail, enhanced the effects of exercise and weight lifting all those years.

We passed an open door, and Jim waved. "Hey, George. How-how's it going?" An older man sitting in the bed grinned and flashed the okay signal.

"Why is he wearing a helmet?" I asked after turning a corner.

"They cut out a three-by-three-inch section of his skull to do brain surgery—a craniectomy. They can't put the bony plate back on until the tissue below heals. He has to wear that helmet all the time, even when he's sleeping."

"If the piece of skull isn't attached, where is it?"

"It's in a special refrigerator, being kept alive, so they can stitch it back on when the swelling's down. At first, I didn't believe him when he told me that was the plan."

"Remarkable."

"It's crazy what he's going through," Jim said. "He's a real trouper, out here all the time learning to walk again—like me." His mood had returned to normal—inclusive. "The big difference is, if he falls and hits, or even jars, his head, he's in deep doo-doo. When I see George, I realize my situation's not so bad." He spoke over his shoulder, voice lowered. "Most of the people in here aren't going back home. They'll end up somewhere else like this." He shook his head. "No way I'm doing that."

On the fifth floor, we looped around several times before returning to rehab. There, I spotted Dr. Zenkel talking to one of his staff. He gave a friendly nod and said, "I'll be right down."

Jim and I got situated in the room.

Dr. Zenkel walked in. "Hey, Jim. Beth. Good to see you both." He swung a chair out from the wall, creating a close circle, Jim in his wheelchair, me seated at the foot of his bed. He looked like someone who played racquetball after extra hours at work. Zenkel lifted the two halves of his eyeglasses from a stiff cord around his neck and clicked them together over his nose. Clipboard on his lap, he said, "I've reviewed your progress with my staff. You lost some ground with the blood pressure episode, but you're gaining it back. You're on target for what we'd expect. Do you have any questions?"

Jim cleared his throat. With one vocal cord paralyzed, he did this often. This clearing, however, was more statesman-like. "Um, yes." He looked at me. "We do have a question."

Even though my inner self wanted to shrink to the size of a fly, I liked that he said *we*.

"As you know, I've got a lot of issues related to the stroke. I-I can't tell the difference between hot and cold on my right side and I sweat more on that side. When I look at a book, I can make out individual words, but I can't read sentences. They have me playing catch with my son to rewire those reflexes. We're also reading about how effective it is to stimulate the nervous system, to challenge yourself."

"Yes. That's all so important."

"As you might guess." Jim cleared his throat again. "I'd like to make love with my wife."

My cheeks grew warm.

"I-I need to know if those nerves have been damaged."

Zenkel nodded as if pondering a request for advice on an automotive issue. No big deal. No looks of surprise or squirming. "I understand. Those are natural feelings and concerns." He stroked his goatee. "But . . . I'm afraid we have rules in the hospital."

Oh no, I thought. He thinks we want to do it here.

Jim smiled. "I'm . . . not asking for that. Beth and Glen have moved from the hotel into an apartment down the street. I'd like permission to go with her for an afternoon."

For a second, I thought Jim had forgotten our earlier conversation.

"We also need to know," he continued, "if you think there would be any issues for me—if it might cause a problem."

The doctor listened and nodded.

Jim's not being explicit enough, I thought, a bit riled. Without forethought, I interjected, "I'm afraid making love could damage his healing blood vessels or trigger another stroke." The words came out shaky, but certain.

Dr. Zenkel nodded. "I appreciate your concern about those possibilities. But those aren't issues for your husband. It's two flights of steps."

"What?" Was he referring to our apartment? There were three.

He continued. "Most men exert the same effort walking briskly up two flights of stairs as they do to achieve orgasm. It would be good to test the water, so to speak. What you're learning is correct—more and more data support the use-it-or-lose-it hypothesis."

My cheeks stayed warm but my shoulders loosened.

"A bureaucratic issue," the doctor said, "is you have to sign a release before you can leave the campus. I'll check on that and get back to you." He stood up.

"One more thing," Jim said.

"What's that?"

"So." Jim looked at me then the doctor. "Is this the first time one of your patients has asked about this?"

Zenkel's smile spread into his eyes. "You are not the first."

When Glen and I walked in the next morning, Jim sat tall on the bed. He pulled out his earbuds. "Hey, good to see you." He sounded like his normal self. "I was listening to an excellent podcast on global health by Hans Rosling. I'd like you both to hear it." He'd showered and shaved.

During our kiss, he wrapped an arm around me and held me longer than usual.

"Last night I slept seven whole hours—straight through." He lifted an eyebrow, demonstrating a sense of humor I hadn't seen in weeks. "Th-the miracle was that no one woke me in the middle of the night to weigh me."

Jim tossed the green ball to Glen. "I heard your new place has a VCR. There are some videos and cartoons in the exercise room. Why don't you pick out a few?"

Glen's face lit up. "Sure." He disappeared out the door.

Jim slid three fingers into my front pants pocket and pulled me close. I recognized the look.

"Zenkel got the release."

"I thought that might be your news."

Midafternoon, the three of us took the elevator down, woven gait belt and video in tow. Glen wheeled his father through the hall and up to the dark-haired guard, who caught my eye and tipped his head. Did he know?

We waited for the light. The sky was low and gray, as if it might rain any minute. Jim gazed out across the street. "It's so great to be outside." Glen and I pushed him up the hill. When the sidewalk leveled, Glen skipped ahead, dragging the video case against rough brick, producing a playful *rat-a-tat-a-tat*.

At the entrance to the Baroness, Glen held the door for us. Built in the 1930s, the inn exuded quaint charm—until that moment. When I rolled the chair across the lobby's burgundy carpet to an alcove, the charm of narrow halls and irregular flooring morphed into handicapped unfriendly. The elevator's half-door slid open, but the boxy chair was too big for the tight corner. As the door was closing, Jim shoved his foot out to block it. The metal slab bumped open with a blaring, *Ding! Ding! Ding!*

I backed us out of the cul-de-sac, scraping a wall.

Jim had Glen press the Open Door button. "I'll stand while Beth tilts the chair in." His plan worked.

In the apartment, Jim scanned the small kitchen, drab couch, television, and skinny-legged desk.

"Look, Dad, we even have our own refrigerator." Glen swung

the refrigerator door wide, beaming as if we'd secured a penthouse suite.

"Nice."

I torqued Jim's chair around and into the living room.

"What video did you bring?" Jim asked.

"*Tom and Jerry*. Can we watch it now?"

"Sure."

Glen turned on the TV, pressed the video into the slot, pushed several buttons, and sat on the soft couch.

Jim stood, hand on a couch arm, stepped in, and sank into the middle spot.

We watched two episodes, as Tom's best-laid cat plans were again and again foiled by the conniving mouse.

"Hey, Glen," Jim said. "Your mom and I are going to lie down for a while."

"Okay," he answered, eyes fixed on the screen.

Leaving our son in the room to watch cartoons by himself made me feel guilty. As Jim rose, Glen remained mesmerized by the madcap goofiness as Tom lit the fuse of a round bomb, forcing Jerry out of a mouse hole.

Together, Jim and I made our way to the room. He sat on one of the twin beds covered with straw-colored spreads. I locked the door.

"Should we move them together?" I asked, hands on hips.

He surveyed the room. There was barely space to lift the table and lamp out of the way.

"We'll be fine here." He patted the nubby fabric. "Thank you for this." He gestured to the spare accommodations.

We took our time undressing each other. At first, I was skittish. Even with Dr. Zenkel's *all's clear*, part of me worried this might harm him. Soon, though, focused on his needs, I took the lead as we moved gingerly across familiar—but altered—terrain.

From the other side of the wall, the louder-than-necessary

soundtrack was punctuated with our son's laughter. Enveloped in Jim's arms, our son on the other side of the wall, a wholeness that had been shattered returned. We'd taken a step forward—up and over the deep pit where the blood pressure knockdown left us—back to a place where hope could root again.

16

HOLLOWED OUT

Two mornings later, on a Tuesday, Glen and I waited for breakfast at a familiar restaurant. He read *Hatchet,* Gary Paulsen's coming-of-age book Britta's mother had given him, while I skimmed a newspaper left on our table. I read that Senator Barack Obama had won North Carolina's Democratic primary and that the subprime mortgage crisis had worsened. I stared out the window, wondering if there was anything I should do about our plummeting savings. I took a sip of coffee, chose to ignore that issue, and instead wrote in my journal: *Three weeks of hell. Everything inside feels tense, on edge. Outside, I'm maintaining. Why is our food taking so long?*

The stroke, and the setback, had each punctured a Tuesday morning. We'd made it through two weeks, to the third Tuesday without a new calamity. Yet Jim was beaten down. His therapists were back to holding his belt when he walked, and his vertigo was worse.

When we returned to his room, we asked how his lunch had been.

"Okay. But you know what I crave more than anything?"

"What?" Glen squared his shoulders.

"A large, cool glass of water." Jim held an imaginary glass in front of his face and tipped his head back. "All. At. Once."

135

⟩ ⟩ ⟩

Back at the apartment. I opened the kitchen window. "Whoa. I am tired," I announced to yellow leaf tips emerging on a young sycamore below.

Glen curled into the overstuffed chair with his book.

"I think I'll lie down for a bit."

He glanced up. "Have a good nap."

I closed the door and flopped onto the bed. A couple of hours later, I woke as if coming out of drugged sleep. Glen was clacking away on my laptop. I drew my legs to the edge of the bed and sat, waiting for the grogginess to dissipate. I longed to crawl under the covers until the next morning, but it was late afternoon. I wanted to see Jim again. I needed to check email. A chill rippled through my body, a recurring symptom I'd been ignoring. I can't be sick, I thought. I hadn't been sick in years.

I took a long, hot shower and pulled on fresh clothes. We left the apartment and walked down the street. The uniformed hospital guard stepped aside. A week earlier, he'd stopped checking my ID.

It wasn't long before we saw him again. After we played three hands of Gin Rummy with Jim, I announced I needed to get to bed early.

As we put our takeout dinner boxes in the trash, Glen asked if he could call his friend Jonah. "He doesn't know why I've been gone so long," he pointed out.

I said yes, sat back down at the table, and opened a booklet on signing up for family leave.

Glen stood next to the couch, receiver in hand. "Hey, Jonah!" His face lit up. "I'm in Seattle with my mom and dad." He twirled the phone cord, listening. "Yeah. Well. The bad news is my dad had a stroke. Do you know what that is?"

I reached for my blue notebook and started transcribing. I'd never heard our son talk about what had happened.

"It's when the blood doesn't go to your brain and your nerves almost die."

Glen listened, then said, "Painting our skylight."

More silence and fidgeting on our end. "Your arteries are blood vessels that go to your brain . . . they actually thread through the bones in your neck. It's a dumb design."

He remembered Dr. Neilsen's description.

"While my dad was looking up . . ." Glen flapped the phone coil against the coffee table with his own head tilted back, and continued, "those arteries got rubbed against the edges of the bones, and they broke. That's why the blood stopped flowing to his brain."

I pretended not to listen, but my chest grew tight as love and sorrow crested and broke against each other like ocean swells colliding in a cross sea.

Outside, a garbage truck rumbled and clanged. Emerging from a thick dream, I rolled onto my side. How could I have slept until eight forty and still be so tired? I'd gone to bed at nine. I showered and dressed, made a cup of strong coffee, then woke Glen. At the round table next to the curtained window, we ate raisin bran cereal with sliced bananas.

"Can you wash these bowls, please? I'd like to rest a few minutes before we go."

"Sure."

I knew a cold had been threatening—some crud with a cough and chills—but I kept expecting it to be done. I flopped back on the unmade bed and pulled the blankets to my chin.

In what seemed moments later, something pushed against my shoulder.

"Mom, wake up," Glen said. "It's ten thirty. Dad called. He's worried."

I struggled upright. "Sorry about that." I rubbed my face. "Give me a minute and we'll go."

Half an hour later, we arrived on Jim's floor and someone called Glen's name. It was Rebecca, one of his physical therapists. Hold on, she signaled from down the hall.

He waved back. The day before, she'd brought two of her son's books for him to borrow.

"Close your eyes, Glen," she called. She ducked into the central station, then emerged with a gray-and-black, gold-flecked Australian shepherd prancing at her side. When she reached us, she said to Glen, "Put your hand out."

When he did, the dog nuzzled his palm.

"What?" He opened his eyes, then dropped to his knees. "Is this your dog?"

"Yes. This is Toby."

Toby wagged his feathery tail as Glen patted his neck.

Caressing his ears, I asked, "How can you have him here?"

"He's a service dog. He can stay with you a while if you like."

Glen smiled. "I'd like that a lot."

My eyes welled with tears of appreciation. I wanted to adopt Rebecca and Toby.

She passed him the leash.

"Thanks!" The click of Toby's nails on linoleum and Glen's cheerful stride as he headed down the hall made it feel like a new day.

"Dad, look!"

Glen explained how he'd gotten the handsome dog.

Kneeling in front of Toby, hands on his soft white ruff, our son peered into a face framed by a cinnamon mask. "Dad, look at his eyes. They're like those blue marbles."

In the afternoon, while Jim worked with the speech therapist and Glen hung out with Toby in the waiting room, I lay on the bed to read the next chapter about brain plasticity.

Jim jiggled my thigh. "Hey, honey." I'd fallen asleep. "You've been coughing and dragging for several days." He peered at me from the wheelchair. "Now you're falling asleep on my hospital bed. Something's not right. Get yourself tested."

"I'm okay, just tired." The words came out slurred. "I'll get a good night's sleep and be fine."

"I want you to see a doctor today."

"But it's after five. There's no doctor to go to." I kept my head on the pillow. I didn't want to move.

He put his palm on my forehead. "You're warm. I want you to check into the emergency room now."

A nurse wrapped fabric tape around my arm to secure an IV needle. Head elevated, I lay on a hospital bed, the scent of disinfectant and bleach more noticeable than usual.

"It's a good thing you came in. You don't want to mess around with pneumonia, especially the type you've got."

"What kind is that?"

"Hospital-acquired—HAP for short—a bacterial strain of pneumonia you caught here, not out in the community."

"How can you tell?" My voice trailed off.

"Chest X-ray and symptoms, plus you've been here visiting someone close to a month." She adjusted a valve on the IV tubing. "How's that feel?"

"Fine."

"Have you been admitted for the night?"

"I can't stay here," I blurted. The thought of being too sick to leave, both of us patients at Virginia Mason, made the dimly lit cubicle spin.

"But you'll need another round of antibiotics in eight hours."

"The doctor said I could come back as an outpatient."

She frowned as if disagreeing.

"I'm with my son—he's only nine. We're staying at the

139

Baroness. My husband's upstairs." I took three shallow breaths. "Recovering from a stroke." I had not said those words before. "I can't be sick."

"Ma'am." She looked over her glasses at me. "You *are* sick."

"I can't—" I stopped to collect myself. "I *can't* be sick." The curtained room, eerie buzz of fluorescent fixtures, Jim's stroke—and now this—distorted my fevered vision of our family. The two of us dangled from a cliff's edge, leaving our son to fend for himself.

"It'll be okay, honey. You're a strong healthy woman. But pneumonia's nothing to mess with." She laid a second blanket over my legs. "We'll get your lab tests and work with you."

I blew my nose. "Is it okay to see my son? He's in the waiting room." I'd never felt so listless, a paper version of myself.

"Sure. I'll get him."

Glen parted the fabric and came to my side. "How're you doing?" He patted my forearm. "What's going on?"

"I'm doing okay." I hesitated. "But I've got pneumonia."

His face drew in with concern. Thinner than when we'd left Alaska, he seemed taller.

I tapped the clear tubing. "These antibiotics will help." I swallowed and blinked. I did not want to cry in front of him. "I probably caught it in the hospital. Go tell your father. Let him know you and I are going to the apartment together. Tell him I'll be fine."

Glen lingered, gently rubbing my arm, then turned to leave the ER stall. Before passing through the curtain, he looked over his shoulder at me. "I'll be right back. Love you."

Never had I craved sleep so much. Tucked in bed at the Baroness, I slid into zombie slumber, broken by bouts of jagged coughing. Glen dragged his bedding to the living room couch.

Midmorning, he delivered a plate of butter-scrambled eggs and toast, glasses of orange juice and water. Gone were the constraints on how long he played computer games. Later, Glen's repeated question finally penetrated, muffled by a thick, bleak dream overloading my senses. "Can I visit Dad now?"

I rolled over to face him. "Call first." My mouth was dry as chalk, voice distant.

"I know," he said. "Don't worry. Dad said the same thing."

After the second intravenous dose of cephalosporin, the ER doctor started me on a ten-day oral course of antibiotics.

In the afternoon, I sat next to the bedside phone, elbows propped on knees as I struggled to catch my breath. Outside, a siren wailed, crested, and faded. My body ached to lie back down. I dialed my cousin Nan and asked if she could come from Tacoma and get Glen for the weekend. Sometime later, she arrived and helped Glen pack. They came into the bedroom to say goodbye. I thanked Nan in desiccated words. Had I made sense?

I knew it was best for him to leave, but something—the fever's haze? the hum of traffic?—made me afraid to be alone. It welled in me as if I were a little girl again. Hot and thrashing in the dark bedroom, I yearned to feel my mother's fingertips stroke my hair, the cool damp cloth she'd pat across my forehead, her kisses on my cheek.

I feared the silence of an empty apartment. Is this why the dying ask for someone to sit with them? Hours passed. I drifted in and out. Hot, then cold. What time was it? Dreary light filtered through drawn curtains. An ocean surge of traffic announced it was the last hour before evening takes shape. The weight of nothing ahead loomed. No dinner with Glen. No conversation with Jim. None of my son's shoulder pats, no squeeze of my husband's hand.

Two days later at noon, I crawled out from under the covers. A deep thirst drove me to water. I drank like a desert survivor. In the kitchen, I peeled back foil and consumed eight ounces of blueberry yogurt by the cool spoonful.

In the shower, I lathered my hair, savoring the warm water dousing my skin, the scent of lavender, as if it had been weeks since I'd bathed. The desire for more than sleep from the budding day arose as a gift I wanted never to forget.

In Jim's hospital room, I climbed on top of him, wrapped my arms tight around him. Each of his inhalations lifted me. That's when the tears came, like a spring rain.

"It's okay," he said. "You're here. You're okay." He held me, rubbing my back, stroking my hair. In the time I'd been gone, he'd grown stronger. "You're better now," he said. And later, "Goddamn, you scared me."

17

ACTION HERO

Two days after I felt whole again and before Glen returned, Jim and I ventured off campus, as Dr. Zenkel called it, for our second conjugal visit.

Once inside the apartment, giddy like teenagers sneaking off to neck in the woods, I threw back the chenille bedspread and covers. We stood face to face, his muscled biker's calves braced against the bed. He pulled me in for a slow kiss in light the color of pale straw. Arms around him, I massaged his spine. His hand slid up my back. As he coaxed one of the hooks of my bra free, his body trembled. His fingers puzzled over the second one, like a first-time lover. I nibbled his ear. "It's okay," I whispered. "There's no rush."

Sunday afternoon, Nan and Ina brought Glen back to us and delivered a tub of baba ghanoush for Jim. While he relished each bite of the Mediterranean spread, we learned Glen had helped care for their chickens, driven a go-cart with Ina, and played chess with Nan.

"We've been doing some reading about lateral medullary strokes," Ina said. She was a doctor. "In addition to painting ceilings, one of the top causes, especially in people under forty-five, is chiropractic treatments of the neck."

"No kidding," Jim said. "I hadn't heard that one."

, , ,

A day later, Jodie walked in with a clipboard. "Well, sir. You've won the Goldilocks clotting lottery."

We looked at each other, not understanding.

"Your levels are finally low enough—just right, for the vocal cord procedure. You're scheduled for three fifteen this afternoon."

"I-I'd rather not do that today."

His answer confused me. We'd agreed the procedures, stretching his esophagus and plumping the paralyzed cord, could help the throat clearing and reduce choking.

"Well, I'm only here to explain what happens. They're going to dilate your esophagus to see if that improves your swallowing. The other procedure is for your paralyzed vocal cord. Depending on what they see, they may do an injection laryngoplasty, as it's called. That means no food or liquids before then."

Jim squirmed. "I'm not interested in having a tube shoved down my throat."

"You'll have a local anesthetic. He'll use a special camera to guide the needle to the exact spot in the vocal fold. He's very skilled at this."

"I'd sure appreciate it," I said, looking firmly at him, "if you lowered your risk of choking."

"If this goes well," she said, "we can move you from thick liquids to a more varied diet."

Jim scowled. "What about water?"

"The sooner your swallowing improves, the sooner you can drink water."

"Well." His shoulders curled forward. "I'll think about it."

In a windowless room in Virginia Mason's gastroenterology wing, I watched the video screen above Jim's head. The ENT doctor and a technician adjusted a monitor and endoscope with a fiber-optic camera at one end.

Jim sat in what looked like a dentist's chair. He was awake, although they'd administered a mild anesthetic and a drug cocktail to decrease anxiety and temporarily block his ability to create new memories.

"Open wide," the doctor said. "I'm going to numb your throat."

My nasal passages hurt watching them feed the gastroscope tube up a nostril and down his esophagus. On the screen, his vocal cords, or folds as I'd learned they were called, looked something like hands clapping if they were hinged together at the base of the palms. The doctor explained that normally each fold, or side, moves to the midline. But the paralyzed left one remained open, leaving a V-shaped gap where food and liquids could enter his lungs.

"Esophagus looks normal." The doctor maneuvered the camera-tipped scope deeper. "No sign of acid reflux. Let's dilate that upper section, though," he said to the technician.

Jim's grip tightened on the chair's padded arm. I massaged his forearm, tipping my head to watch the projected video. It was strange to be touching him while viewing, so vividly, his shiny pink, moving larynx.

"You doing okay?" the technician asked.

"Uhmm-um," was all he managed with the metal snake in his throat.

"I understand," the doctor said to me, "your husband doesn't want us to do the plumping injection at this time. Is that correct?"

"What are the chances of his paralyzed cord recovering?"

"We sometimes see spontaneous recoveries, but they're not common. We inject collagen or another inert filler to bring the inactive fold closer to the working one, so there's less risk of asphyxiation and choking, and it helps with voice control."

Watching Jim in profile lying back on the chair, groggy and vulnerable, I had an urge to ask him again if they could go ahead with the plumping. He might say yes. They were all set up and could do it right then. I squeezed his hand, formulating a manner to ask again in a way he might agree to. He tensed up as they adjusted the metal snake. What was I thinking? I can't trick him into the procedure. "Thanks for asking, but he's not ready for that."

Toward the end of the exam, I let Jim know I was leaving to check on Glen.

He raised two fingers in acknowledgment.

Later, Glen and I found Jim in his room. "Hey, hon," I said. "That seemed to go well."

He cut me off with a glare. "*That* was the most god-awful procedure I've ever experienced."

Caught off guard, I said I thought the doctor and his assistant were good.

Glen listened, turning his head as we each spoke, as if watching a heated tennis match.

"No way I'm ever having a tube down my nose and throat again."

So much for that memory-blurring drug cocktail, I thought. "The doctor thought plumping your vocal cord could really help."

"No friggin' way."

After a moment of silence, Jim patted his hand on the sheet signaling Glen. "Hey." Glen slid his hand forward. Jim took it, and closed his eyes. "I-I'm sorry. My swallowing's getting better, and I don't care about my voice. What matters is walking again."

Back in the room after lunch, Glen squeezed past me to lift a package on Jim's bedside table. "It's from Juneau—from Tenzing's mom and dad!"

Inside were two more of Jim's short-sleeved cotton shirts. "Honey, look. Your favorite batik shirt." When we'd learned we'd have to stay two more weeks, Kim offered to send our mail and other items.

Glen pawed deeper into the box. "Hey, here's something for me from Tenzing." He lifted three dog-eared Erin Hunter *Warriors* books, gazing at them as if they were live kittens.

I passed Jim an envelope from the box. "This has your name on it."

He fumbled with the edge, ripped the seal, and opened a note folded around three rectangles of paper.

"What is it?"

"Th-they sent us their Alaska Airlines mileage coupons." His chest rose and fell several times. "For our flight home." He handed me the frequent flyer vouchers for travel anywhere in the United States.

"Wow," I said, stunned. Tenzing's family lived on a tight budget. They could have used the vouchers to visit Kim's aging parents on the East Coast or take a much-deserved vacation.

"Very thoughtful." Jim stared out the window. Instead of conveying gratitude, he'd tensed up like he was about to throw something.

"What's wrong?" I asked. Why in the world would he be mad about such a gift?

His expression hardened. "If I hadn't had that damn setback, we'd already *be* home."

Three weeks after the Learjet hurled us from Alaska to Seattle, Jim stood in the hall outside the hospital room, feet in a wide stance, hands on a walker. Glen and I watched from the far end of the hall.

"Okay, Jim. Today's the day." Annika faced him exuding confidence, shiny black hair pulled into a short tail. Finally, the moment he would take his first steps without assistance had arrived.

He wore the navy polo shirt with tan cargo shorts. Aside from the hospital-issued gray socks with anti-skid bottoms, he was dressed like he was about to grill salmon on our deck in Alaska. His leg muscles were still defined like that day in grad school when he rode up to me on his bike and we first spoke to each other in a parking lot.

"Ready?" Annika asked.

"The whole way?"

"Yep. We'll keep this on." She patted the gait belt snugged around his waist.

How many times had he struggled back and forth down the rehab hall, fighting to regain a simple balanced stride? He'd practiced using parallel bars in the exercise room, and again and again with the walker. He'd sweated through some fifty sessions with one of several strong women coaching, guiding, retraining. Annika, Rebecca, and Mary had become key advocates, hailing each small success and ignoring setbacks.

Annika skidded the walker aside and backed away.

I stood watching, fist pressed to my mouth, Glen at my side. This man had climbed mountains in winter, ridden his bike across the country, and carried a stranger with broken ankles down a mountain through the night in Guatemala.

He lifted a foot. One, two, then three steps. A pause and six more, unsteady. He held his feet farther apart than before, arms slightly bent, like a plastic action hero. He sped up, fighting to counter his body's tilt. His left leg stalled. He faltered.

Annika grabbed the belt to center him. "Look ahead."

His chest rose and fell. He started again toward us, forehead glistening. He staggered along that austere, too-familiar hall, past the nurses' station, the bulletin board thumbtacked with cards and photos from former patients, past the room of the man with a trapdoor cut out of his skull.

Glen called out, "Good job, Dad!"

His feet brushed and landed on the tiles with a step-sway rhythm and, briefly, something smoother.

And then he was there—in our arms. Glen, Annika, and I whooped and congratulated him. We heard clapping and a "Way to go, Jim." Staff and patients who'd witnessed him waver past their doors had emerged and were applauding. I hugged him and kissed his neck. The smell of his sharp sweat sparked a memory of a winter afternoon in Alaska after he'd cut, hauled, and split a half cord of firewood.

The next morning, I washed breakfast dishes and then gathered items for the day. Glen was taking longer than usual. I slung on my backpack on and leaned against the wall. "Let's get going." It was mid-May.

He paused to stare up at the crown molding. "Oh yeah. Wait a minute."

"Honey. We need to go." I said, exasperated.

He dug around in his orange pack. "For you." He held out a piece of folded green construction paper.

I set my bags on the floor and followed him to the armchair.

He placed the hand-cut creation on my lap. On one side was pasted an image of mountains reflected in a calm lake clipped from a magazine. "I love this picture. What's this for?" I asked.

"Read it."

Along an edge of the rectangle, he'd taped a red strip of paper into a loop, like a short strap on a purse. On the side, he'd written, "Rip here" with an arrow. I carefully slit open the taped green edge. He leaned against my thigh. Watching. Smiling. The green sides fell away from each other, held half open by the red strap.

I tilted the V-shaped structure to see inside. In brown crayon, he'd written, *Step 1. Pull each edge away from the other and, Tada! A paper Viking Boat!* The next line read, *Step 2. Important, but easy. Have a Happy Mother's Day! Love, Glen!! P.S. Results may vary.*

"Oh, sweetheart. I forgot. Thank you." I pulled him in for a long hug, swallowing hard to contain a surge of love so potent it made me cry.

"Remarkable." Jim stabbed another cube of gray meatloaf. He'd passed the barium exam for consuming solids.

Jodie stood nearby, hands on hips. "You sure look happy. Glen and Beth, you can help by reminding him to take small bites, chew longer, and tuck his chin." His left vocal cord remained paralyzed and showed signs of atrophy. The throat doctor had again recommended plumping it. Again, Jim declined.

"Man, this tastes good," he muttered.

"We saved the best for last," Jodie said. "Glen, bring in the surprise."

He jumped up and headed out the door.

"What's the surprise?" Jim asked. "A leg of lamb?"

Glen returned, walking awkwardly, hip canted to one side, balancing something behind his back with both hands. "Ta-da!" He brought an arm around and set a tall glass on Jim's tray. "You can have water now," he said.

"Oh, wow." Jim stared at it. He lifted the glass to his nose and inhaled as if it was a snifter of prized cognac. "I've dreamed about this moment." He tilted the glass to his lips, eyes closed. For twenty-four days he'd consumed water as chips of ice. He took a slow sip and swallowed.

Glen watched, hands on hips, smiling.

"Man," Jim said. "This is way better than lamb."

18

MOVING TARGET

On the board in Jim's room, someone had smudged out *May 7*, his discharge date before the setback, and written *May 21*. Could we trust the new five-day countdown?

Later, returning from faxing my grades to the university, my step was light. Closing out the semester felt good.

During Dr. Zenkel's visit, Jim asked about his release.

"The twenty-first sounds reasonable. For the most part, you're on target. Have you done much work on stairs yet?"

"Not yet."

The doctor stroked his goatee. "Are you going to buy a walker for the trip or rent one in Juneau?"

"I'm going to bring the cane."

Jim's use of *bring* and not *use* caught my attention.

"Let's see what your therapy team recommends. We don't want you to take a fall after coming this far." Zenkel turned to me. "You'll need to reserve a walker and a wheelchair in Juneau."

I pulled out my notebook, avoiding eye contact with Jim. "What else?"

"Annika will go over the equipment list and appointments to schedule."

My neck grew warm. I was acting like a confident spouse, despite insecurities rumbling inside. Would the rentals be covered by insurance? Back at work, how will I manage his care? He'll be downgrading from some twenty professionals' round-the-clock help to Glen and me.

In the days that followed, Jim's swallowing improved, but choking and coughing fits persisted. Midweek, Chuck called to invite Glen and me out for the weekend.

"You should go." Jim straightened his back against the bed rail.

"I don't think so," I said slowly.

"You need to get away. Every day here is the same as the one before. I'm like Bill Murray in that movie *Groundhog Day*. Same routine every day. You two deserve a break."

I squinted at him.

"Don't be ridiculous. I'll be pissed if you don't."

Chuck drove Glen and me through heavy southbound traffic, then broke free of the pack onto a Pierce County highway. Farm properties lined the road. Horses and cattle grazed along green slopes. Plowed fields stretched so far you could see the rows converging.

"We host a TGIF potluck with Randy and Sally on Fridays, like we did in Alaska," Chuck said. "Are you up for that tonight?"

"Yeah, sure." We knew Randy and Sally and their family from Glacier Bay.

Chuck parked, and Glen disappeared with Kiana and Skyler. After exchanging hugs and greetings, we five adults gathered around the expansive kitchen counter. Over drinks and snacks, peeling and chopping vegetables, I answered questions about how Jim was doing.

"Remember that Christmas swim when Jim rigged your sailboat's spinnaker pole," Chuck said. We'd all met at Glacier Bay National Park, which had a long-standing winter tradition for families with kids to shove themselves into bright orange US Coast Guard immersion suits. Gumby suits, as they're called, can keep someone floating and alive for up to three days in the open ocean if their boat goes down. We'd swim and laze in the cove beneath a winter sky, playing keep-away with a ball, learning about water safety while having fun.

"And then Jim showed everybody," Chuck continued, "how to swing out over the water on a rope from *IJsselmeer's* bow and drop. The kids had a blast doing that."

"So did Randy," Sally said. We laughed remembering how her husband had swung out in his bulky Gumby suit over ice-cold water and and impressed even the kids with a flamboyant, big-splash flip.

We were loosening up, immersed in reliving good times in Alaska. Our memories took us to a connected place. Like volleyball players, we served memories back and forth, laughing one minute, serious the next. For long moments, I forgot the hospital—forgot my husband was altered from the physically capable man he'd been in the Glacier Bay stories. The wine glow washed through me, pressing my worry doors shut. Chuck, Fawn, Sally, and Randy made me feel as if I'd come home.

I envied their easy banter over federal bureaucracy; their victories and frustrations of working in a national park. What I'd give to return to a similar stage, where Jim's and my lives once again fanned out, each into our own professional realms with few overlapping stressors. The stroke had funneled all our worry onto one spot, like a giant jabbing his stout thumb into a single pressure point and not letting up.

I slept well and woke to chickadees chattering, hens clucking, and horses nickering. Beneath an overcast sky, Glen—brightened to normal energy levels—headed outdoors after breakfast with Kiana and both dogs.

Midday, Chuck and Kiana saddled up her handsome chestnut

mare. I rubbed Karma's forehead and fed her yanked-up wads of grass. The mare's velvet lips probed my palm for the last blades.

The fragrance of alfalfa, mud, and manure triggered buried memories. My girlhood obsession was to have my own horse. For three summers, my best friend and I saved our allowance and babysitting dollars in a Mason jar. Oblivious to the costs beyond purchase—not to mention parental buy-in—we never realized our dream of owning a hot-blooded, hoof-stomping horse.

Chuck tightened Karma's front cinch. "She tried to throw me the other day," he said. "Let her know you're in charge."

It had been more than a decade since I'd ridden. Chuck had to help my left foot reach the stirrup before I could hoist myself up. *Wow.* I'd forgotten how wonderful it was to be on a horse. The potential for connection, sense of power, and escape lit within me as Karma cantered around the large corral.

Chuck and Fawn were living my childhood dream. They were like the farm families I'd drawn on large sheets of paper: children slamming out of screen doors to climb trees or race across green acres filled with siblings, horses, spindle-legged colts, dogs, and chickens. I'd finally abandoned that dream when I moved to Alaska with Jim. What if I hadn't? I tried to visualize my life if I'd pursued the small-farm path. But that meant I wouldn't be with Jim. I would not have Glen. Full. Stop. I would not be the same person without Jim as my partner. The arrogance of pining for some alternate future, of tinkering with the past, jolted me. I would not revise my life. Not ever. Jim was my rock. Yes, we had our spats, but he knew and believed in me. He helped me be the best version of myself.

The next morning, before anyone was up, I laced on my shoes and went for a run on the winding road. Still regaining strength, the country air and open space invigorated me. Soon my mind locked onto Jim. Worries invaded as if I needed to compensate for the time off. How can I go back to work with him not walking?

I didn't want to leave him home alone. The questions piled up until there was no more room in my head. I ran harder.

The morning after we returned from our weekend adventure, the date on Jim's message board had been rubbed out again. Another four days had been added. My heart fell. "What's up with this?" I tapped the board.

"I saw it, too." He sounded defensive as if I'd accused him of not being observant. "They think I need more work on stairs and with the cane inside and outside since I'll be home alone." He glared out the window, wearing his pissed-at-the-world look.

I exhaled loudly, a show of solidarity for his frustration. Inside, though, I felt at once relieved for the delay and ashamed of my relief. The night before, I'd filled a page in my spiral notebook with things to do, a nervous slant to my handwriting. I'd lain awake worried he might fall on the trip home. I wondered how we'd cope with his mealtime choking. Away from the hospital scene, he might not tolerate our reminding him to take small bites, chew and swallow carefully.

I remembered his vasectomy reversal surgery eleven years earlier. Afterward, he'd spent a day in the Seattle hotel room on his back, ice packs draped over his aching groin. I was so grateful he'd agreed to the surgery, but he refused to let me baby him. Normally companionable, he'd said, "Just leave me for the day. Go to a museum. I need to be grumpy on my own."

I called Alaska Airlines and rescheduled our flight for Monday morning, May 26.

"Look at you go," I said, stretching forward on a floor mat. Jim pedaled the rehab exercise bike up to a pulsing hum. "How's that feel?"

"All right." Breathing hard, sweat spread around his shoulder blades. It was only the second time he'd ridden.

A woman in sky-blue scrubs walked in. She looked at the bike then at me. "Is that Jim?"

"Yes."

"I'm Callie. I was one of the nurses in ICU the day he had that horrific headache and high blood pressure. I almost didn't recognize him."

"I thought you looked familiar." I stood.

Glen was draped over a giant exercise ball in the corner. He waved.

"Jim," I said loudly above the thrumming bike. "Callie was with you during your blood pressure blowout."

"That," she said, "was one helluva long day."

He kept pedaling, but said, "You got that right."

"I'd never seen a patient in that much pain for so long."

Jim's eyes narrowed and grew distant as if he were crossing a wide-open prairie.

Callie's relief at seeing Jim—and her comment that his situation had been off the scale for her too—seemed incongruous with her professional demeanor through the ordeal. I appreciated her frankness.

Before leaving, she said to Jim, "Seeing you ride like that makes my week."

He thanked her and pedaled harder. A bead of sweat dripped from his nose.

19

A DRUNK

"He always falls to the left," the therapist said, "so that's the side you'll be on."

I slid my fingers between the snug fabric belt and his spine.

"Grab from underneath." Susan's no-nonsense attention to detail made me wish she could come home with us. I switched my handhold.

"O-okay," Jim said. "Let's do it."

My right hip pressed against his left, arm tight around his waist. The position triggered summer camp memories of three-legged races—minus the burlap sack. His concentration was like electricity humming.

Two laps in, Susan had him switch to the cane.

His brisk pace and the cane's odd angle alarmed me. Every so often his foot swung out beyond its normal arc. Without physical contact, I wouldn't have time to catch him if he stumbled. I wanted him to slow down, but Susan was in charge, and he was in a pissy mood.

As we passed the nurses' station, someone called out, playfully, "You're gonna wear her out."

"Nice work," Susan said. "Tomorrow, you two can take a stroll outside with the cane. Let's do stairs next." This mattered—our living area and bedrooms were on the second floor, office, laundry, and garage at ground level.

The stairwell door closed behind us with a heavy sigh.

"Beth, hold the belt again." Susan's voice reverberated in the concrete tower.

Jim marched up, stopping with feet together on each step, like a toddler learning.

We take so much for granted, I thought. At home, I trot up the stairs, view obscured by laundry heaped in a basket. Left-right-left, up-up-up, feet and legs coordinated by the master computer, no hand on a rail.

"You've got that," she said. "Let's switch directions. Jim, remember: good hand on rail. Bad foot leads going down; strong leg holds your weight. Beth, stay one step below and keep him close."

I repositioned.

Jim stared down the stairs, calculating. The pungent scent of his concentrated effort was familiar but unlike that of yard work or a long run.

Without asking if I was ready, his foot lurched forward, too far, aimed to descend two steps at a time. My mind pulsed a video of his plunge down the concrete stairs. "Jim! Slow down." I leaned hard into him.

"S-sorry."

My heart pounded at the tumble he'd nearly taken.

"Beth, nice job. You corrected his overshoot. Jim, take your time."

With practice, the exercise became like a stiff dance with Jim leading. But the rhythm of bracing and releasing remained awkward, more like crabs scuttling than Fred Astaire and Ginger Rogers.

"You two are doing it. You're quite the team."

Another milestone, I thought, wishing it felt more like he wanted me on his team.

The next morning, on our first walk outdoors without a wheelchair, fragrant air greeted us. Leaves rustled. Seattle in spring is a sight to inhale. Locals say it arrives early and leaves late. While purple and yellow crocuses emerged in Washington, mounds of gray snow lingered on Juneau's sidewalks.

"How's it feel to be outside?" I asked.

"Unbelievably good. I've never spent so much friggin' time inside."

"I've made some calls about renting a wheelchair in Juneau. Annika recommended reserving one since they sometimes run out."

"I don't need a wheelchair."

"You're supposed to have one." Both therapists had told me he'd need one as soon as we got home.

"I'm not going to use a fucking wheelchair." He dropped my hand and picked up his pace, charging ahead with the cane jabbing concrete. Two businessmen walking on the other side of the street glanced at us. It might have been my imagination, but they seemed to be checking in with me.

For the first time, I witnessed my husband's purposeful, swaying gait out in public. A female jogger approached him. She kept her pace but stepped off the curb, offering a wide berth for him to swagger on. He looked like someone who'd spent the morning in a tavern. His behavior made me want to return to the apartment and read a book. Yet, his rejection of the chair and not caring what strangers thought were traits helping him push through this. Can I be this stubborn man's caregiver?

I watched him, hands on my hips, shook my head, then chased him up the hill.

, , ,

The next morning was jacket-cool beneath low clouds. "You're doing great with that cane." I stepped off the sidewalk and low-ered a leathery branch from a magnolia tree. "Smell these."

We'd left the cavernous safety of the hospital for another test outing. Back at the hospital, he'd apologized for his brusque reaction the day before.

He inhaled above the showy pink blossom. "Nice. Like lemons."

"Yeah, with a hint of plumeria." I wrapped my arms around his waist and pressed my cheek to his collar bone. His scent, free of hospital overtones, transported me. "Can you believe we'll be home in a week?"

"I-I sure want to believe it."

"What do you look forward to most?"

"Well. That's easy. Sleeping with you."

Elbows linked, we continued down the sidewalk in tight synchrony, the cane tucked under his other arm. His words and good mood made me want to skip. I wondered whether any of the other care-giving partners on the rehab floor were experienc-ing ups and downs as extreme as mine. One minute, I could be impressed by, and fiercely in love with, my husband. The next I might question everything about us.

"Hey," he lit up. "Did I tell you Annika had me cook a meal while you and Glen were gone?"

"No. Where?"

"First, we walked to the store."

"Cane or walker?"

"Walker. But inside, I used a grocery cart."

"Who chose the menu?"

"I did. They let me pick anything I wanted. I went for my spaghetti. Bought lots of garlic. And mushrooms, pasilla pep-pers, that range-fed ground beef we get in Juneau—they had that same brand—and grated fresh Romano. Not quite all the stuff I throw in at home."

As he spoke, his stride grew stronger. "And who ate your gourmet concoction?"

"Just the two of us."

"Why did they have you do that?"

"I don't know. I guess I mentioned I cook a lot of our dinners. Something I've noticed about Zenkel is he's always testing me. Every conversation, he's on the lookout for a weakness, something else they might help me relearn. His whole team constantly surveys how I'll navigate normal life. Can I shower? Piss? Walk? Shop for food? Shave? Cook? That kind of thing."

"Make love?"

He flashed his old-self smile.

"Hey, let's get coffee." He tipped his head toward a Starbucks.

Inside, we made our way to a table, passing people hunched over laptops and slanted together in conversation. Warm air infused with hints of roasting beans, cinnamon, and steamed milk triggered a memory of our first work date, twenty years earlier when he lived in Berkeley. We'd met at Peet's café to discuss the summer field research course on humpback whales we'd been hired to teach. He rode up on his bike, wearing shorts, his thick hair wild from the wind. I couldn't help noticing his muscled calves. Back then, I'd classified him as a timid scientist, never imagining we'd end up together.

To claim our table at the café, I set my pack on a chair. Jim hooked his cane onto the back of the other seat while I dug out my wallet.

"Don't you want this?" I touched the cane's handle.

"I don't need that here."

I cringed but said nothing. His gruff answer dampened the sultry feeling I'd savored since we'd embraced beneath the blooming magnolia.

He strode ahead to the counter. Outside the confines of the hospital, his wide-apart gait tripped a twinge of self-consciousness. After two women paid for vanilla low-fat lattes, he stepped forward to study the menu board on the wall.

The young man behind the counter smiled, waited several seconds, then said, "May I help you?"

"Uh, y-yes." Above planted feet, hands on the counter, Jim's body wavered in small circles.

A half dozen people had filed in behind us.

As he hesitated, the cashier's brows tensed together.

"I'll-I'll h-have—" His voice crawled out like gravel.

Shooshhh! The espresso machine blasted steam.

Flustered, Jim's gaze went back up to the board.

"Sir." The cashier's voice was now loud. "May I take your order?" The welcome had drained from his face. His look warned, *You better not misbehave.*

I was sure he thought my husband was drunk or crazy.

Swaying like that, Jim's behavior was, in fact, unusual. My impulse was to interrupt on his behalf, but he had made it clear he wanted to do this on his own. I needed to remind him a cane provided an important social cue. People using one were typically treated with respect.

Jim ordered an Americano.

The cashier's disdain persisted.

I stepped forward, suppressing the urge to explain my husband was recovering from a stroke. I wanted to tell the young man this weird-assed stroke he did not deserve had trashed his balance, screwed with his vision, and torn his voice in half—but not his intellect. I wanted to say how proud I was of my husband's fight and stamina. And, yes, sometimes he seemed like a jerk. But he was not a jerk.

He was my hero.

❯ ❯ ❯

On the fifth Tuesday, Jim's sisters Adelle and Sheila flew in from Idaho and Utah. Adelle reached to embrace her seated brother. "Jim! You look great. Sheila, don't you think he looks good?"

Sheila hugged him. "You do."

In anticipation of their visit, Jim had showered and shaved. Seeing their brother in a wheelchair must have startled them. Here was the person who had led them into mountains, up and down favorite trails, carried each of the family's two German shepherds over rocky pinnacles—the lean young man who ran track in high school and rode his bike across the country—unable to stand and greet them.

Their positive outlooks and love for him—for our family—flooded the room.

"I didn't know what to expect," Adelle said. "Beth, we've been so worried. We lived for your updates."

His sisters spent their one full day in Seattle with him. I ducked out and took Glen for an overdue haircut. Afterward, I dropped him off to join his father and aunts so I could make phone calls from the secretary desk in our apartment.

"And why does he need a wheelchair," the insurance agent in Juneau asked, "if he's been in rehab a month and can use a cane?"

"He still has serious balance issues, and he'll be home alone on the second floor."

"A walker usually suffices."

Heat crawled across the back of my neck. Her tone had shifted from interview to interrogation. "He only learned how to walk again two weeks ago."

Silence.

"And his rehab doctor ordered one."

"All right. I get it," she said. "The chair has to be a medical necessity."

Guilt spiked my conscience. I did not mention the patient did not consider the chair a necessity.

The next morning, before his sisters caught their flights home, Sheila snapped a photo of Glen and me standing behind Jim seated in the wheelchair.

When she emailed the family portrait, I noticed the weight I'd lost and the droop in Jim's left eye which I'd stopped seeing.

20

FLIGHT PLAN

"**W**here've you been?" Jim's voice was hoarse, blue eyes dejected.

The paper bag in my arm crinkled as I leaned in to kiss him. "I'm sorry I'm late. I made some calls, and there was a line at the grocery store." I set down fruit and snacks he couldn't eat. "Glen's at the apartment."

Seated on the bed, legs straight ahead, he looked different, as if his fighter's will had drained away.

"What's going on, hon?" I ran my fingers through his hair. Seeing him like this made me ache inside.

"I-uh . . . I don't know why, but this morning, I've been missing you bad. Yesterday was a big day. I haven't had a chance to tell you about it."

The day before, cousin Nan and partner Ina had taken Glen and me to some of their favorite places in Seattle, including a city amusement park. It was our son's repeated request, "Please can we go? I've *never* gotten to ride bumper cars," that got me to accept their invitation. His use of the word *ride* versus *drive* revealed the barren truth of my parental neglect: At age nine, he had never operated a bumper car.

Glen's giddy smiles as he spun the helm of his red car, doctor Ina's flying hair, and Nan's tricky maneuvers as the four of us bumped and bounced off each other, had left no room for my chronic angst. The outing reinvigorated Glen and me, but we'd missed our normal hospital visits.

I sat on the bed and rubbed my hand along Jim's shin. "Tell me."

"Yesterday, Annika took me for my first car ride—part of my therapy plan. We went on a field trip to the Aerospace Museum." He stared out the window.

"That must have been interesting."

"It-it was strange." He twisted his mouth. "The sensory overload was too much. Cars were passing and coming so fast."

"She let *you* drive?"

"No. No." He shook his head. "Annika drove. She was driving and talking. The radio was on. Normal stuff. But it felt like a lot. Cars speeding by. We made it to the museum—middle of the day—a throng of students swarmed around us."

"Did you have your cane?"

"Yeah."

"Did they notice? Give you room?"

"Not really. They were just kids. Maybe they did, but it wasn't enough. It was dis-disorienting. So much noise. The vertigo keeps coming back. I was on the verge of telling Annika I wasn't ready." He cleared his throat. "That I-I needed to leave."

As he swallowed through a hiccup, I sensed his shame about being afraid. This strong, solid man—who had stood up to a charging brown bear by jabbing an empty rifle barrel at her snarling head—had been unnerved by middle schoolers.

Describing the situation, he was shaky. "B-But I stayed. We stayed."

I squeezed his leg, eyes brimming. "Oh, honey, I'm proud of you." Implicit in his account was the realization his team had been right to postpone his release.

He cleared his throat. "Annika's helped me a lot." He blinked through a strong emotion and swallowed. "I had no idea I'd be overwhelmed by traffic and a bunch of kids."

Later, Jim's bedside phone rang and I answered.

"Hey, Bethlet," a familiar voice said.

"Hello, Bill!"

Jim waved at me and I mouthed, "Bill Brown." We'd grown close over campus politics, dinner parties, fishing, and supporting him through a divorce. He and Glen had a special connection. When Glen turned one, Bill announced he thought our son was going to be the next Buddha.

"I heard you're coming home soon," he said.

"We are."

"I'm calling to find out if you have a grab bar in your shower?"

"We don't."

"I've lined up a friend to install one."

How in the world had Bill thought of this? I swallowed to keep my voice from cracking. "You don't have to do that."

"I know. But I want to."

Jim cocked his head at me, and mouthed "What's up?"

Moved by Bill's thoughtful offer, I turned away from Jim. "Have your friend leave the paperwork so we can pay him."

"Well. I don't know about that."

"Bill?" I shook my head.

"We'll discuss it later. Give Jim and Glen my best. Tell Glen to check the refrigerator for smoked salmon when he gets home."

I hung up, tears rolling down my cheeks.

"What's wrong?" Jim asked. "Is Bill okay?"

"Yes." I yanked a tissue from the box and blew hard. "Very okay. He's arranged to have a grab bar installed in our shower for you."

, , ,

The next morning, the three of us strolled together down the hall, Jim click-walking with a cane. We'd been discussing what needed to be done for his release when he said, "You two should go to the Flight Museum today."

"Oh, I don't think so," I said.

"I've got therapy and tests all day. Take the Blazer."

Chuck and Fawn had loaned us their car. It had been parked all week in the hospital garage.

"Glen, you'll love it," Jim said. "They have flight simulators. You gotta try one."

"Sounds cool," Glen said. "Can you come?"

"No. I can't." Jim shot me a glance. Glen didn't know about the unsettling experience during his field trip with Annika.

I hesitated. On top of not feeling ready to be home, I wasn't keen to tackle Seattle's six-lane traffic.

"Go. I'm out of here in two days. Today's your only chance."

I steered down the exit ramp off I-5. "What's next?"

Glen held the highlighted map across his lap. "Left on East Marginal Way," he said. "We're close."

At a stoplight, I pulled behind several cars, shifted into neutral, and leaned down to draw a pebble out of my shoe. Ahead, the T-intersection joined a busy four-lane street.

"It's green," Glen said, impatient.

I shifted into first and pressed the accelerator. Nothing happened.

"Mom. Light's green."

"I know. Something's wrong." Clutch in, shift into first again. Still no traction.

The driver behind us honked.

What's going on? I thought. I turned the ignition off and

back on, shifted into first—nothing. Horns blared. I opened the door.

"Don't get out," Glen said.

"We've got to get help moving the car to the shoulder." Our light turned red. Cars and trucks whooshed through the intersection.

I knew it, I thought. Something was bound to happen. Why now? I simply want to take my son to a museum. Standing on the floorboard within the wing of the open door, I waved an arm. A battered truck passing in the adjacent lane made the wide left turn and slowed. The man parked, then dashed across the intersection.

"*No gasolina?*" he asked.

"No. It just stopped running."

"I help you push." He gestured to the intersection.

"I can help, too," Glen said.

"No, honey, you stay inside." As the man pushed from the rear, I steered and shoved from behind the open door. We inched into the intersection.

Another car pulled over. A tall man with a short Afro hopped out and joined us. The two men pushed from the tailgate.

Leaning hard against the door frame, I aimed for the curb.

A silver Lexus pulled around us and parked. A middle-aged woman climbed out, dressed like she was on her way to meet with a CEO. Or maybe she was the CEO.

"You all right?" she called.

"I think we've got it." I waved. "Thank you."

Finally, parallel to the curb, I set the brake.

On high heels the woman *tick-tacked* back to us. "These are for you all—your little boy, too." She passed out four bottles of water.

I thanked her and shook hands with each of the men longer than their comfort levels. As they drove off, I leaned back against the SUV. Gratitude obliterated the day's wobbly angst. I thought about all Chuck and Fawn had done, other friends and family who had helped us inch our way through this quagmire—these three strangers stopping to help. Soon we'd all be on an airplane—flying home. Life *was* good. People *were* good. We would get through this.

The day before Jim's scheduled release, Dr. Cortez dropped by to review our plans for his treatment in Juneau. "Do either of you have any questions?"

Jim leaned forward. "What-what about swimming?"

"What do you mean?"

"Will I be able to swim once we're home or scuba dive later?"

I almost said, *He can't answer that*, but held back.

"I haven't read anything about swimming specifically, but what happened was an accident. The probability of you having another lateral medullary stroke is as close to zero as it could be for someone else your age and fitness." He checked his notes. "You do have unresolved issues but there aren't any follow-up studies that would address this." He mentioned an older study in which five of forty-three lateral medullary stroke patients didn't survive, and two had another stroke later. "Since then," he said, "with advances in imaging and targeted treatment, few people who are treated die." Although next to nothing was known about long-term outcomes he thought it would be okay for Jim to swim.

Seattle's skyline glowed orange as the coffee maker hissed and spattered. Like most mornings, I showered, woke Glen, and we ate breakfast at the Formica table. On this morning, instead of zipping over to be with Jim, we packed up. I stared at the small bed where Jim and I had made love, grateful for his foresight in pressing for that. While descending in the groaning elevator, an unexpected sadness about leaving the meager apartment struck. What would we have done without it? It had provided quiet shelter, a haven where our son could be a kid, and where I blocked out all but what mattered most to support Jim's recovery. I would miss the front-desk cowboy's good morning greetings, the Baroness's old-country charm. Our month there had been an eternity—and a blur.

We found Jim perched on the edge of the hospital bed, dressed in the faded blue polo shirt and canvas shorts.

Dr. Zenkel dropped by to finalize his release. My thank-you felt inadequate. Here was the man who had thoughtfully held the tiller on the long first leg of my husband's recovery journey. He'd never let us down.

"It's been a pleasure working with you," he said as he and Jim shook hands. "You've been a model patient. We all wish you the best."

From the metal locker, I handed Jim shirts and shorts and a pair of unworn long pants. He folded and stacked them into the small duffel.

"There's not as much as I thought." I scooped up loose items from the bedside table drawer. A note from Jim's sister caught my eye. *Mom and Dad gave us many things during their lives, but I remember them saying the best thing they gave us was each other.* I resisted an urge to reread all the cards and tucked them in the bag.

"Good morning!" Rebecca entered, cheerfully rolling a wheelchair.

"What is that for?" Jim asked as if she'd arrived with a pogo stick.

"Your grand exit."

"What?" He scowled.

She told us she had to take him in it to the front door. "It's an insurance thing. Once you're all checked out, if you fall and get hurt inside the hospital, it would make the paper pushers crazy."

Jim zipped his bag sharply, stood, pivoted, and sat down hard in the chair. After adjusting the footrests, he pulled the duffel onto his lap and laid the cane across it, like a shotgun, I thought, in case anyone tried to stop him on the way out.

"Glen," Rebecca said, "how about if you take the helm?"

"Sure."

I gathered up a jacket and Jim's other bag.

Glen maneuvered his father out of the room where he'd spent twenty-six of the thirty-seven days since *the accident,* as Jim preferred to call the stroke.

As we trundled down the hall, a man's thin voice called, "Good luck, Jim!" It was George, with the helmet.

Jim's hand shot up in a wave, but his expression faltered—as if he'd tripped. He changed his open-handed hello to George into a determined OK signal.

When we reached the nurses' station, Mary stepped out to say goodbye. "Send us a card. We'll want to know how you're doing."

On the ground floor, Glen angled his lean weight into the chair, speeding up toward the triangular spaces of the familiar revolving door. "Use the regular door," I called to his back, thinking the wheelchair might get stuck.

"No way—this will be more fun."

I followed his lead and from a revolving capsule behind them, we *schloop, schlooped* through the cylinder and emerged onto the sidewalk.

Once outside, Jim stood and slowly reached his arms to the bright sky, like a released prisoner. In seconds, an out-of-breath Annika emerged. "Oh, Jim. There you are. I was afraid I'd missed you."

Jim blinked. In daylight, he looked even more pale. "Thanks for coming."

"We're so glad you're going home. But we'll miss you."

Rebecca tousled Glen's hair. "And what are we going to do without this young man?"

As a truck drove by, Jim startled.

I hugged Rebecca and Annika. "You've all done so much to make this day possible. Thank you for your hard work—your positive attitudes—sharing your son's books *and* Toby with Glen." My throat tightened.

After they left, Jim, Glen, and I made our way to a metal bench where we sat close together. High, thin clouds scattered white light. I patted Jim's thigh. "How's it feel?"

Squinting, he rocked forward on stiffened arms, hands grasping the bench edge. Jaw set, he gazed at the street ahead and said, "Ho-holy moly."

Part Two:
SHIFTING GEARS

Oh be swift to love, make haste to be kind.

~ Henri-Frédéric Amiel

21

JEKYLL AND HYDE

Forehead pressed on a cool oval window, I stared at the Alaska Panhandle thirty thousand feet below. To the east, the Pacific Coast Range rose, its ridgeline the boundary between Alaska and Canada. Below, the Inside Passage snaked and branched around islands and into steep-walled fjords, etched twenty thousand years earlier by a mile-thick slab of ice.

We were in the home stretch over the Alexander Archipelago, high above teal-blue ocean channels, swirled milky with glacial runoff. Straining to see a cove below, I tapped Jim's shoulder, pointing down at Gambier Bay. "Isn't that Good Island?"

He unbuckled and leaned across me.

"Where we anchored last year with Sherry and Bob and their kids?" I liked the feel of his shoulder pressing against me as he scrutinized the land below. "You and Bob went deer hunting."

"It is. Nice spotting."

We settled back, and I took his hand into mine. An image of him striding out through waist-high grass in a camo jacket, rain pants, and rubber boots—frame backpack loaded with gear, food, and his gun held against a shoulder—made me wonder if he'd ever hunt again.

We'd never flown first class as a family. At the last minute, Brendan had upgraded our tickets with frequent flyer mileage.

Asleep in the wide leather seat across the aisle, Glen looked so small. There are times when I look at my son and cannot believe my good fortune. We'd beaten my ticking clock by months. Watching him sleep—head tipped at an awkward angle, pant legs too short—filled me with over-arching desire to protect him from harm and heartache.

The state capital of Alaska has no road access. Residents and visitors come and go by planes, boats, ferries, or cruise ships. As the jet shed altitude, I gazed at familiar mountains that rose from the Mendenhall Valley where we lived. In winter, we took Glen and his friends sledding on a steep hill that protruded into the frozen glacial lake. We'd compete to see who could coast the farthest, nursing sleds and saucers forward to eke out extra inches, cheeks rosy and fingers numb.

The plane jolted, triggering a collective gasp. Legendary for white-knuckle landings, flights into Juneau often abort after tense minutes of anticipatory circling. In certain conditions, wind funneling northwest up Gastineau Channel and cold, dense air flowing down glaciers and snow-capped mountains collided, creating turbulence and wind shear at the airport runway. But on Memorial Day, when our pilots eased us down between the mountains, we landed in minimal crosswind.

We strapped on packs and pulled down carry-on bags. Jim led us, using alternate headrests to steady himself. He strode down the sloped ramp, cane in hand. Eager to see Dianne, who'd offered to meet us, I resisted the urge to sprint around him.

When he entered the main concourse, whoops erupted as Dianne and Kim, Sherry and Bob flocked toward us. The six of us huddled and bumped around Jim, our reunion a collective bear hug.

"You're home." Kim's soft words caressed my ear like velvet.

"We are home," I said. Arms around friends, I did not want to let go.

"Look at this young man," Bob said, setting a hand on Glen's shoulder. "You've grown."

Outside, we piled into the van. "We weren't sure if Jim would need the wheelchair," Dianne said, "so I asked Bob and Sherry if we could bring it in their van. Bill delivered it with a walker to your house yesterday," she added.

I thanked them. Jim's silence—his lack of gratitude—troubled me.

"Jim," Bob said over his shoulder as he drove. "You seem to be doing great."

"I-I've still got a ways to go, but I'll tell ya, I'm damn glad to be out of the hospital. What a nightmare."

"You've been through the wringer." Bob's voice was low. Sherry's husband and Jim had connected over their keen interest in fishing and boating.

As we pulled into our driveway, I noticed a flurry of purple and orange petunias growing around our mailbox. "Who planted those?"

Dianne leaned forward from the back seat. "Brooke asked if she and another neighbor could. Of course, I gave them the green light. They also mowed your lawn."

I stepped out onto the driveway and turned around to take it all in, pressure building in my throat. Our yard looked as good as it ever had. We didn't know our neighbors well. Inhaling the familiar fragrance of cut grass, spruce and hemlock, and warming deck wood, I shut my eyes to accommodate the surge of gratitude.

Jim scooted across the van seat.

"I'll get that chair for you." Bob hopped out of the van.

I cringed, afraid Jim might say something harsh.

He hesitated, then said, "Thanks. Go ahead and bring it, but I'll walk."

We stood in a circle next to the flowers. Dianne took my

hand, looping her other arm through Jim's elbow. "We're so glad you're all home, especially you, sir." She nodded at Jim.

I flashed back to our first hour at Bartlett Hospital in Juneau and those agonizing hours Dianne had stood at Jim's bedside, comforting him and shoring me up during the blood pressure blowout in Seattle, when we almost lost him a second time.

"You've had a long day," she said. "Kim and I are going to take off unless there's anything else you need."

We thanked them and waved as they drove away.

Cane tucked under an elbow, Jim made his way toward the house using a wide stride. He step-stop-stepped up the entry stairs, one hand strong on the rail. Inside the front door, he stared up at the skylight. Ladder and paint supplies were gone, entry swept and mopped. The house felt fresh and lived in, not hastily abandoned.

"Who cleaned up?" I asked, recalling that morning, the paint chips on the floor, as vividly as if it were the day before.

"Kim and several others helped," Sherry said.

Jim leaned the cane in a corner and exhaled through puffed cheeks. With a hand on the banister, he looked around. "It is damn good to be here."

We climbed the half flight of stairs and settled around the living room coffee table. Glen opened our cockatiel's cage and lifted Mango out on his finger. He stroked her back, and she lowered her yellow-crested head, flaring her wings, welcoming his delicate massage. While we were gone, Sherry and Bob's daughter had cared for her.

"Would anyone like a glass of wine?" I asked, as Mango took flight and landed on my shoulder. I reached up to return her welcome chirps and beak nuzzles with thumb and forefinger wing massages.

"I sure as hell would," Jim said.

We laughed, but I felt a twinge of uncertainty. Did the Coumadin brochure permit one or two glasses?

Later, Jim lifted a spoonful of Thai massaman curry we'd ordered from the local restaurant. "Man," he said. "This tastes so damn good. You know you're in the pits when you can't tell lasagna from pablum."

Over dinner, our friends entertained us with stories of spring outings we'd missed—hikes on Mount Roberts, fishing for king salmon, and the annual potluck BBQ on Douglas Island's Sandy Beach. Sherry, a crab physiologist who collaborated with Jim's research team, made us laugh and cringe over outlandish university politics I was glad to have missed. When they left, Jim looked content but worn out.

At last in our own bed, his breathing rolled in and out like calm waves against a shore. I slid an arm around him and pulled myself against his radiant back. He reached back and massaged my thigh. I secured my hand on top of his. "Not tonight," I whispered, assuming we were both too tired. "I have to be at work tomorrow."

He moved his hand to my inner thigh. His body lean and strong, his touch just right, my resistance dissolved. No symptoms interfered.

We'd made it home.

Awake before the alarm, I stared at shadows on the ceiling, wondering how day-to-day life would feel. I lingered, aware of our refrigerator's hum, Mango's low, sweet chortles, and my husband's steady snoring. I slipped the bedcovers aside, lifted my robe off the hook, and tiptoed out.

Later, while Glen ate breakfast and Jim slept, Kim and Tenzing arrived. Glen dropped his spoon, hopped off his stool, and ran to greet Tenzing. The two trotted into Glen's room, picking up where they'd left off five weeks earlier. Kim and I embraced, sharing relief for a bad storm passed. "Thank you for everything," I said. "For this." I waved my hand toward the stocked refrigerator and the rooms her family and other friends had cleaned and brightened with flowers and fresh air. She stayed for a cup of tea and left with our sons, their animated focus on each other impenetrable. I went to our bedroom where Jim rested, eyes open, arms folded behind his head.

"Hey, hon, coffee?"

"You bet." He sat up. "I can't tell you how good it feels to wake up here."

In the shower, I lathered his back. At close range, holding onto the stainless bar, he seemed fit and normal. "Everybody should have one of these." He patted the grab bar.

I liked seeing the bits of shaving foam spotting his jaw. A cloak of steam enveloped us.

I toweled off and dressed, suppressing a mounting urgency to get to my office.

We cooked together and ate eggs and salsa on flour tortillas at the table, knees touching.

Somewhere in the forest, two ravens exchanged deep-throated calls as if in conversation.

"The ravens," I said. "I love hearing them."

"There's so much we forget to appreciate," he said. "Like eating normal food and taking a shower with no technician standing by. And no one—*no one*—woke me up in the middle of the night to weigh me."

While he finished eating, I washed dishes. "Your first appointment's not until tomorrow," I said, drying my hands. After twenty-five therapy sessions a week, he would now have two. "I'll set up the wheelchair for you."

"I don't-don't need that chair." His voice was suddenly gruff.

"Dr. Zenkel said you'd need it for at least a couple of weeks." He scowled.

"Honey," I pleaded. "I have to go to work today. If you fall, things could get worse." I didn't add *down the stairs*. I could not shake the image of him tumbling onto our hardwood entry. In the hospital stairwell, I'd witnessed his foot lurch forward—too far. "Your balance is better, but it's still not great. Please use it to get from room to room, for now, while I'm gone. You can stand wherever you have handholds. But don't go downstairs today. Don't worry about the laundry."

His scowl deepened. "I can walk down our stairs." He brandished the sentence like a sword.

"I'll set it up." Ignoring his rebuff, I pulled the folded wheelchair out from the wall and yanked the two sides apart. The maroon vinyl seat drooped into place. I parked it between the kitchen and the living room. "Please use it while I'm at work."

I caught the flash of white as he rolled his eyes.

"Sure." His voice was flat.

Are we really arguing about this? I thought. I picked up my briefcase and stood, searching for, but not finding, words to soften the impasse. Before I rounded the corner to the lower level, I heard him exhale in what seemed like a sarcastic *Whatever.*

As I turned the keys in the ignition, my mind screamed: Why is this so hard? How am I supposed to concentrate at work with him like this?

The following Thursday, I left my office to take him to his second physical therapy session. "Hi, honey." I reached across the console to take his cane as he climbed into the car. "How's your morning been?" I looked over my shoulder and backed out of the driveway.

"Pr-pretty good," he said. "I did those balance exercises, then cleaned the kitchen and rested. The real estate agent phoned again about the house. I-I didn't pick up, though."

While waiting for the light to change, I remembered an important call I needed to make. I mentally engraved a reminder to contact the retreat center once I returned to my office.

"Did you even hear what I said?" he asked.

"What?" I flashed an eyebrows-up, I'm-sorry look. "I was thinking about something I need to do for the students."

"Jan needs you to call her about canceling the house sale." He was agitated. "I could tell you'd wandered off. You're so distractible. It's the two of us here, and your mind's somewhere else." He waved his hand up toward Thunder Mountain as if that was where I'd been. "You're always multitasking." He had a pursed-lip, angry expression that made me want to be far away.

"What do you expect?" I snapped. "What else would you call this?" I threw my hands up, open wide. "I'm the bill-payer, real-estate liaison, mother, wife, scheduler, chauffeur. And, in case you haven't noticed, I have a full-time job. Do you think this is how I want it to be?"

I tapped the steering wheel. I hate this, I thought. Why are we arguing? One last salvo propelled itself out of my mouth. "I'm doing everything I can to support you, and you're mad at me?"

We stared ahead. When the light changed, I resisted the urge to squeal ahead of the pack.

"I'm not mad at you. It-it's just not how I thought we'd be. I want quality time with you."

I inhaled and exhaled slowly, deflating my pumped-up, defensive stance.

"We-we need it—more than ever."

"But there's so much to take care of." My face grew warm. "There's nothing I can drop. I'm behind schedule for recruiting students for the summer program, there's so much to do to get ready for them, and I can't even find therapists in this town to help you."

He turned away and gazed out the window. We sat in silence as the highway hissed by. Finally, he spoke. "Please make time for me."

I released the breath I'd been holding. "As soon as I'm caught up at work, it'll be better."

We're becoming some Jekyll and Hyde couple, I thoug
love birds by night, snapping turtles by day.

Friday night, after my husband and son were in bed, I covered
Mango's cage and turned off all but one light before sitting at
the kitchen counter. We'd stumbled through the week, ending
it over a quiet dinner of Jim's spaghetti and meatballs, Glen's
favorite.

I was not prepared for how fragmented being home would
feel. In Seattle, my priorities had been to help Jim and care for
Glen. Now I craved what I'd lost: the comfort of my son's con-
stant company, our shared mornings and evenings in the small
apartment, the freedom to be with my husband during the day,
witnessing and supporting his struggles and victories. For five
weeks, we'd worked as a team toward a single, desperate goal.
That goal remained, but I could no longer stave off the backlog
of personal and professional responsibilities.

I'd survived the week by compartmentalizing. In the mornings and at bedtimes, I focused on Glen. Jim got more attention
in the evening. On campus, teaching, advising, and writing provided islands of relief but left a guilty residue, like oil-spill tar.
The feeling I had when I left Jim home alone each morning triggered uncomfortable memories of the first weeks of dropping our
son off at preschool. The dread of separation created pressure on
my chest and throat. My eyes hurt. Jim needed me to trust him
when he was on his own, like Glen had. And, as hard as it was to
admit, I needed to do a better job of being emotionally available
when we were together.

I opened my journal and wrote a letter to my daytime self.

The week's demands are blocking you from feeling and
doing what is most important: loving and spending time
with your husband and son. Jim knows and accepts all of

you: the good, the bad, and the insecure. Do not forget: Any rejected embrace, terse conversation, or uncorrected slight could be your last. Had that morning six weeks ago been his last, these days would be gouged with unimaginable sorrow and unrelenting regret.

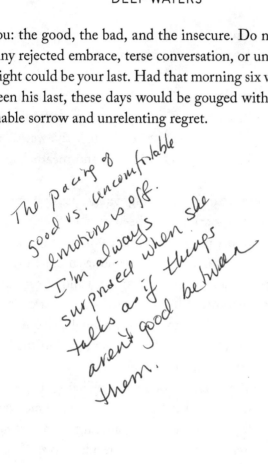

The pacing of good vs. uncomfortable emotions is off. I'm always surprised when she talks as if things aren't good between them.

22

ICE CYCLE

It was Jim's idea to go hiking our first weekend back in Juneau. Saturday morning, with Glen and Tenzing in tow, we wore light jackets over fleece. The lush forest trail meandered, then rose beside a magnificent glacier. The half-mile-wide river of ice was sustained by a fifteen-hundred-square-mile icefield above. Like all glaciers, the Mendenhall Glacier appeared solid but behaved like a slow-motion liquid. Along its exposed face, turquoise spires as tall as the White House occasionally broke away and plunged into the meltwater lake. Around 1732, when George Washington was born, our lot three miles away would have been underneath the retreating glacier. In recent years, geologists used a laser-beam altimeter during aerial surveys along the glacier's midline to precisely measure ice sheet elevations. They described the rapid thinning and retreat of the glacier since 1995 as dramatic and primarily due to climate change.

The unpaved trail was slick and pocked by patches of melting snow. Glassy panes of ice capped most puddles. Glen and Tenzing dashed ahead, disappearing behind thickets of lanky alders and scruffy willows. Jim's cane made sucking noises as he flung it forward and pulled it from the mud with each stride. He stumbled.

"You okay?"

"I'm fine." He regained his footing. His tone made it clear I shouldn't have asked.

The sky was Alaska blue, air brisk and pure.

He moved to one side of the path where he could plant the cane on higher ground. The angle made his gait more irregular, but his progress improved. I stayed behind, watching him labor across the terrain. This is good for his nervous system, I thought. Thank God he's such a trouper. He normally outpaced us all with easy smooth strides. When the path widened, I sped up to hike beside him, slowing to match his pace.

"This is great," he said, winded. "I-I've got to get out. There's only so much I can do at home."

"Have you noticed the cottonwoods?"

He glanced around.

"Smell."

"Oh, right." He inhaled deeply. "That's such a funky smell, totally connected to spring."

We crossed a burbling creek where the path became steeper. After fifteen minutes, I asked if he wanted to rest or turn back. "Coming down is likely to be harder."

"No. I'm fine. Let's get to the falls."

"Okay," I said in a curt, have-your-way voice I instantly regretted. "I'll catch up to the boys, and we'll meet you there." I lengthened my stride, jogging where the trail leveled. It felt good to run on the wooded trail. I couldn't help it; watching him struggle threw me into a protective mode.

I caught sight of the boys and called ahead, "We're going to the falls." They waited for me to catch up.

"Where's Dad?" Glen looked concerned.

"He's coming."

We turned off the main route, toward the sound of tumbling water. Near the steep waterfall, Glen and Tenzing climbed onto a granite boulder the size of an overturned van. While they played king of the mountain, I found a smooth rock to sit on. Chickadees bustled branch to branch while a hermit thrush whistled clear, flute tones. The sounds of boys, birds, and cascading water quieted my mind. I leaned back and shut my eyes. This was what I needed, too.

The power of time—on a massively different scale from that of glaciers—was on my mind. In six weeks, Jim had gone from blaring ambulance to hiking. Yet, some days and nights in Seattle had moved at the pace of a glacier. Why can't I be more gracious and calm, like Dianne?

Soon Jim approached beneath filtered light, expression determined.

Glen slid off the boulder. "Hey Dad. How're you doing?"

"O-okay." He trudged toward me and stopped, waving the boys over. "I have a new idea."

They joined us.

"It-it's so obvious. I can't believe I didn't think of it before." A smudge of dirt decorated one of his knees, and the lower half of his cane was coated with mud. He'd perked up since I'd left him.

"What is it?" asked Glen.

"What I need are hiking poles."

Back then, we rarely saw anyone using them.

"Great idea," I said. "Let's order a pair today."

Halfway down, we stopped to take in a view of the lake in front of the glacier. Water closest to the retreating glacier was frozen. A half-dozen townhouse-sized turquoise chunks of ice pierced the wide lake. Standing with an arm around my husband's waist, I remembered a winter day a year earlier. *No.* A quick calculation told me it was merely five months ago—January—when Jim had pulled Glen and me around the frozen lake on a small plastic sled tethered to his bike. We'd laughed uncontrollably as Jim pedaled and turned, zipping us in wide, slippery-fast arcs behind him. Who else would ride a bike across a frozen lake? Onlookers might have thought my husband was a crazy man, instead of someone fully prepared to have some fun.

Jim's two-wheel sleigh ride was unusual enough to catch the eye of photographer Michael Penn from the local paper. He'd snapped a shot that landed on the *Juneau Empire's* front page. Entitled "Ice Cycle," the caption read, "Jim Taggart pulls Beth Mathews and their son, Glen, 9, on his bicycle Sunday over Mendenhall Lake. 'I wouldn't try this without studded tires,' Taggart said."

I wondered if Jim was thinking about that day too. Would he ever be able to ride a bike again on normal pavement?

I looked back on the special day, all of us bundled up, Glen kneeling in front of me on the sled, and my giddiness at the absurdity of it. Who would have predicted Jim would have a stroke exactly three months later? The memory hurt, like freezing air flooding lungs too fast.

In southeastern Alaska's sharp, clear air, each exhalation a visible puff, the energetic boys racing up and back like border collies, I felt hopeful again. During our hike back down the trail, Jim faltered twice.

Each time, I reacted less.

"We gotta have a garden," Jim announced, responding to my suggestion that we skip planting vegetables that year. When we first moved in, we'd hacked and peeled away slabs of grass from the back corner of our yard. Four truckloads of composted Alaskan Brewery hops, nine years of kitchen compost, and many days of Jim's labor, hand turning and cultivating the medley, had transformed rock dust from thousands of years of glacial scouring into dark soil. Midmorning on Sunday, the first of June, Dianne and Gretchen arrived to help us plant the twenty-by-seventy-foot plot.

The same day, ten college students traveled to Juneau from

around the country for the Research Experiences for Undergraduates program Brendan and I led. For the ninth summer, we had a grant from the National Science Foundation for the program. I was the detail person, Brendan the big-idea leader. Along with other science faculty, we mentored students in topics ranging from the effects of climate change on ringed seal pupping to testing whether antifouling boat paint, leached into the ocean, triggered sex changes in marine snails. My students studied harbor porpoises that frequented a small cove near campus. In other years, I met our students at the airport, but having promised Jim I'd take the weekend off, I delegated the greetings to an assistant.

Jim drove the shovel blade into winter-crusted soil, leveraging moist wedges of chocolate-colored dirt into upside-down heaps, one after the other. He was focused like an athlete trying to break someone else's record. Gretchen, a Juneau master gardener, and I followed him, digging trenches, while Dianne raked the wide rows into smooth beds. We could not keep up with him.

Sweat dripping from his brow, he rested against the handle. "Our goal's not perfection. If we aim for that, we'll never finish in a weekend."

Dianne ran a trowel tip through the turned soil, creating small furrows. She and I poured tiny lettuce seeds into cupped hands and drizzled them down our lifeline creases, guiding them into the soil as we scooted along on our haunches. Packet by packet we planted dwarf blue kale, arugula, radishes, collards, carrots, Swiss chard, and Japanese peas—proven varieties in Alaska's short but intense growing season.

A low sun promised warmth to come. We talked about politics, favorite books, and memories of other gardens planted. We worked within an easy rhythm of silence punctuated by lively conversation. In the background, squirrels chattered as a light wind feathered towering spruce limbs. The comfort of close friends gave me permission to let go of work concerns. But it was seeing Jim turning the earth, a shovel in place of the cane, that offered deep solace.

I tapped broccoli starts into small holes and snugged loose soil around their roots. As the others finished the third row of potato sets, Jim stopped digging to stand, one hand on the handle. He asked Gretchen and Dianne if they'd heard the story of Glen's first gardening experience.

Neither had.

"His first spring was our wettest ever. That year, we'd delayed planting because of the rain. It was still spitting, but I zipped Glen into a thick fleece bodysuit."

"How old was he?" Gretchen asked.

"About seven months—not walking. I set him on the grass. While I dug in the sludge, he crawled around. I was making trenches to drain the soil. When I turned to check on him, he'd crawled up a chunky mound, scootin' along like some fleece-covered four-wheeler."

Jim's stance was casual and certain, gestures and face animated—like his former self.

"Glen was over there on his belly, smeared with mud, focused and in his element. A little while later, I noticed he was waving his arms and had this odd expression—not bad, but-but curious—mouth turned down, eyes all wide." Jim imitated baby Glen. "I went over, picked him up—twenty pounds, still nursing. It was like he was chewing on something—but he had no teeth. I stuck my finger in his mouth." Jim's smile crinkled up into his eyes. "I pulled something out. It-it was a slug!"

Laughing nearly to tears, he said, "My tough son's first solid food—and it's *a slug!*"

"You did what?" Home from work later that week, I held the refrigerator door open. The shelves were full. Cool air spilled onto my arms.

Jim stood at the counter, chopping vegetables, his back to me. "I-I walked to the grocery store."

"You walked to the store today?" I asked, my voice as incriminating as some lawyer about to pounce. "I could've stopped on my way home."

"I wanted to. It's not far."

In the ten years we'd lived there, neither of us had ever walked the two miles to the grocery store.

"How did you carry everything?"

"Frame pack."

I turned to face his back. "But we've only been home two weeks." Why was I taking a prosecutorial stance?

"I used the new poles." His tone remained brusque.

"Are you ready to walk on roads?" The image of him striding with that wider sway of trekking poles, cars passing, alarmed me. I knew my fears were overblown, but they weren't trivial. I stepped forward and slid my arms around his chest.

He kept chopping garlic.

"It scares me," I said, voice soft.

"Why?"

"What if you fall down—into traffic?"

"I won't fall."

"You could."

"If I do, I'll get up."

I tightened my embrace. Why was it so hard to not worry?

23

UNCOUPLED

Glen spit toothpaste foam into the sink as I cheered him on. "That's three out of five." He'd already eaten breakfast and dressed. It was day two of his fine arts summer camp, which he liked. But getting him out the door on time was a challenge, not because he was difficult, but because he was cheerfully distractible.

Task four. Feet on a stool, head bent over the sink, he flushed his sinuses with saline to tame allergy-induced asthma. Growing up, I'd never done anything like that. When I got sick, my father force-fed me pills by shoving them down my throat.

Next was an inhalation treatment to dilate and relax his lungs. I led him into the living room where he plugged in the shoe-box-sized nebulizer. "Hop up." I patted the couch.

"Can I watch cartoons while it runs?" He flashed a hopeful smile.

"Not now, sweetie. Your dad's sleeping." Our television lived in the bedroom cabinet. I stretched the mouth-cup's strap around his head, thankful the doctor had said there was a good chance he'd outgrow the asthma. The nebulizer hummed as vapor delivered a bronchiole-dilating drug.

"Can we play Gobblet?" The mouthpiece garbled his voice.

"You sound like a cartoon character."

He held cupped hands in front of his face like rabbit paws. "What's up, Doc?" he squawked.

Laughing, I tickled him. "You goof. Sabrina and her grandmother will be here soon. I've got to get ready for work."

"Please," he pleaded. "One game?"

I checked my watch. "After this treatment's done, we'll have time for a short game before they arrive."

"Okeydokey." He reached for a book.

"Hey, mor-morning." Jim's gravelly voice startled me. With the nebulizer buzzing, I hadn't heard him come down the hall. He stood across the room in T-shirt and boxers, hair tousled. It was unusual to see him up this early—since the stroke.

"Good morning, sweetheart." I left Glen on the couch and briefed Jim on the morning plan. While he listened, sipping coffee, the phone rang.

It was my assistant reporting that the boating center didn't have enough kayaks for the student training I'd scheduled. I had an hour to find two singles to rent and deliver to the cove. I put my hand over the receiver. "Hon, can you help Glen finish up and get ready for the pickup?"

I was discussing solutions for the kayak snafu with my assistant, when Jim's gruff voice boomed out. "There's no time for that. Get your shoes on *now*," he huffed.

Had he even said good morning?

I told my assistant I'd find kayaks and hung up. "What is going on?" Our son sat with arms folded tight, close to tears. What could've happened? We'd navigated a demanding morning and he'd been wonderful.

"I-I've got it under control," Jim said, not taming his brusque stance. "*Get* your shoes on," he repeated, looming over our son.

"No." Glen's mouth was tight, cheeks blotchy from the mouthpiece. "We were going to play one game first."

"There isn't time," Jim said.

My insides churned. Everything was fine before he walked in. I heard my stern voice say, "If you're mad at me because I took a work call, take it out on me. Not our son."

The doorbell rang.

Jim rinsed dinner plates and stacked them in the dishwasher while I transferred leftovers into containers and wiped counters. Consistent with the morning, we'd had a tense evening. It was ten o'clock. Twilight would linger until sunrise. His clipped responses to my attempts at small talk signaled he was angry with me—still. Or again? I wanted to give up on the night, abandon my share of the cleanup, and huff off to bed. Why couldn't he understand how unfair he'd been that morning?

I lifted a pan from the rack to dry. "Please, tell me what's going on." He shut the dishwasher and stood, back to me. After several seconds, I spoke again. "I hate how we're not communicating." He turned and leaned against the sink. I stared at him, my arms around the skillet as if it were an emotional shield.

His eyes jittered. It was the nystagmus flaring, yet his unsteady gaze pushed me away like a thrust-out arm. His silent treatment led me to guess at my shortcomings: I'm too distracted by my job, work more hours than I'm paid for, don't make love often enough.

He clamped his eyes shut.

"What am I doing wrong now?" I blurted, all filters gone.

"It-it's not that. It's the double vision." He rubbed his forehead. "Sometimes it just hurts."

For two decades I'd interpreted this man's body language well. Now I had to learn when a scowl was not meant for me.

I was doing as much as I could, supporting my husband to heal, keeping Glen's life on track, shouldering our finances, but Jim's irritability—new since leaving his job and amplified by the stroke—made me feel like none of that mattered.

"Tell me." I tapped the cast-iron skillet, losing patience.

He didn't speak, so I took another tack. "When you get up in the morning, it feels like you're already mad at me. Your mood is like a dark vibration. It makes me want to leave, to be somewhere else—anywhere but here." I hesitated, not sure what I wanted from him. Then it came to me. "I need you to be more friendly." As the words spilled out, they sounded pitiful—so petty. Another voice countered: He's trying to recover from a stroke, you idiot.

He tensed as if I'd hit him.

He's going to tell me to cut back at work, again. That's what he wants. We can't afford it. We need my income more than ever. And I *like* working with my students. None of them make me feel unwanted or bad.

His words emerged slowly. "For seven weeks, I-I have not felt good when I wake up. Not a single day. My body's screwed up—pain shoots into my eye, this foot goes numb, hot feels cold, sometimes the skin across half my back burns. I can't fucking read." He looked away. "And I goddamned can't walk right."

I needed more air. "Oh, honey. I didn't know all that was still happening." For weeks, he hadn't complained. How had I gotten this so wrong?

"It-it's like the bad dream never ends." His jaw muscles tensed. "But when you touch me. . . ." He inhaled and exhaled hard. "Wherever you touch me, I feel better. I need you. But I. . . ." He shifted his weight to the other foot. "When I wake up, I reach for you, and you're never there."

At last, Friday arrived, and I got home from work on time. After showering, I put on the purple-and-blue dress Jim had bought for me years earlier in Mexico. Cooking our first planned dinner for guests since returning from Seattle, we slid into our entertaining routine like practiced dancers, each knowing what to do.

We'd invited Alex and his family. Alex, a former student of mine and, more recently, Jim's employee, also owned a sailboat. We'd shared many outings with his young family. When I'd called to invite them, Alex insisted on preparing the main course.

"That would be wonderful," I'd said. "What would you like to bring?" Alex was also an avid hunter and fisherman, so I'd assumed salmon, halibut, or deer.

"It'll be a surprise." I could visualize his boyish grin.

Jim rinsed garden greens, while I layered sliced tomatoes, mozzarella, and basil leaves into a ceramic dish for the appetizer. As I drizzled balsamic vinaigrette across the rows of red, white, and green, a giddy lightness swelled at the prospect of a social evening at home. With the stroke looming in our rearview mirrors and the week's misunderstanding, having friends over was a step toward coercing life back onto a normal track.

The doorbell rang. "Let's get it." I took his hand and led the way. I opened the door to cool night air and what felt like glowing light from Alex, Ellen, and their son, Tristan. We had not seen them since before Jim's stroke. Our embraces were intensified by all that had happened. Ellen's warmth emanated from her sparkling eyes. A counselor at Juneau's women's shelter, she'd won our hearts years earlier, when Alex brought her over for dinner on one of their first dates.

Ellen and I held each other tight for several heartbeats. Stepping back, hands on her forearms, our eyes locked, and it seemed she understood all we'd been through. We both laughed, in that crazy way when laughing substitutes for crying. Cradled in her arm was a canvas bag with a loaf of French bread, a bottle of wine, and a baking dish tucked under a blue-checkered cloth.

I scooped up eight-year-old Tristan, still light enough to straddle my hip. "When did you get so tall, young man?"

He flashed a bashful smile and asked, "Where's Glen?"

"On the trampoline, waiting for you."

He hopped down and flew out the door.

Later, when the six of us were seated, Alex placed his covered mystery dish on the table in front of Jim. "Okay," he announced, eyes twinkling. "Everybody ready?"

Glen and Tristan stood on their chairs to watch.

With a magician's "Ta da!" Alex pulled off the checkered cover. "Venison meatloaf!"

"Oh, wow." Jim's eyes lit up. "This looks great."

"In honor of your first real meal at Virginia Mason," Alex said. "But. Full disclosure: I added a bunch of stuff not on the menu there—garlic, spices, and hot peppers—to make sure you don't have any spooky hospital flashbacks."

Jim smiled. "No way I'll confuse this."

During dinner, Alex and I refilled wine glasses. Jim relaxed and became talkative. The boys finished first and left the table. As Alex and Ellen asked questions about the stroke, I realized there were aspects of the ordeal I'd never heard. Other than a few times when I'd probed, Jim hadn't shared many details of his experience with me. When others asked what happened, I'd done most of the answering.

"So Jim," Alex said. "What was that blood pressure blowout like? You had us totally scared."

"Again," Ellen added.

"It-it was the worst freaking thing I've ever been through."

"Worse than being charged by that brown bear?" Alex quipped.

The fall before, on separate deer hunting trips, Jim and Alex each had close calls with a grizzly bear, possibly the same female.

Alex, like Jim, had been hunting alone on Admiralty Island. The bear Alex startled ran off.

In Jim's encounter, he pulled our kayak up through the intertidal zone to secure it in tall ryegrass. It was Thanksgiving weekend, when Alaska's coastal brown bears, larger versions of Alaska's interior grizzlies, were typically hibernating.

With storm conditions prevailing, we'd anchored in the lee of Point Young. Warm mug clasped in both hands, I watched Jim kayak to shore, knowing if he made it paddling upwind, he could get back to the boat. When I saw he was safely ashore, I went below, where one-month-old Glen slept. Assuming all was well, I pulled out a shoebox of family photos to add to a scrapbook.

Meanwhile, Jim lugged the kayak up the sandy berm and began removing hunting gear. Suddenly, a five-hundred-pound bear thundered toward him. A couple feet away, she skidded to a stop, huffing steamy air. Caught off guard, he jabbed at her snarling muzzle with his not-yet-loaded gun, using it like a spear. On the third thrust, the riled bear snorted, turned, and galloped off.

"It sure came out of the blue," Jim said, "just like that bear. But the blood pressure blowout was more like a mauling."

"Geez!" Alex said, sawing off a slice of bread. "What do you remember?"

Jim inhaled and exhaled forcefully through his nostrils. "Around one that morning, this headache came on, kept intensifying. Like nothing I've ever experienced. Pounding. I buzzed the nurse. She put the cuff on. Wrote something down. Pumped it back up. Read it again, then left in a hurry."

This was new. Jim was opening up, willing to tell the story with a glimmer in his eye, even though the experience was still raw.

His breathing at the dinner table became more labored as if remembering demanded more oxygen. "Suddenly, six doctors gathered around me. They leaned in, discussing my symptoms. Their name tags jittered so much I couldn't read them. One lifted my hand, turned it over. I missed most of what they were saying. Their grim faces and voices drifted in and out. The pain came in tunnel vision waves so intense, I was almost blind and deaf from it."

Alex ignored a forkful of meatloaf, eyes glued on Jim.

"Dr. Royal, the night-shift neurologist, was inches away, hands on my arm—firm. He looked like Robin Williams with a thick beard—but serious." Jim grabbed his own forearm. "Royal entered my shrunken visual zone. He seemed to understand that was the only way to reach me. He said my name. The delay between his mouth moving and his voice made it seem like he was far away. He enunciated each word. "We . . . do . . . not . . . know . . . what is causing your pain or high blood pressure. We've ordered a CT scan to make sure there's nothing nasty happening inside your skull.' I remember those exact words."

"When the nurse asked where my wife was staying, I told her next door at the Baroness She asked if I wanted her to call you." He leaned on folded forearms, and looked at me. "I said to wait until morning."

I had not heard that detail. He let me sleep, I thought, while all hell broke loose inside his head. I shut my eyes against a building pressure. Ellen squeezed my shoulder. While I was typing my first CaringBridge post to friends at the secretary desk, describing Jim's initial recovery, he was four hours into this ordeal.

During dessert we shifted to light reminiscing, prompting peals of laughter. Jim was in his element, sharing food, wine, and stories with friends.

After our friends left, I did a minimal cleanup, then found Jim standing at the bathroom sink, about to wash his face. I reached around him from behind. He took my forearms into his hands, and we held each other in front of the mirror for a long time. I eased away to massage his shoulders and back.

"Tell me what's good," I said. "I don't always know what you want anymore." For years, he'd been the one more likely to ask.

It was my turn.

24

WHITE FLAG

I poured two glasses of chardonnay and carried them through the French doors to the deck. Jim, wearing cargo shorts and a navy T-shirt, squirted lighter fluid onto a pyramid of charcoal briquets. A whiff of solvent triggered fond memories of other weekend barbecues. On a plate, steaks from one of three deer he'd shot the previous fall were marinating.

I set his glass on the rail and gazed out at the sea of evergreen spires, a living edge of our country's largest national forest. "The garden's taking off. Half of tonight's salad is baby greens."

"It sure feels like summer." He carried his glass to the patio table and pulled out two chairs.

Relaxed, I filled him in on Glen's camp activities and my work at the university. "The REU program's off to a good start. I like the students. Two will do their scuba checkout dives tomorrow."

He swirled his wine. "I'd like to dive again."

What? I thought. He must mean in the distant future. He loved being in the ocean and was certified as a research diver. He and his Glacier Bay research team would suit up in quilted underwear, hood, and booties, and shove themselves into stiff, coated-nylon dry suits equipped with O-ring seals customized for a snug fit around ankles, wrists, and neck. They swam along the seafloor, wearing headlamps and holding clipboards of waterproof datasheets. Their search target was usually Dungeness crab, but they recorded other invertebrates and fish as well.

"Like . . . in a year?" I asked.

"No. This summer."

"No way. You're not ready." The words avalanched out of my mouth, too fast, too strong. But I couldn't help thinking about his paralyzed vocal cord and balance issues. I pictured him choking underwater through a bubbling regulator.

He bristled. "I-I'm talking about recreational diving. Not research scuba."

"I'm not okay with that either. Not yet."

He glared at me, then stood. The metal chair grated backward. He strode to the grill, picked up the tongs. Back toward me, he rearranged red-hot coals.

I waited a minute and went inside. If that's the way he's going to be, I thought, I'll check on Glen.

After cooling down, I returned carrying place settings and the salad.

"Hey," he said over his shoulder. "I've been meaning to tell you how much I like those hiking poles you ordered." We knew each other well enough to recognize implicit apologies. I refilled his empty glass. He cleared his throat and said, "I agree it's too soon to think about scuba, but I'd like free dive, and Cortez said I could swim."

I pressed my lips together. I needed to erase the images in my head, and I knew not to reject his revised proposal outright—a guaranteed backfire. From behind, I slid my arms around his waist. "That's . . . sort of true. As I recall, though, he wasn't aware of any reason why you couldn't swim. He only knew of basic survival data for lateral medullary strokes—nothing on how survivors handled swimming specifically."

The steaks sizzled as he lowered them onto the grill. His

silence suggested he was chewing on my comment. "I-I'd like to get out on the boat this weekend."

Three weeks earlier he'd emerged through wide hospital doors into Seattle's noon light, pale and fifteen pounds below normal. Compared to scuba diving, taking our sailboat a few miles down Stephens Passage seemed reasonable. Since we'd been home, the walker and wheelchair had remained folded against a wall. He'd hiked several mountain trails with the poles. Every day he pushed the limits of his damaged nervous system, striding across town to stores, riding the bus, stretching, striking odd yoga poses—one foot tucked against a thigh—promoting new neurons to replace those destroyed.

Still, I contained my honest reaction. The nystagmus prevented him from reading for more than a few minutes. Bolts of eye pain struck at the dinner table, on the bus, in bed at night—anywhere, any time. Vision and neuromuscular issues had kept driving a car out of reach. Could operating a forty-two-foot ketch be safe when he couldn't drive?

"Do you think we're ready to go boating?" My tone sounded more open to the idea than I was.

"We could go to Taku Harbor. Motor, not sail. It's an easy run—twenty miles. We've done it lots of times."

"But you've still got issues. Your balance is off."

"On a boat, everyone's off-balance. It'll be easier than being at home. Boats are designed so you can get around when it's rough, handholds everywhere. I want to spend time on the water with you and Glen."

"But what if something happens? Once we turn the corner at the end of Gastineau Channel, we won't be able to reach anyone in Juneau."

By *anyone* I meant the medics in jumpsuits, the rescue floatplane we might need to fly him to safety. I tried to imagine being on our boat. We'd shared mainly good, but also stressful, times on the water. Simply docking in a crosscurrent with wind required hand–eye coordination and clear verbal directions. He was our captain and mechanic. I could do a lot, but I was not up to running the boat without him. If the engine failed, and he was incapacitated, could Glen and I set the sails and keep *Ijsselmeer* from going aground? Could I deliver him to help in time?

My calmer self recognized alarmist voices. I'd copiloted boats out of dire circumstances more times than I wanted to remember. But I didn't have all the skills to be *Ijsselmeer's* solo captain if something happened to Jim. Even so, it was summer. Other boats would be on the water. If we had trouble, someone would help. Over the years, we'd responded to Mayday calls. The boating community was like that. And *Ijsselmeer's* engine was more reliable than most because of his meticulous care.

"Dr. Cortez said my chance of having another stroke was no higher than anyone else's."

The neurologist had mentioned he had the blood vessels of a young man, but surely he hadn't meant for Jim to operate a large boat this soon. "I don't like not being able to contact Juneau if something happens," I said. "The marine operator network is shutting down. Everyone's switching to cell phones."

"I'll install the new wifi booster. It came right before—" He paused. "Before Seattle."

"But there aren't any repeaters in Stephens Passage."

"We'll have coverage most of the time. Let's go for the weekend. We need to get away. I need quality time with you and Glen."

I let his words sink in. "Okay . . . but only if the forecast is good and the booster is working."

His solutions and logic softened my resistance, but it was the look in his eyes—a caged animal begging for freedom—that won me over.

❥ ❥ ❥

A couple of mornings later, a jolt against the mattress woke me. "Jim?" Heavy shades kept our bedroom dark long after the four o'clock sunrise.

From below the foot of the bed, he muttered, "I-I'm okay."

I sat up. "What happened?"

"I lost my balance." He rose from the floor and sat on the bed. "When I first wake up, my foot's a bit numb."

"But you've never fallen down before."

"My balance isn't so great when it's dark—when I can't see. I didn't want to wake you with the light."

"You sure you're okay?"

"I-I'm fine. Can I bring you coffee?"

It was six o'clock—a workday. "That'd be wonderful."

In the month since our return, it was the first time he'd gotten up ahead of me.

Thursday afternoon at the harbor, the three of us transferred gear and food down the ramp to the boat. We unpacked groceries and duffels into lockers and spaces below floorboards and filled the tiny refrigerator with perishables. Glen and I topped off water tanks and hosed the deck, and Jim stowed engine oil and gear. He and Glen installed the booster antenna on top of the mizzen-mast while I made dinner.

To streamline the morning departure, we slept on board at the dock. The forecast was good—no big winds or storms. Glen settled in the forepeak bunk with a book, and Jim said goodnight.

In the aft cabin, I lifted the covers and slipped around the mast post into our double berth. Radiating warmth, Jim pulled me close. Only twelve miles from home, the pressures of work and our uncertain future faded. Being on our sailboat oasis simplified life to what was essential, creating space to appreciate and love each other.

I woke to water sloshing against the hull. Gulls exchanged strident calls. When the lapping became irregular, I whispered, "Could that be a river otter?" They'd swum around our boat before. Inches from our faces—separated only by the hull—an otter snuffled, splashed, and dove. We listened to several rounds of quick breaths in between dives.

I was tempted to linger but sat up and said, "We need to catch the tide." This was our first post-stroke test run with the boat: no room for mistakes.

I ground French roast beans and boiled water while Jim crouched in front of the engine room to check oil, coolant, and fuel filters. He climbed to the cockpit and started the diesel engine. "Hey, Glen," he called out over the low rumble. "Time to wake up and help us get underway."

We put on life jackets, Jim took the helm, and Glen and I climbed down onto the dock. "Beth, you cover the stern. Glen, you handle the bow." Jim shifted into gear. The boat inched forward. Glen and I leaned against the hull, pushing her twenty-eight thousand pounds into a light wind. I signaled Glen to climb on board.

"You get on first," he said. "I've got it."

I hesitated, then grabbed the lifeline, and hoisted myself up. Glen continued easing us off the dock, walking his hands back along the moving boat, body angled over the water. Seconds before the stern would clear the last piling, he sprang like Spiderman onto the side of the hull and climbed aboard. Our son had never before executed the departure push-off.

Jim powered up to cruising, seven knots, and set our course down Gastineau Channel toward the rising sun. Miles ahead, a fishing boat motored in the same direction. Our bow split smooth water, leaving two rippling trails. The engine hummed. As we gained speed, optimism pushed aside lingering tension, opening my mind to the day ahead. Facing the sea breeze, I felt like I was blossoming into the present, shedding stiff outer petals of worry one by one into our frothy wake.

Ahead, a pair of marbled murrelets paddled across the water. At closer range, they took off, dangling legs slapping wavelets until their small football-shaped bodies lifted clear. Improbable creatures, I thought. A pair lays one egg high in an old-growth forest within the mossy crook of a conifer limb. After the chick hatches, one parent flies on wings optimized for diving, not flight, some twenty miles, up to eight times a day, from forest to ocean to forest. Each trip, the returning adult delivers a calorie-rich fish to a downy youngster, hunkered beneath its mate. Before sunrise, the parents silently swap roles. A month after hatching, the fledgling rises from its treetop moss bed, scooches to a higher edge, stretches, and flaps its wings, exercising and preening for a day or so. Then—without any practice—the chick lurches off the branch and flies those twenty miles by itself on stubby wings, a wobbly torpedo aimed for the sea.

Standing tall at the helm, hair blown back, Jim looked relaxed. Normal. It struck me he was like one of those murrelet chicks: wide open to expeditions never before tried. At the foot of Mount Roberts, we motored past a row of beachfront homes with expansive decks and big windows. I used to want to own one of them. If we'd taken that path, we couldn't have afforded *Ijsselmeer.* I stepped into the cockpit onto the teak bench behind Jim and draped my arms around his shoulders, chin nestled in the crook of his neck.

"God, this feels good," he said. "This morning, I woke up and didn't think about the stroke until I was out of bed."

"I've had moments of forgetting, too."

"I keep expecting to learn it's been a bad dream—a terrible, long nightmare."

I held him tighter. "I'll start breakfast and more coffee."

"Don't go yet." He reached a hand back to hold my

We leaned into each other, admiring emerald mountains aiid the glassy sea.

Later, in the cockpit, the three of us ate scrambled eggs on flour tortillas. Afterward, I tested the new cell phone booster. Skeptical, I wrote a test email to Brendan and watched it swoosh off. I let him know we were heading to Taku Harbor and when we were due back. I didn't mention my concerns about Jim's health, but if something happened, Brendan would be the person I'd contact.

After we turned south into Stephens Passage, I took the helm while Jim rested.

We passed a salmon troller motoring north, too far away to ck. notice my wave. As we approached Grand Island, I spotted a wispy blow. I reached for my binoculars.

"Glen! Come check this out. There's a humpback—close." The baleen whale was working the shoreline, using a rocky ledge to concentrate small schooling fish, possibly herring or capelin.

He poked his head up through the companionway. "Cool."

"It's a small one, probably a yearling."

We watched the whale surface close to a kelp bed.

"Can I use your digital camera?" he asked.

He'd never tried to photograph a whale. Excited for his interest, I said, "Sure. It's in the cubbie, below the chart table.

"Thanks!"

"Be sure to zoom in."

"Oh . . . it's not for the whale. I'm going to make a claymation video."

From the helm, I watched him pinch off pieces of clay, roll and shape colored bits. He climbed up to show me a stick-figure cowboy and little clay dog. He set them up on the table, shot a few frames, repositioned the figures, filmed a few seconds again, and on he went. He'd learned the stop-action filming technique at the fine arts camp. I'd failed to pique his interest in a feeding whale, but at least he was happily entertaining himself.

Around noon Jim took the helm. Taku Harbor, once home to a bustling salmon cannery, is a favorite wilderness getaway for Juneau boaters. He eased us alongside the pier, reversing the engine in the last seconds for a smooth docking. A couple of fishing tugs, a small sailboat, and a twenty-foot aluminum cabin cruiser were tied up. While Glen worked on his video, we rested in the aft cabin. Jim fell asleep fast. As the boat lolled in the water, I listened to a Steller's jay screeching and the buzzy mono-tones of varied thrushes. Summer in Alaska was hard to top.

Midafternoon, we pulled on Xtratuf rubber boots and went ashore. Glen and I each carried a casting pole. Jim maneuvered ahead, trekking pole in each fist. The floating dock rocked with his shifting weight.

"Remember the time we were here when Glen was a tod-dler?" I said. "Glen, right about here, you ran ahead. You turned around to get our attention, but kept stepping back. Before we knew it, you'd hit the dock edge and flipped over backward. You plopped into the water headfirst. Right here. Your dad yanked you out by your life jacket."

"You looked so surprised." Jim grinned.

"Yeah, I remember," Glen said. "The water was *really* cold."

Jim swayed ahead on the trail. A thick stand of lichen-draped hemlock and spruce reached out over the path. At ground level, lime-green devil's club, lush ferns, and brambles grew in dap-pled shade. The scent of a temperate forest in full production sweetened the air: moist soil, seeds germinating, life erupting. We followed Jim onto rocky mudflats, exposed by the low tide. I slipped on an algae-covered rock, but caught my balance by flinging out my arms.

Ta-lick, ta-lack, ta-lick. His trekking poles made a rhythm against the stones. He was getting the knack, moving across irregular terrain. He squatted to examine something. "Hey, come look at this," he called.

We joined him as he turned over a rock to show us a swarm of amphipods and a writhing, blood-red ribbon worm.

I wished his doctors could see him. At the hospital, they told me he'd need the walker for at least a month. We'd been home three weeks.

Taku Harbor had also been a seasonal, and later year-round, home to the Taku people—a regional tribe within Alaska's Native Tlingits—a trading post, a salmon salting operation, and a major salmon cannery. At one time, around 270 people lived on its shores, harvesting fish from the river and ocean, berries from the forest. Dilapidated houses with red tin roofs and weathered outbuildings stood at odd angles along the overgrown northeast bank. Abandoned decades earlier and declared a National Historic Landmark in 1978, we had the cove to ourselves. Large skeletons of rusted canning machinery and boiler parts loomed along the shore, like avant-garde statues. The beach was scattered with clam shells, purple mussel beds, and shards of blue-and-white pottery.

We picked our way to a familiar rock outcropping. Jim set down his poles and helped Glen bait his rig. Twenty feet ahead, a grebe paddled past us and dove in clear water. The *whoosh-plunks* of my husband's and son's lures hitting water were music to my ears.

"Dad's got one!" Glen shouted, cranking his own line in.

Holding a wide stance in sandy mud, Jim reeled in a shimmering trout. "It's a beautiful little cutthroat."

Glen knelt nearby while Jim cleaned the trout at the water's edge.

Encouraged, I picked up a pole. Several casts later, I shouted, "I've got something." I wound the reel, watching a speckled fish swerve through the water. In one glimpse, I saw the rosy blush on its gills. "Another cutthroat." I backed up, bringing the foot-long fish onto beach gravel.

Glen waved a high five.

"Nice job." Jim stepped toward me, wobbly without poles, but determined. He dropped to his knees and pounced on the flapping trout seconds after it thrashed free of my hook. My catch was no trophy, but we cheered like our lives depended on it.

While Jim and Glen fished, I sat on a boulder and watched the horned grebe surface and dive. Twice I saw the little bird swimming on his side through the water, lobed feet propelling him this way and that as he snatched invisible prey. I tried to predict where he'd pop up next. I was always wrong. I thought about Jim's comment back at home that he wanted to free-dive for crab on this trip. Catching these fish, I hoped, would make him drop that food-gathering plan.

"Hey, you guys," Jim called from his casting post. "I'm going to head back." It was unusual for him to leave first. That was normally my role.

"I'll go with you," Glen said.

The sun warm on my face, I said I'd stay a while longer.

Jim urged me to take my time then started back.

Glen passed me his rod and scampered across boulders like a mountain goat, passing his father. I tried to imagine where we'd go from here. What would Jim's future look like? Would he be able to do research as an independent contractor as planned? Would we recover from the lost vision of building a home at Lena Point? Could I find a less demanding job I liked that would support us?

I positioned the leader beneath my index finger and flung the pole overhead, releasing at the apex as he'd taught me seventeen years earlier. The line played out with a faint *ker-plunk* as the weight hit water. After several casts, I felt a tug and glimpsed a kelp greenling, about four times the size of the cutthroats. I imagined the excitement back at the boat—too soon. The fish broke free. A small pollock bit, and I kept it for bait. As the sun set, a burst of orange backlit a stand of spruce along the cove's western rim. I thought of the endless days in the hospital when I could not see ahead. Watching the little grebe forage while Jim and Glen fished, running *IJsselmeer* down Stephens Passage, seeing Jim click his way across the rocky intertidal with our son—and casting by myself—calmed and centered me.

A swarm of no-see-um insects found me. Soon they were the only things biting. I gave up casting and headed back to my family.

Walking back across the intertidal, I remembered an outing the summer before on our boat to Hawk Inlet when our nephew was with us. Jim had been keen to try out his new free-diving wetsuit. After he'd been snorkeling in the cove, he crocodile-crawled up to my half-submerged boots, inhalations whistling into the snorkel. I squatted to greet him. The mask amplified his grin. He raised a mesh goodie bag, offering his clacking bounty of Dungeness crabs like other men deliver a dozen roses.

Back in the cockpit, I pulled off my boots. The evening air had cooled. I climbed down the companionway ladder into the warm galley and aroma of basmati rice cooking.

"Welcome back." Jim and I embraced. Two teak spice shelves were laid on the counter. "Can you give me a hand?" he asked.

While the rice cooked, we installed the new racks along the galley wall, a project interrupted by the stroke. On a boat, every cubic inch of space is valued. While I put away tools, Jim dipped trout fillets in beaten egg and cornmeal-paprika breading. I poured water while Glen added bowls of broccoli, rice, and salad.

The smoking skillet sizzled as Jim set it on the table.

"The trout's fantastic," I said. "Jim, what was your favorite part of the day?"

He'd taken a bite of fish when he started to answer.

"Finish chewing," Glen said.

He swallowed. "I-I love being out on the boat again. Everything's familiar. I also really liked—" He coughed several times.

"Finish before you talk," Glen insisted.

"—hiking and fishing," Jim continued. "And tomorrow, I'm going to get us some Dungies."

"Oh, really?" I thought he knew I didn't want him to snorkel yet.

Moments later, he had to clear his throat after a drink of water. Glen urged him again to be careful. By dinner's end, Jim was annoyed with the interruptions. For seven weeks, our son's well-intentioned cautions had punctuated most meals.

Jim's difficulty swallowing also sparked my concerns, but I kept quiet. What troubled me was whether I would be able to talk him out of free-diving the next day.

25

DON'T LIMIT ME

"Good morning." Jim set a mug of coffee and bowl of oatmeal on the pullout table next to our berth.

Golden light streamed through the hatch. I stretched and sat up. "It is."

"We're comin' up on low tide. Stay here, if you like. There's no wind. Glen's sleeping. I can get us off the dock and anchored mid-cove."

"What's your plan?"

"I-I'd like to snorkel and see if I can get us some Dungies."

My hands tightened on the mug. "Are you sure? It's only been two months."

"It's no big deal. My wet suit's like flotation. I won't wear much weight. It'll be fine. Water's clear and it's a minus tide—perfect for free-diving."

I stared sideways at him.

"I'll be *fine.*" He shook his head, radiating a *don't limit me* look.

"Okay, then. I'll help get us off the dock and anchored."

As the tide dropped, the boat behind us would block us in. The departure would be tricky in the shallow inner cove with limited space to turn around.

He left the cabin, and the engine started with a familiar

thu–rumm. I dressed and went up top. While releasing dock lines, Jim tossed me a life vest. I zipped it on. The air was cool on my arms and face. Small waves sloshed onto the beach where a faint mist rose in front of the lush forest.

Jim shifted into gear. I pushed the bow away from the dock and climbed on. We inched forward. Nearby, a loon peered underwater, arched, and dove.

Helm hard to port, he powered up and shifted, forward-neutral-reverse, through a four-point turn, turning the boat around in the tight space.

Bleep! Bleep! Bleep! The depth sounder blared. Programmed with two feet to spare, the alarm still kicked up my heart rate. Watching Jim pivot our forty-two-foot ketch 180 degrees, I saw no impairment. A jumble of pride and awe welled up in my chest.

We slid past the other boat and rounded the end float. The depth flashed from six to seven, then nine feet. "Impressive," I said, relieved to be beyond the risk of going aground. "How did that feel?"

He stared out across the shimmering cove. "I-I have to concentrate more. But it feels good." He squinted, then muttered, "It's easier than walking."

After we'd anchored, he undressed in the cockpit, dusted his skin with cornstarch, and tugged on neoprene Farmer Johns. I took off my life vest and hung it with the others, then helped him stretch the hooded top down over his torso.

"I'd like to have the kayak ready in case you need help," I said. "And to photograph that loon if it sticks around. Can you give me a hand launching it?"

We went forward, lifted the double kayak over the rail and tied it midship.

"Hey!" Glen poked his head up from the companionway.

"Good morning, Mr. Sleepy." I ruffled his hair. "Your dad made oatmeal the way you like—with raisins and vanilla."

"Mornin' Glen," Jim said, then turned to me. "I need to get in the water. This suit's cooking me."

At the stern, he held my shoulder and strapped on long, free-diving flippers. He bent over to buckle his weight belt and attach a mesh bag.

It seemed too soon for him to free-dive for crab. But his neurologist said swimming should be fine.

I unhooked the lifeline above the ladder. He stretched the mask onto his face, smoothed his mustache out of the way, then positioned the snorkel, a familiar routine.

I slid out a few hairs caught beneath the mask's rim and kissed him on the cheek. "Don't overdo it. Okay?"

He nodded, lips expanded, chimp-like, around the snorkel mouthpiece.

One hand on a halyard, he lifted each flippered foot over the stern rail and balanced on his heels, four feet above rippling water. I knew he'd use the giant stride entry method, rather than descend the ladder. When suited up, it's easier to jump in than maneuver down the narrow rungs. He hesitated, a hand holding his mask against his face.

"Take your time." I liked how he looked in his black wetsuit—normal.

He stepped out over the water, legs in a deep stride, ready to execute the entry scissor kick as soon as he hit water. I can still see him there, as if I'd snapped a photo, catching him midair, strong legs in a wide stride. A research diver, he'd done the entry many times. He dropped and splashed in. His head disappeared. Normally, right after the closing kick, the diver pops back up.

Seconds ticked off as I stared at the ocean's surface. Mirage-like through teal water, I saw him kicking, but he was on his side, head underwater, swimming parallel to the surface, like the grebe. His flippers pulsed the sea to a froth, steering him away from the boat. He hadn't taken a breath.

"Jim!" I called out, confused.

Twenty feet from the stern, he lurched sideways, breaking free. His mouth opened, gasping. It was as if a demon had speared him from below and was dragging his body away from us inches below the surface. For a second, then, his face—submerged—flashed into view. I glimpsed the fear.

Glen appeared. "What's going on?" he asked, alarmed.

Our eyes met and I saw Glen understood his father was in trouble.

Then, by chance it seemed, Jim's kicking curved him back toward the stern.

All I could think was, Get his head out of the water. Damn. I'm not wearing a life jacket. He'll pull me under. No time. He was coming my way. I scrambled down the ladder, gripped the top rung. Knees bent tight, feet on the bottom step, I leaned out. Ready.

"Get him!" Glen shouted.

Every edge of his 180-pound body was smooth black neoprene—no handholds.

His arms flew about, fighting for life. His strong legs kicked and kicked—driving him away from air.

Cold water lapped my feet. *Lean farther. Hold tight.*

Glen clenched my wrist.

As Jim lurched toward the stern, I took aim. My strike hit his shoulder. I clutched a fistful of neoprene, but he kept kicking. I tensed my arm, bicep straining to keep him. Our eyes met, but his jittered side to side. He didn't see me. His next kick ripped the slick neoprene out of my hand. He was yanked back under and away.

What the hell was going on?

"Jim!" I yelled. Glen's shouts joined mine. "Jim! *Jim!*"

The splashes seemed to be circling back.

I braced as Jim thrashed toward the stern.

"Grab him!" Glen yelled.

I struck out, cuffing his neck with all my force. I pulled. His head came up, eyes unfocused, confused. He gasped.

"Jim. It's me. I have you. I have you."

His legs fought me. My arm quivered.

"Glen, throw me the floating line."

The yellow line appeared.

My plan was to tie it around his chest—secure him. I instantly realized that wouldn't work. Suspended by one arm over the water, I couldn't loop the line without letting him go.

Face inches from his, I spoke firmly, "I've got you."

He shook his head, inhaled, and coughed. "I'm-I'm okay." His kicking slowed, then stopped. Deep inhale, exhale. "I'm okay."

I did not trust his words. I pulled him closer. "Hook your arm on the ladder," I commanded.

He brought an arm up through a low rung as if he was in a trance. His chest rose and fell. "I-I'm okay."

"Can you hold on while we put a line around you?"

He stared ahead, catching his breath. "Yeah."

I scrambled up. Glen handed me a lifejacket. I zipped it on, climbed down, and we secured a line around Jim.

Jim removed his flippers and raised them, one by one, to Glen. While I kept tension on his tether he climbed the ladder like an old man then stumbled onto the deck. We grabbed him and hugged him tight.

"My God. What happened?"

"Dad? What were you doing?"

He shook his head. "I-I can't tell you now. It-it was awful."

We released him and he staggered to the cockpit. He lay down on his back, forearm over eyes. A moment later, he said, "I've got to get out of this suit."

We helped extract him from the long-sleeved top and Farmer Johns. While he soaped up and hosed off in the cockpit, his expression remained distant.

"What happened?" I asked again.

"I need to rest." Towel around his waist, he made his way to the aft cabin.

An hour later, I touched his arm. "Would you like some lunch?" He drew me onto the bed, on top of him. We held each other.

"Holy shit," he said.

I stroked his hair. "If you want to tell me now, Glen's napping." I slid alongside him, head in the curve of his arm. From the beginning, he'd coaxed me beyond my comfort zone—lured me to Alaska, taught me how to sail. No part of me wanted to rail at him for snorkeling too soon—play that pointless I-told-you-so card.

He stared at the cabin ceiling, where reflected light danced. "I remember doing my weight belt check, holding the halyard to balance. Lifting my flippers over the rail was hard, but I kept thinking, one leap and I'm free. Screw this walking crap. In the water, my legs won't have to be coordinated. When I hit water, I knew something was wrong. I did the scissor kick, expecting the euphoria of weightlessness. Instead, some alarm went off. I thought maybe I'd hit my head or gotten hung up in a fishing line—"

"Were you?"

"No. That wasn't it. As soon as I went under—" He winced as if in physical pain. "I-I couldn't tell where up was. I told myself, 'Go to the surface!' I wasn't deep, but I could *not* find it."

"Oh, geez."

"First thing you learn in scuba if you get disoriented: follow your bubbles. But I'd knocked my mask off. I couldn't see. I started kicking for the surface. My right hand found and released my weight belt clip. It dropped off. That's my training. Then I finally broke the surface. But-but, oh, my God." He winced. "Our sixty-foot mast was horizontal."

"What?"

"The ocean was friggin' vertical. I panicked. I couldn't tell what was real. For a split second, I thought, 'Oh, I get it. This is a nightmare.' But I knew I was in trouble. My brain wasn't working. Everything I learned about following bubbles—not possible. 'Swim hard!' I told myself. That's what I did. I kicked."

I squeezed my arms around him.

"I wasn't scared. I just thought, 'Swim hard! The plane's going down. Holy shit. The plane's crashing.'"

"Do you remember needing to breathe? You didn't come up for air."

"I don't. I swam as hard as I could. If I'd had the wherewithal, I could've simply relaxed. Without the weight belt, I was buoyant. I knew the surface wasn't vertical. But logic was totally gone. I think the cold water hitting my face screwed up my ability to tell up from down."

We held each other as waves sloshed against the hull.

"I remember you grabbing me," he said. "Oh, my God. Thank God."

"I grabbed you *twice*." I trembled. "You couldn't see me. You scared me so bad." I buried my face in his T-shirt and hugged him hard.

Later, at the cockpit table, the three of us ate grilled cheese sandwiches and sliced cantaloupe.

"Tell me what happened," Glen said for the third time.

Jim wiped his mustache and cleared his throat. "Something went wrong with my bal-balance."

Glen stared at his father. "Why were you kicking so hard?"

"I couldn't tell up from down. I'm okay now. I won't jump in like that again."

It was our last morning at Taku Harbor. As I extracted myself from bed, not wanting to wake Jim, I froze each time he stirred, like one of Glen's clay animation figures. After Jim coughed and rolled over, I eased out and went forward through the main salon to close our son's door. The plan was to return home later that day. After scanning the cove for wildlife I returned to the warmth below, cued classical music, made coffee, and wrote in my journal, grateful for time to myself.

Twenty minutes later, Glen's door popped open. There goes my alone time, I thought. "Good morning, pumpkin!"

"Hey," he said, hair wild, eyes puffy. With no further words, he climbed across the cushioned settee and nestled into my lap.

I wrapped my arms around his lanky body. He has my grandmother's long legs and toes, I noticed for the first time. Savor this. One day he'll no longer choose to curl against your core. Your arms will ache to hold his goodness. Smoothing the hair around his ear, I leaned into the magic of my son's drowsy love.

26

BOTTLENECK

"How's that going to work?" I asked. "My REU program doesn't end for another month—in August."

At home weeks later, over a glass of wine, Jim had announced his plan to take our boat on a three-week expedition around Admiralty Island, some three hundred miles.

"You can take some time off," he said. "I've mapped it out. You and Glen will crew the first leg from Juneau to Hoonah over a weekend. From there, you take the ferry back to Juneau to finish up."

Three months earlier, the day everything changed, we were a week from moving on board to begin a similar trip. We'd planned to spend the summer mainly on the boat, which would have made it easier for the realtor to show the house. I would travel back and forth as work allowed. Jim's new plan was shorter, but mirrored the aborted one—except for one glaring difference: he was recovering from a stroke. His proposal made me edgy.

"But you can't be out alone with Glen."

He bristled. "I've invited Brendan and Corwin."

My face grew warm. He'd set this trip in motion without consulting me.

"They'll replace you in Hoonah for the middle leg. You can then join us for the last two weeks after your students leave."

Why was I resisting his plan? There was no one else I trusted more as crew than Brendan, and his son, at age thirteen, had more experience on the water than anyone else we knew his age. Plus, Glen and Corwin got along famously. But I didn't like not being with them for the whole trip.

"We'll have a great time sailing down Chatham Strait, up Stephens Passage," he spoke as if my concern hadn't registered. "We need this—as a family—before Glen goes back to school."

Later in the week, during an evening walk around the neighborhood, our conversation migrated to fine-tuning the August expedition. We realized there would be a few days between when Brendan and Corwin left and my return.

"Just how long *are* you planning to stay in Juneau?"

"We already talked about that. I'll need eight days." I tried to keep my voice steady. "That leaves three with only you and Glen. After they leave, you'll stay at the dock, right?"

He let go of my hand. "No, we'll be out."

I stopped walking.

He turned back to face me. "We'll anchor in Neka Bay. It's only thirty minutes from the dock, but it's a world away. You and I anchored there through a winter storm. It's bomb-proof."

"It's not the weather that worries me." He knew what I was getting at. He had to have another adult on board. Why was he making me be explicit? "I need you to stay at the dock."

"Why don't you come back sooner?"

"I can't." I let out a long sigh.

He frowned, lips tight.

"You have to work with me," I said. "I can't ignore what's happened."

He shoved his hands into his jacket pockets. "All right."

"And please, no swimming. No snorkeling when it's only you two."

Navigating his recovery and moodiness was straining our

relationship. Although I didn't like the idea of leaving the expedition midway, time apart might help us through this bottleneck.

Monday morning, the week we were to begin the Admiralty trip, I left home early and drove to a café near campus. Steaming mug beside my laptop, I chipped away at my list for the last stretch of the undergraduate research program. Enveloped by the cozy aroma of crisping waffles and rhythmic soundtracks, I sent emails to students who still owed me research abstracts, created a flyer for the final seminar and barbecue, and consulted with my colleague Matt to firm up how we'd share student introductions during the seminar. At ten, I called Kim to make sure Glen had arrived as planned for a play date with Tenzing.

"They're in the treehouse," she said, "hammering something."

Back at my office, I settled in to finish an important letter. As chair of the Alaska Scientific Review Group, an advisory board of a dozen scientists mandated by the Marine Mammal Protection Act, my team and I were urging the National Marine Fisheries Service (NMFS) and the Alaska Native Harbor Seal Commission to update federal population boundaries for harbor seals. Because both agencies had ignored this responsibility for thirteen years, the species was at risk of being over-hunted through localized depletions.

Our letter urged NMFS to implement harvest guidelines based on the best available scientific data, including genetics and ecological sustainability. This was the most important conservation document I'd coauthored.

Favorite blue-ink pen in hand, I signed my name: Elizabeth A. Mathews. Our team's letter could potentially winch the National Oceanic and Atmospheric Administration out of a deep political ditch.

On Thursday, I led a seminar and met with students for one-on-one advising. Teaching and answering questions invigorated me. Next, I added a section to a research proposal due before I joined Jim and Glen.

Midafternoon, I reviewed an unusual accident report. One of our research skiffs had collided with a humpback whale. My job was to determine if we needed to revise safety protocols. From their account, it appeared the whale was not seriously injured. I concluded the accident primarily reflected a recent increase in the Northeast Pacific population of humpbacks with reduced visibility and a bit of bad luck stirred in. Students had followed all safety procedures, quickly retrieved the boat operator—who had been knocked overboard into cold water—minimizing what could have been a much more serious accident.

Before leaving, I straightened stacks of folders, notes, and research papers. They could wait. I'd tackled what was most pressing. Yet, part of me did not want to go boating. The impulse to stay and work on a paper I hoped to publish, read colleague Jan Straley's recent article describing how sperm whales stole squid from fishermen's longlines, or take care of one more important email was strong. The desire to back out of the Admiralty trip ran counter to my desire for Jim to succeed in leading the expedition.

Jim was right: my job pulled me in many directions. But it was also deeply fulfilling with measurable short- and long-term successes. In contrast, some of the hurdles at home seemed insurmountable.

27

BACK IN THE SADDLE

Saturday morning, south of Douglas Island, we pulled anchor beneath low, dense clouds. We'd left the Juneau dock late afternoon the day before. Glen slept, and I took the helm, while Jim bled an air bubble out of the heater's fuel line. Even in August, we needed a functioning heater to keep *IJsselmeer* comfortable and provide hot—albeit short—showers. He finished the job as we motored toward Scull Island, a small rocky outcropping. Stephens Passage was outside my aerial survey range for Glacier Bay, but I liked to check a section on the island commonly occupied by harbor seals during low tides. En route, Glen climbed into the cockpit, blue robe wrapped tight and its hood up against the morning chill. His response to our greetings was flat. He hadn't wanted to leave his friends in Juneau.

Something caught my eye as I scanned the exposed rocky shoreline. A Steller sea lion was emerging from the water within ten feet of several seals. In seventeen years, I'd only observed a sea lion on the same beach as harbor seals once. I pulled out my good camera and long lens. Until recent years, Steller sea lion predation on harbor seals was considered extremely rare. Since 1997, though, my team and I had documented thirteen lethal attacks by Stellers on harbor seals in Glacier Bay, where we'd also been tracking a steep decline in the seal population. In a library search, I found no other mention of direct observations of sea lions attacking harbor seals, but suggestive circumstances turned up in two publications. Harbor seal remains were reported in the stomachs of three dead Steller sea lions, two mentioned in a 1975 report and one from a study published in 1755—two accounts in two hundred years before our observations.

I remembered my disbelief and excitement the first time I witnessed a male Steller sea lion attack a harbor seal pup. Adult male sea lions weigh around twelve hundred pounds, compared to a month-old harbor seal at fifty. My field assistant and I were camped on an island a half mile west of Spider Island in Glacier Bay National Park, a primary breeding site for several hundred harbor seals and their pups. We were monitoring the effects of boaters on resting seals. When motorists or kayakers passed too close to the haul-out, they sometimes spooked seals into the water. At seven fifteen that morning, we began surveying every thirty minutes. We sat in low camp chairs with powerful binoculars mounted on tripods between our knees. In between staring through binoculars, I recorded our observations in a notebook propped on my lap, and later summarized:

25 July, 1997

3:40 p.m.: 204 harbor seals were bunched together on two strips of beach not yet covered by the rising tide. At 3:59, all seals stampeded into the water. Moments later, we spotted a large, adult male Steller sea lion between us and the haulout with a small harbor seal in its mouth. The sea lion bit onto the head of the seal and began slinging it side to side. About twenty gulls flocked to the scene, swooping down to the water, snatching bits of tissue. At 4:15, a subadult Steller sea lion approached the bull, who continued to fling the seal about. By 4:16 the seal pup was clearly dead after rigorous thrashing. The smaller sea lion was about a yard from the bull, highly attentive to his activities. The bull disappeared from view and resurfaced, chewing and breathing hard—we could easily hear it huffing from our observation site. At 4:23, a third sea lion, another subadult, approached, and the two younger animals remained close to the big male and appeared to consume scraps of tissue. When the bull began thrashing the seal over his head again, the other two departed. By 4:32, there was no more evidence of the seal pup, the gulls had dispersed, and we watched the big bull swim off to the southwest.

As the Scull Island haulout beach came into view, I lifted my camera and squeezed off a series of overlapping photos of the seals and the lone sea lion. I waited, perched for action. Minutes later, the sea lion ambled back into the water and swam away. Both disappointed and relieved there'd been no predation attempt, I counted the seals through binoculars. Mid-count, one undulated its chubby body up the beach. Another adult in its path flipper-waved as the newcomer approached as if signaling, *Don't get so close.*

"How many?" Jim asked.

"Ninety-five, maybe a hundred, including several older pups." Straddling the cockpit edge, I recorded my count. I never grew tired of observing seals and other wildlife. The focus required was my version of meditation.

"Okay to go?" Jim asked.

I wanted to linger but agreed to leave. A half-dozen surf scoters took flight, necks outstretched, wings humming as they gained altitude. Images of seals on the rocky beach still vivid, Jim at the helm, our son down below, I felt whole in a way I could not remember.

, , ,

After a calm night in Swanson Harbor's craggy embrace, we pulled anchor at daybreak beneath a gray veil. Once beyond Point Couverdon, the boat rose and fell in a lazy three-foot swell. While Jim rifled through his triple-decker tackle box, I navigated to Rocky Island. The day before, I'd counted sixty-nine Steller sea lions resting, jousting, and roaring on the smooth ledge, one of their regular haulouts. I searched with binoculars, but none were on the ledge.

"We're coming up on slack tide," Jim said. "Plus, no wind. It's perfect."

"For what?" Distracted, I was wondering why there were no sea lions on the haulout.

"Fishing the seamount. So we won't drift off."

"Oh right." I remembered our conversation the night before. I traced my fingers across the worn paper chart to the shallow spot. The halibut hill, as some locals called mounts like this, rose from a depth of 150 feet and peaked at twenty-four, shallow enough for sportfishing gear. When the current was running the pinnacle's steep slopes generated eddies, ideal habitat for flatfish to lie in wait for their prey to be delivered. I adjusted the helm ten degrees.

"I'll see if I can rouse Glen. It's clear ahead."

Jim nodded as he baited a circle hook.

Below deck, I gazed at our son's face, marveling how he'd slept through the *clang-cling-chunking* of a hundred feet of steel chain dropping into the bow locker adjacent to his bunk.

"Hey, hon." I jiggled his foot. "It's a gorgeous morning. Fog's burned off."

He rolled over and blinked, flashing a sleepy smile. I reached out to smooth his hair, overcome by a desire to scoop him up and cover him with kisses as if he were still a toddler. Instead,

I leaned in to plant one on his forehead. "Come join us. We're going to fish soon."

Back at the helm, I refined our course. "We're almost there." I read the depths: "Thirty-seven, thirty-two, twenty-six." After a pulse of reverse, I shifted to neutral. We were the only boat near the well-known mount.

His legs wide to balance, Jim handed me a herring-baited pole. "Start jigging while I get the other rig set up."

Arm hooked around a mast shroud, I released the line. Unlike Jim, my patience for fishing was limited. I released line until the bait touched bottom, then established a haphazard up-down-up rhythm of tapping the seafloor. A few minutes in, my attention shifted to searching for birds.

Znngggg! My line peeled out, pulling the pole down and jamming the rod end into my abdomen. "Whoa!" Hands clenched and knees bent, I steadied myself against the force. "I've got something!"

Jim was already clambering my way, shouting, "Glen, fish on!" Then to me, "Loosen your drag. Let it run." His voice was excited but calming.

I fumbled for the metal lever, but couldn't make it move. He reached me, slipped his hand over mine, toggled the lever to reduce friction. The tugging force dropped as the line screamed out faster.

Glen climbed into the cockpit. "What's up?"

"Your mom's caught something," Jim said over his shoulder.

"All right, Mom!"

"Something big," Jim added.

Glen zipped on his life jacket and joined me.

"When it slows down," Jim coached, "reel in. Keep your tip up."

I'd never felt so much weight or strength on a rod. I lowered the pole, cranking the reel, eating up slack. At the bottom of each arc, I stopped reeling and leaned back, lifting rod and fish.

After several down-crank, pull-up cycles, I was smiling.

Zingggg! Whatever it was swam hard again, stealing back my progress.

"Glen, get the fighting belt—in the milk crate." Jim was in the zone, excited, helpful, anticipating what I might need.

Glen dug out the padded purple belt with plastic rod holder Bill Brown had given us.

Jim fastened the device around my hips and buckled it in the back. "Now give it a bit of slack before you move the rod onto the belt."

From behind, Glen grabbed the belt, holding me inbound. The fish and I fought each other for another twenty minutes. Adding the belt improved my leverage, but after several more rounds of cranking, my back muscles quivered. Too much tension and the line could break. Not enough and the beast might twist free.

"Jim," I said, breathing hard, "you should bring it in."

"You've got it. You're wearing him out."

I shook my head. "It's the other way around."

Eventually, a shadowy diamond shape appeared.

"Geez," Jim said. "That's one mother of a fish."

A foot below the surface, the huge army-camo flatfish glided by, both eyes aimed at us. We could release her, I thought. Cut the hook. We knew the reproductive rates of large females like this one increased exponentially. In other years, we'd released big halibut. In that instant, my conservation intellect collided with my provisioning sensibility. Not only did I want to fill the freezer with healthy fillets, but I wanted the success of this trip to smudge the edges of our bad experience in Taku Harbor. My hunter-gatherer genes won out. I held my thoughts and kept working the rod and reel.

"Careful, now," Jim said. "This is when it's easy to lose 'em. Walk your rod to the stern while I get the harpoon." Hand over hand, he used the rigging to stabilize himself as he stepped to the locker. "Let her run if she tries," he added. The way he moved about the swaying boat, no observer would guess he'd learned to walk again three months earlier.

Crowded together at the stern, Glen held my belt from behind as Jim leaned out over the water, homemade harpoon in hand. My job was to guide the big fish in close. If we tried to lift her all six feet to get her on deck with the circle hook alone, she would almost certainly break free. Sailboats were not designed for deep-sea fishing.

"Here goes." Jim struck and the fish veered off, deflecting the harpoon.

After the missed attempt from the deck, Jim climbed down and got into position on the ladder instead, one hand on the rail above, adopting the same crouched position I'd taken in Taku Harbor.

"Careful, Dad."

A pulse of worry mirrored the concern I sensed in Glen's voice. We were adrift in deep water, no other boats nearby. I did a mental inventory: We were all wearing flotation. Jim had a strong grip on the rail and the harpoon wasn't attached to him. "He's okay, hon," I said to Glen. "Let's get this fish."

Crouched below us, Jim was ready. I reeled in, steering the prize toward him. This time, he plunged the spear clear through the gills. On impact, the halibut arched and kicked hard, making a desperate run. My reel screamed again but stopped short the instant she reached the end of the harpoon tether.

It took the three of us to hoist the heavy fish on board, with Jim lifting most of the weight.

"Holy moly!" he said, as she flopped onto, and almost covered, the back deck. He grinned. "That's a hundred-and-fifty-pound fish you caught, woman."

My body tingled with his praise. "I didn't catch this halibut. We did."

❯ ❯ ❯

Swish–swash–swish. Jim stood on deck sharpening his fillet knife. "You know, your mom might've broken this year's halibut rod-hour record."

Glen looked up from the cockpit where we were setting up the vacuum packer. "What's a rod hour?"

"Average time bringing in and landing a fish." Jim straddled the halibut and made a clean cut down the length. "Average for halibut here is close to five hours. Your mom's time was thirty, forty minutes, max."

"Cool," Glen said.

"*Our* time," I corrected.

Jim passed us a metal bowl heaped with two-pound pieces of translucent white meat. I wrapped each in plastic, and Glen ran the vacu-sealer. The motor hummed while the machine sucked the air out of each packet and heat-sealed the opening. The three of us developed a rhythm. When we emptied one bowl, we swapped it with Jim's next batch. Glen enjoyed controlling the buttons. Between the vacu-sealer's loud hum, we talked and laughed.

The first time I ate fresh ocean fish was on Vancouver Island. I was in my late twenties, and that was day one of my love affair with wild salmon and halibut. I thought back to a morning nine years earlier in Juneau, feeling the bumpy edge of Glen's first tooth. That's when it dawned on me that most of the calcium in it had come from Alaskan salmon, Pacific halibut, and Sitka black-tailed deer.

"I bet you there's a hundred pounds of steaks here." Jim stood to stretch his back.

"You think?" I wiped my slimed hands on a paper towel. "That's dinner twice a week for a year."

During the three hours adrift above the ocean mount, far

234

from city distractions, *IJsselmeer* and the sea's bounty became our universe, and no thoughts of email, proposal writing, or computer games interfered.

We loaded the steaks in the cooler. Jim asked Glen to take the helm and get us back underway, while he doused the deck with buckets of seawater and put away gear. He signaled me to be the backup navigator. Standing on the teak-slatted bench, hands on the helm, Glen peered over the canvas dodger at the ocean ahead. He glanced at the chart and back at the horizon. "Is that Sisters?" he asked, pointing to distant islands.

"Yep. Keep them to port until they're off your beam. We'll anchor here," I tapped the paper chart. "Off Halibut Island, not far from Hoonah."

The week before, Glen helped Jim install our first GPS navigation system linked to electronic charts. Our son had figured out how to make the marine chart software communicate with the GPS device and taught us how to use it. That Sunday, Glen ran the boat for an hour—a first. His track-line wobbled but followed the intended course.

At anchor, Jim showered while I started dinner. It was my last night out. The next day I'd return to Juneau alone. While I showered, he pan-fried three halibut steaks. Before our first bite, we raised our glasses and toasted, "To the beautiful halibut."

During the toast, it struck me that my husband as captain and fisherman was as able-bodied as he needed to be.

Later, in the aft cabin behind closed doors, Jim gently traced his fingertips over a bruise on my abdomen from the fishing pole. "I don't want to hurt you," he said.

"You won't." I pulled him close.

28

HUNGRY HEART

Jim set my mug on the table next to our bed in the aft cabin and cleared his throat.

I opened my eyes. "Good morning."

"Before you leave," he said, "I-I have a list for Juneau."

I reached for my notebook and pen.

"Two Perkins fuel filters, four gallons of Delco oil, a new macerator pump. Harri's Plumbing carries those. Fifty feet of dock line—double braid nylon three-quarter-inch."

Transcribing his words fired up thoughts of my lists. Over the weekend, I'd been living in the moment on our floating haven. Responsibilities at work and home now rumbled to life.

"And a metric tape measure."

"Don't we have one on board?"

"We do, but I'd like a metric one."

"We can't just buy things we already have," I said. "We're spending more than I'm making."

He stared at me.

I resisted an impulse to add, "especially without you working." Instead, I blurted, "Last week, I paid Bruce twenty-eight grand to finish the foundation and driveway." I hated where I was steering the conversation, but I'd already stepped off the rationality cliff edge.

Before the stroke, Jim managed our long-range financial planning, creating twenty-year projection spreadsheets to convince me we could pull off selling our house and building a new one while we rented an apartment, as long as he did a lot of the construction. We had both put as much as we could into retirement savings. Since the stroke, I hadn't expected him to revise spreadsheets, but he'd been checked out, unwilling to even discuss financial matters.

To meet Brendan and Corwin's ferry on time, we dropped the conversation, pulled anchor, and motored toward Hoonah in silence. Steam tendrils rose from fifteen wet harbor seals resting on a rocky islet. En route, my colleague Matt called to discuss an issue with the REU program we needed to resolve. I hung up in time to help secure the boat at the dock. Cars leaving the ferry thundered up the ramp. Glen trotted ahead with my duffel, scanning arriving pedestrians for our friends. Jim and I each lifted a handle of the cooler loaded with halibut. A stiff silence clogged the air between us as we walked toward the station, still bristling from the morning's bad start. His irregular stride disrupted our four-legged gait.

"Your comments about the tape measure make me feel like I'm not doing enough," he said, his voice gruff. "I had a plan to reduce our expenses by building a smaller house, but those were knocked apart in April. I'm sorry I can't do more."

"Obviously it's not the tape measure. It's our overall finances—the mortgage crisis has slammed our savings. I've stopped opening bank statements." I set my half of the cooler down. "I'm sorry I went off like that."

"Then this morning," he added, not registering my apology, "immediately after you were on the phone about work, you left us. I felt you go away."

Brendan and Corwin strode up the ramp, Glen in the middle. Arms wide, Glen was telling them about the halibut. Their hugs and broad smiles shoved aside our ongoing tiff, a welcome transition. While saying goodbye, I realized I did not want to leave.

Three hours later, the ferry glided toward the Juneau terminal. I loaded the cooler onto a cart and walked to where Brendan told me he'd parked our car. What would it feel like to be home alone? For weeks I'd craved time to myself, but now insecurities surfaced like chickweed in a garden. As I unlocked the door and heaved the cooler into the back seat, I was anxious leaving Jim and Glen behind, the opposite of the confident, light-footed person I'd planned to be.

At the university, four afternoons later, I flipped the microphone switch. "Are we on?" The technician at the back of the auditorium nodded. Reassured by my notes, I began, "Welcome to the ninth annual Research Experiences for Undergraduates seminar." Our students sat in the front row, ready to deliver presentations on topics ranging from glacial hydrology and red king crab reproductive biology to the detrimental effects of earlier and earlier spring thaws on Arctic ringed seal pups born in snow caves. In the audience were their mentors and other faculty and students, agency biologists, and the university's chancellor and provost, and—the person who would have the final say in my promotion request—the dean of my department.

At home that evening, happy both with the outcome of the seminar and, equally, to have it behind me, I cued up a Bruce Springsteen CD on the stereo, cracked two eggs into a heated skillet, and dropped a slice of wheat bread into the toaster. My voice melded with Bruce's, singing, "Everybody's got a hungry heart." My body rocked to his bass as I tore romaine leaves into a bowl.

After eating, I moved to the other end of the dining table where I'd set up my laptop and file folders. I worked until midnight on our proposal to fund the undergraduate program for another three years.

Lying in bed, I felt good about the summer session. But my mind refused sleep, instead reviewing what remained to be done: double-check the proposal budget, tie up loose ends from the program, and prepare for the fall semester. What worried me the most was my meeting with Frank Stafford, the chair of the Natural Sciences Department to ask him to support my promotion request. He was a wildcard. I switched the light on and scrawled reminders on a notepad.

Having an unfettered week to work had been good, like surfing a cresting wave. But alone in bed, concerns swirled in. Was I incapable of maintaining a work–life balance without my family nearby? Our son's childhood was racing by. In two months, he would be ten. I needed to give Jim more attention. I rolled over onto my other side and counted backward from a hundred. Outside of the dark abyss of my thoughts, a clock ticked, a neighbor's garage door opened and closed, an ice tray emptied.

The next afternoon, I ran into Brendan outside the campus library, the day after he and Corwin had left Jim and Glen on the boat in Hoonah.

When I asked how their leg of the trip had gone, he said Jim was doing well. He told me about an enormous skate his son had hooked, which they eventually decided to release, despite his son's protestations. "We had a great time."

"I'm so glad it went well. How's Glen?"

"He's doing fine." Brendan folded his arms. "But there was a situation."

Oh no, I thought.

"We were anchored in Neka Bay to snorkel for Dungies. We all got suited up. Jim and Glen took the inflatable kayak. Corwin and I loaded into your dory. We paddled up the river until we started seeing Dungies everywhere. Clear water. Lots of them. When Jim was about to get in, Glen got very upset."

"What did he do?"

"He told Jim not to go in. He was distraught." Brendan looked directly at me. "He's worrying too much about his dad. Taking on an adult role. He overreacted."

Brendan's comments set off a defensive flare. "Did Jim tell you what happened in Taku Harbor?" Glen had good reason to be worried about his father.

"He mentioned some trouble when he jumped in, but that's no reason for Glen to worry like this. Jim talked to him, but Glen couldn't let it go. Every time Jim's flippers tipped up when he dove for a crab, Glen freaked out."

"I understand why he was so worried," I said.

"It's inappropriate for him to dictate what his father does."

My face grew hot. "There's more to what happened in Taku than Jim told you."

I wanted to describe the incident, but it was too personal to discuss at work. Brendan had levied judgment based on a sliver of the story. He thought he was acting on behalf of his close friend who needed to get out and explore—live as fully as ever. I understood coddling Jim would be counterproductive, and a nine-year-old shouldn't have to take responsibility for a parent, but it was not fair to criticize our son for wanting to protect his father. Glen's instinct, his near-crazy drive to prevent Jim from free-diving again—to keep him safe—made sense to me. I was proud of our son. My feeling was Jim should have done more to reassure Glen. Instead, it sounded like he'd downplayed how rattled we all had been by the free-diving incident.

As I rushed off to a meeting, a wave of anger and disappointment in Jim hit me. Brendan had no idea what actually happened. Brendan's belief that Glen and I had overreacted to a small snorkeling incident burned a hole in my trust in Jim's perception of reality and sense of fairness.

, , ,

Two days later, I stood in front of an office door on the second floor of the science building. I raised my fist and hesitated. After another deep breath, I knocked. Nothing. I knocked harder.

"Come in." Dr. Stafford's low monotone sent my heart pounding faster. I was prepared, I reassured myself. My case was solid. I opened the door to the head of the Natural Sciences Department and stepped into the corner office with its expansive view of Auke Bay. He continued writing, head down. I greeted him.

He looked up and said, "What do you want?"

"I set up a meeting with you to talk about my position." He'd forgotten. His desk and the three extra chairs in his office were stacked high with scientific journals, books, papers, and student notebooks.

"Oh." He lowered his glasses as if to clarify who I was. "Right." I'd been in our small department seventeen years, longer than any of the other biology faculty. He gestured to a pile on the chair across from his desk. "You can put those on the floor."

Frank Stafford, a chemist, was smart and hard-working, but his manner was often condescending. Over the years, I'd experienced rare connections with him through our senses of humor. During faculty meetings, his sarcastic and witty jabs provoked spotty laughter around the conference table. I enjoyed hearing, and especially making, him laugh. He was, however, more often brusque than funny.

"Go ahead." He reached for a pad of paper.

I summarized my years at the university, the awards and favorable student evaluations I'd earned, my research on harbor seals and Steller sea lions in Glacier Bay, and the Research Experiences for Undergraduates program Brendan and I had led for nine years.

He jotted a few notes.

"I publish my research and present it at professional conferences."

"Okay," he said, in a flat, get-to-the-point tone.

I glanced at my notes and sat taller to release tension. I mentioned I'd never asked for a promotion. I did not explain why. One reason was Jim had earned almost twice my salary. The second was I had a fanciful notion if I did good work it would be rewarded without having to ask.

"When I submit my three-year review to the dean," I continued, "I plan to request a promotion from Assistant to Associate Professor. I'd like your support."

He inhaled hard and looked out the window. "Well." He fingered his mustache. "Without a PhD, I don't think you'll succeed."

I swallowed, although my mouth was dry.

"Have you thought of getting one?"

I held his gaze. Was he serious? He knew about my husband's stroke.

"You could do it through Fairbanks."

He *was* serious. My mind raced. Yes. I'd love to go back to grad school for a PhD—indulge in research without the extra work of teaching, grading, and faculty meetings. But I needed to earn more money, not less.

"In two or three years," he added.

I held my expression without speaking. My blinking rate, however, increased. Maybe a biochemist can complete a PhD in two years, I thought. Collecting enough data on a population of marine mammals in Alaska for a doctorate would take many more. Coursework and securing funding alone would eat up a whole year.

He was telling me, as the chair of my department, he wouldn't support a promotion because I didn't have a PhD. Without his endorsement, as I understood, my request could not move up the chain. Blood drained from my head. "Thank you, Frank." I stood to leave.

"Think about it," he said.

A few days later, during lunch in the campus cafeteria with a senior colleague from another department, I told him about the meeting.

"That's bullshit," he said. "Gary doesn't have a PhD. He's in the exact same position as you, and he was recently promoted. Since you're not tenure-track, it's not even up to Stafford. It's up to the dean and the provost. Take your case to them."

29

WATCH THE BIRDS

With the summer program behind me, I hurried up the ferry ramp toward Jim and Glen, starved for their company. Jim lifted me off my feet and swung me around like he'd done in our courting days, somehow keeping his balance. Glen stood back and watched, then joined in a family embrace. Tears of joy threatened as we walked hand in hand to *IJsselmeer's* slip. That night, we anchored east of Hoonah in Whitestone Harbor, a protected cove used mainly by loggers and fishermen.

The next morning, the pitter-patter of raindrops pulled me from a gauzy dream. I rolled over and stared at Jim's shoulders. How can my need for time apart be as strong as my desire to be with him?

The wind hummed in the rigging, tripping a vivid memory from twelve years earlier—before our son was born. I thought back on our stormy, midnight escape from South Inian Cove, visualizing the two of us performing as a team as if witnessing someone else playing my role. Faced with the same situation now—dragging anchor toward shore in a storm at night—my intuition warned I might lock up with fear and be incapable of doing what I did then. With all our experiences across the years, wasn't I supposed to become more and more confident about boating? Was it normal to feel less secure remembering a successful performance under strain so long after the danger had passed?

The rain continued to splatter the deck above. *IJsselmeer* rolled with the swell, a giant cradle. What had changed?

One factor was obvious. We now had a child. It was one thing to explore Alaska's wilderness edges as a couple, another to bring our son along. But we'd been doing that for nine years—successfully—since Glen was six weeks old. Many of our most memorable family experiences had been on *IJsselmeer*. And we were a cautious boating couple. From the outside, my husband might appear to be a risk seeker, but the opposite was true. His mechanical know-how, willingness to tackle any at-sea engine hiccup or failure, and desire, if not compulsion, to run a safe ship remained intact. He took pains to anticipate and reduce risk. Before the stroke, I'd viewed him as physically invincible. Through many challenges, his body had never failed him—or us. But we'd entered a new phase. No longer could I rely on him pulling us through every situation.

The next time, I might have to lead us out of danger.

Angled light on glassy water backlit the misty blow of a humpback whale far ahead. I adjusted my heading a few degrees. We were motoring down Chatham Strait. Jim napped and Glen read below. I checked the chart: an hour and a half to Baranof Warm Springs. Near where the whale dove, another surfaced. Through binoculars, I watched as two dozen small birds flocked low over the water. Seconds later a whale lunged up, exactly below the swarm of birds, mouth open.

"*Pa-hooohh, shush!*" The slow-exhale, rapid-inhale cycle was followed by two more surfacings. I shifted into neutral. Three decades after my first winter as a research volunteer in Hawaii, observing whales still filled me with awe. As the forty-ton mammal arched and raised its flukes, I clicked off a photo. The boat was well behind—but close enough to capture details on the pigmented underside of the tail. Colleagues might be able to use the unique fluke pattern to figure out if this whale had migrated to Alaska from Hawaii or, less likely, Mexico, after a breeding season. As I scanned the area, several more whales surfaced and dove.

Twenty-six years earlier, I'd volunteered on these same feeding grounds. Back then, I was sorting out who I was, proud of my independence. Grad school at UC Santa Cruz was learning on steroids, and I loved it. I'd been mesmerized by the self-reliant field researchers I'd worked with in Alaska. I missed the tight camaraderie and intense sense of discovery that came with long stretches of camping on a remote island, living and working together as part of a driven team.

Jim and Glen should see this, I thought. "You guys," I called into the boat. "Come check out these whales. There are at least eight ahead."

Waiting for the next surfacing, I zoomed in on those grad-school memories. Wasn't the glossy idea of *being on my own* simply a euphemism for having failed to find a fulfilling relationship? Those days had, in fact, not always been so rosy. Unsure of myself, I'd had a few relationships with men I enjoyed and trusted, but they hadn't worked out. One grad-school boyfriend was fun and funny—but not available on a deep level. I couldn't remember why I'd tried so hard to make that work.

Minutes later, Jim stepped into the cockpit. Hair splayed at the crown like a stubby turkey tail, he reached for the other pair of binoculars. A wave of love for him engulfed me.

Glen nudged up from behind. "What's going on?"

"Watch the birds." I raised my binoculars. "They're red-necked phalaropes. Every year they migrate between the Arctic and South America."

Ahead, a flock of twenty phalaropes swarmed and coalesced

inches above the water. I watched one of the skinny-necked birds, weighing about as much as half a croissant, hover and dance its lobed feet across the water, dipping her needle-thin bill into the water. Suddenly, one of the whales emerged, mouth open wide, lower jaw and expanded throat pleats engulfing 15,000 gallons of seawater teeming with prey. The phalaropes darted out of the way, flitting down and up, snatching prey pushed to the surface by the whale, seawater rolling and tumbling out over the whale's closing jaws.

"Very cool," Jim said, fully engaged.

A smaller whale lunged in tandem with an adult. "There's a calf!" I said.

"What're they eating?" Glen asked.

"They're too far away to tell. The calf's probably still nursing, but it may be learning how to filter feed."

Glen stepped out from the cockpit to join us on the deck.

"The calves have to learn how to use their baleen to feed on schools of small fish, like herring, and invertebrates the size of a fingernail." I clicked my thumbnail. "One day, when it's about seven months old, that calf will have to fend for itself."

While the whales were down, Glen thwapped the end of a line against a rail.

"What if you only had a year to learn everything you need to know from us?" I asked.

He gave me an *oh brother* half smile and quipped, "I'd call Keagan to see if I could move in."

The sun's hint of warmth graced the air as a faint breeze ruffled the water.

"Is that what they're eating?" Glen asked.

I scanned ahead. "Where?"

"Right there. Look."

Binoculars lowered, I leaned out over the rail.

"There! See?" He pointed down at the teal ocean. The water

all around our boat teemed with swarms of inch-long dog-paddling krill, *Euphausia pacifica.*

"Good spotting, hon!" The three of us leaned out over the rail.

"Far out!" Jim said, scooping some up in a net for a closer look.

Later, Jim took the helm, and we continued south to the warm springs. Perched on the cockpit rim, I finished my entry about the feeding whales and Glen's observation. The VHF radio crackled with US Coast Guard alerts.

The three summers I'd spent in Alaska studying humpback whales were among the best and most formative times of my life. What hit me as I sat in the cockpit, sea breeze rushing by, was I did not want to turn back the clock. Raising a child in Alaska was beyond what I could have wished for before I met Jim. These moments of discovery with my husband and son were treasures I would carry to my grave.

30

BARANOF
WARM SPRINGS

L ine in hand, I straddled the railing as we coasted toward the
dock at Warm Springs Bay. To the left, a river cascaded into
the remote bay, fueled by a huge glacially fed lake. Warm Springs
Bay tucks into the east side of Baranof Island. The size of Dela-
ware, Baranof is the tenth largest island in the United States and
home to around a thousand brown bears and nine times as many
people. Almost all human inhabitants live in Sitka, which is on
the other side of the island opposite Warm Springs Bay and not
connected by road.

Two fishing boats and three other private vessels, including
a large tug, were tied to the dock. Jim slowed *IJsselmeer*, aiming
for the one remaining space. I stretched a leg down and stepped
onto the dock, looped the line around a cleat, springing the boat
in snug, then took the bow line from Glen. Jim's expertise in
docking made my job easy.

As soon as the boat was secure, we gathered soap, shampoo,
towels, and fresh clothing in a canvas bag. Into another tote, we
tucked a chunk of cheddar cheese, crackers, bottle of wine, cork-
screw, and three water bottles.

Owners of the fifteen houses and cabins along the community

boardwalk had diverted the nearby hot springs into three private bathhouses. A hand-painted donation box was nailed to a railing. Outside of peak summer weeks, however, the bathhouses were free. A welcoming sign read, "As a courtesy to others after your bath, please: Empty and clean tub with brush." Built on pilings over the cove, each room featured its own galvanized steel cattle-watering trough. The wall facing the opposite shore was open above waist-height, framing a grand view of temperate rainforest. The only voyeurs were raucous ravens and masked ospreys.

We filled the six-foot-long tank by adding a plug to capture the continuous flow of hot water. Jim eased in first, Glen next, then me. Enveloped in sulfury steam, the three of us sat and talked, legs entwined. We reminisced about the week, Glen's improved boating skills, and the whales and birds we'd seen. Outside, ravens exchanged throaty calls.

Seconds after we'd toweled off in cool air, Glen climbed back in the half-drained tank and sloshed back and forth on his belly like a river otter.

On our way back to the boat, we met Kate, who stepped out of the cabin door of a sixty-five-foot wooden boat, *Lazaria*, to introduce herself. She and her husband ran their salmon tender out of Petersburg. Eight-year-old Lizzie peered out from behind her mother's legs and invited Glen aboard. Compared to ours, their vessel was huge, with an upstairs, downstairs, and a main cabin with room for a cupboard full of games. I liked Kate instantly. She welcomed Glen aboard. We did not see him again until dinnertime.

The next day, I woke first. Jim slept in until pancakes and sausages were on the table. Before we finished breakfast, Glen asked to go play with Olive.

"Who's Olive?" Jim and I asked.

"Lizzie's new kitten."

"Oh, nice," I said. "Yes, you may go as soon as you clear the table."

He cleared, then grabbed his Spot It pattern recognition game and headed down the dock.

On our second afternoon in Warm Springs Bay, the three of us hiked together in rubber boots past the bathing cabins, into the inner sanctum of spruce, hemlock, and alder. Jim relied on his trekking poles to navigate the muddy path, gnarled with roots and ruts from other parties of tourists and fishermen. I watched from behind as he faltered and corrected more than usual. With three weeks on the boat, his balance was tuned to counteract ocean swells. My inner ear vestibules also amplified the sensation of undulating more while on shore than on the boat, a temporary neurological condition known as land sickness. The trail soon paralleled the Baranof rapids as they drained from the lake to the ocean. A quarter mile up, we heard distant voices and laughter.

Between the trail and river, magma-heated water bubbled up from thermal springs below. The temperate rainforest framed several steaming pools eroded into rock. I'd never seen anything like it. The thundering river made it possible to have private conversations a dozen feet from strangers. Still, I was glad the naked visitors were dressing in preparation to leave as we stripped down to bathing suits. It had been my idea to wear suits.

Glen maneuvered across slippery rocks. "Wait for us," I called to his back.

The higher pools, closest to the trail, were hottest—up to 120 degrees. Those spilled over several levels toward the torrent of glacial meltwater. We climbed over and around boulders to reach the lowest pool where we eased into clear, hot water. Surrounding the pools were lime-green devil's club and lush ferns. Exposed tree roots ambled over rock and forest duff like a network of veins across a weathered hand.

I laid my head back and closed my eyes. "Did you feel that?" I asked Jim and Glen. "Those splatters from the waterfall?"

"I heard some people tried to raft down these rapids." Jim spoke loudly over the noise.

"Really?" Six feet away, cold water screamed by.

"Yeah, they died trying."

"Glen, don't go so close." I reached out to him.

"He's okay." Jim patted the underwater ledge, coaxing him back in from the icy river.

From opposite sides of the clear pool, Glen and I aligned the soles of our feet and pedaled them back and forth, laughing whenever they slipped apart.

Jim squeezed my hand. "Man, this is great. This-this feels so good. To be out here. Taste that air."

After breakfast the next day, Jim and I peered at the nautical chart of Chatham Strait, Frederick Sound, and Stephens Passage unfolded across the table. We were plotting our route for the next few days. Glen was off playing with Lizzie and Olive.

"So. Tell me again when you have to be back?" he asked.

He should know this, I thought. And why did he say *you* and not *we*? I stared at the back of his weathered hand and reminded him Glen started school on the twenty-seventh. "We need to be home a few days before that." I sensed his frustration building, wisping out his nostrils like dragon smoke. He did not want our trip around Admiralty Island to end. The fall before, we'd enrolled Glen in a new school because the lot we'd purchased was in a different district. We'd stuck with that plan even though the stroke halted construction, because Auke Bay school had a better academic reputation. With all we'd been through since April—Glen had spent half his summer vacation in Seattle—I wanted his first weeks as a fifth grader to be smooth.

"I-I'd like more time together, in Pybus and Gambier Bay." He waved a hand toward the dock and hills, and added, "Like this. This is magical."

"I agree, hon. But let's spend our last night in Taku Harbor, so the final run isn't too long."

He let out an exasperated sigh. "It-it'd be good to catch more fish before we head home."

"Of course it would." Using the chart's scale, I spread the plotting compass to measure seven nautical miles, the average distance *IJsselmeer* covered in an hour of motoring, and walked the points between our current location and Pybus Bay. "It's a full day away."

"We-we can get an early start. Counting back from the twenty-fifth—"

"The twenty-fourth would be better," I interjected. We can't just stop being parents, I thought.

"That doesn't leave much time."

I pinched my lip, ignoring his frown. "The three weeks have been wonderful—"

"You've only been with us eight days," he interrupted.

"But we need to get home. He doesn't even have pants that fit. And we need a buffer day for weather."

The wall clock ticked as Jim scrutinized the map. "Okay. We'll leave tomorrow."

I folded the chart back to a manageable size. "I'm going to clean the hull," I said, wanting to escape the tension.

Without speaking, he turned and tugged both sets of heavy rain bibs off hooks in the forepeak.

I wanted to say, *If you can't do the job with a good attitude, I'd rather do it alone.* Instead, I said, "I'm glad to do it by myself."

"I'll help."

In silence, we pulled on bibs, light jackets, and rubber boots.

Beneath a cloudy sky, I stood on the dock and plunged the long-handled deck brush into a foamy bucket. I scrubbed away at a fur-like growth of algae on the hull at the seawater–sunlight junction.

Jim worked ahead, cleaning the teak rub rails. Later, he looped back to tackle the growth of algae and crustaceans that had resisted my brush. Kneeling on the dock, he reached out and scraped the hull with a rectangle of stiff plastic. "Geez, it's warmed up." He stood and unclipped his shoulder straps, toed off his rubber boots, and wriggled out of his orange rain bibs, down to cargo shorts.

"You look awfully cute in those shorts and Xtratufs," I teased as he pulled his boots back on.

He glanced up. Still no smile but the fuming had stopped.

While I cleaned the midsection, he knelt on the wooden dock scrubbing our bulbous fenders. "I started that audiobook," he said, "by Thomas Friedman, *The World is Flat*."

"What's it about?"

"How globalization, technology, and the internet are changing businesses—flattening hierarchies." The conversation signaled he was retreating from our disagreement about when the trip should end. Being out like this meant so much to him. It was his first chance to test whether he could move beyond the stroke—beyond disability. In the big scheme of things, he was right. He'd done so well. Being out in nature, he seemed normal again. And boating in Alaska with our son promoted something I'd never had with my parents. Glen might not remember his first day of fifth grade, but he will remember the hot springs, catching the big halibut, and Lizzie's kitten. On the boat, we connected more meaningfully than at home. Camping with my students, I'd experienced a similar closeness. Still, my priority was to set Glen up for a successful school year.

As Jim stood to help me reposition the boat, he stumbled.

"You okay?"

"Yeah, I'm fine. That leg sometimes goes numb."

We tightened the bow line to angle the bow in so we could reach the forward quarter. Moments later, Glen trotted toward us. "Can I have lunch on Lizzie's boat? Her mom's making grilled cheese and ginger cookies."

"Of course," I said. "How nice,"

The dock rumbled beneath his feet as he ran back to *Lazaria*.

While we washed the hull, a lanky man with thick brown hair, wearing a navy T-shirt and jeans under yellow fishing bibs approached. "What do you do in Gustavus?" He gestured toward our boat's hailing port. Through a lively exchange, we learned Tony was an electronics specialist who spent several months every year in both the high Arctic and Antarctic helping researchers establish remote monitoring stations. He and Jim discovered a mutual friend from Barrow—Craig George—Jim's college climbing buddy from Utah State. Since those days Craig had become one of the world's experts on bowhead whales.

"Any chance you've come across a guy named Brendan Kelly?" Jim asked.

"Yeah, I know Brendan. Great guy. Helped him with some equipment for his ringed seal work a couple years back."

I loved seeing Jim relaxed and animated as he and Tony discussed fishing, research, and mutual friends. The stroke did not come up.

"You ever come across the journalist, Dan O'Neill, from Fairbanks?" Tony asked.

"He was here a couple of weeks ago," I said. "My students read his book, *The Firecracker Boys*. He's a guest speaker for the summer research program Brendan and I started."

"No way." A grin spread across Tony's face. "Dan's a good family friend."

"Small world," the three of us said in unison.

"Is that your son?" Tony asked. "I've been watching him on the dock here. For a second when he first ran by, I thought he was one of my boys. I usually have the two of 'em with me. We should get them together some day."

We swapped contact information, the steady gush of river water and intermittent raven calls as backdrop.

"You meet some of the most interesting people in places like this," Jim said after Tony left. "Who would guess a guy like that out here trolling for salmon might travel the globe and know three of our closest friends."

We cleaned the other side of the boat and ate a late lunch. While I put away dishes, Jim called down into the companionway. "Can you give me a hand getting these onto the dock?" He gestured to the teak seating and flooring inserts in the cockpit. "They're overdue for a deep clean."

"Maybe you should take a break?"

"I-I'm fine. It feels good to clean her up after all those idle months in that sooty harbor." While he scrubbed the woodwork, kneeling in shorts on the dock, I retreated to the aft cabin to read. Jim's energy is coming back, I thought, but I hope he's not overdoing it. I gave up trying to stay awake and let the book fall onto my chest.

We let Glen sleep as we performed our departure routine, silent in the misty dawn. We motored out of Baranof Warm Springs, and I lingered on the foredeck. I'd defended the sunrise departure, but that did not inoculate me from the sorrow that lodged in my throat. Leaving the magical cove hurt.

After four hours in sloppy seas, buffeted by twenty-five-knot gusts, we rounded the southern tip of Admiralty Island beneath spitting clouds. A mile from Herring Bay, the sea became less confused, the rain stopped, and our course relative to the wind improved.

"Hey, team," Jim said. "Conditions are perfect for sailing. Beth, what do you think?"

I stepped out of the cockpit. Far ahead, a troller motored in a two-foot chop. I turned around, taking it in. "Okay. Sure."

We rolled up the mainsail cover, ran lines, then called Glen up to join us.

As soon as we're pointing dead upwind," Jim said, "you two raise the main."

Glen and I worked our way forward. "You tail. I'll crank," I said.

Since leaving Juneau, we had not sailed. There were several reasons. One was the lack of optimal conditions. The second was Jim's status. Because he was our most avid and skilled sailor, there was an unspoken agreement we'd wait until he was ready. But a third factor was me. I was overly cautious, more inclined to motor unless circumstances were just right. Even though we'd owned *IJsselmeer* sixteen years, an emotional force held my sailing reins in tight check. I didn't like getting overpowered, or into some other calamity, while under sail. My concerns were not entirely logical—we were a seasoned team. And I didn't want to be that woman who holds her husband back. But the trepidations ran deep, up from Midwestern roots, bolstered by a lack of exposure to boating until adulthood, and fueled by a double dose of worry genes from my mother. The stroke, no question, had undermined my hard-earned confidence. What if something happened to him *out there?*

That afternoon, however, with the end of our expedition looming and the shift in weather, I agreed it was time to ride the wind.

I passed the halyard to Glen. "Clockwise wrap," I reminded him as he wound the line around the winch. "Let's start off pulling together."

Our son stood with feet wide to counter the rolling deck. His limbs looked too long for the youth-sized life vest.

"Ready?" Jim called.

"Ready."

Jim steered upwind. "Here it comes. Okay . . . now!"

Glen and I pulled in unison. "One. . . two. . . three." When we could no longer hoist the huge triangle of stiff Dacron with our weight, I cranked the winch handle in big circles as Glen kept tension on the line.

The sail rose fifty-five feet, thwacking side to side.

"You okay?" Glen asked as my breathing grew hard.

I nodded.

"More," Jim called.

We inched the sail up another foot.

"Cleat it," he called. "Good job!" The mainsail billowed and caught.

Next, we launched the jib. Jim cut the engine, and we were there: my favorite moment. Sails aloft on a beam reach, the engine's white roar became a pastel swirl of water along the hull as *IJsselmeer* skimmed across the sea.

Glen positioned himself at the bow pulpit, where the boat rose and fell the most. Hair blown back, with each plunge–splash, he jumped a second before the drop, prolonging each instant of weightlessness.

A mile away, close to shore, two humpbacks threw their tails into the air, as if doing cartwheels with forebodies submerged. Moments later, a third whale in the distance breached. The huge splash erupted as if in slow motion, the action microseconds ahead of the sound. Surrounded by ocean and the Tongass National Forest, sails trimmed, we skimmed across Frederick Sound. One hand on the rigging, I reached the other arm up, closed my eyes, and lifted my face to the wind. There was nowhere else I wanted to be.

31

WINGMEN

Rain spattered the canvas dodger over the cockpit. I opened my eyes. We were anchored in Cannery Cove, two days from Juneau. In a week, fall semester would start. Concerns swarmed, as if the dawn breeze had transported a mood-dampening fog into my bloodstream. What if the dean rejected my promotion request? I needed to sign Glen back up for violin lessons. Should I refinance the house?

While Jim slept, I slid out of bed and pulled my fleece robe over flannel pajamas.

In the galley, I adjusted the flame under the espresso pot's base. Its low gurgle escalated to an energized *cssshhhHHH*! I poured a cup and wrapped the pot with a towel to keep Jim's portion warm. A movement through the small galley portal caught my eye. Leaning over the stove on tiptoes, I saw a young brown bear on shore. I hurried up top to get a better view with binoculars. Alternate shoulder humps jutted as the bear ambled across the intertidal flats, head low, nosing rocks slick with algae. He paused to scrape the earth with claws as long as human fingers, then turned and disappeared into the forest.

The days were shrinking at a detectable pace. Three weeks on the boat had been good for Jim, although balance remained an issue, and his eye pain continued. His reaction time in certain situations seemed slower than before the stroke. Or was I looking too hard? How could I know for sure? Out on the boat, he'd been less moody, and things felt almost normal. He loved being on the water. Even so, I couldn't remember the last time he'd laughed.

I climbed halfway up the companionway ladder and slid the hatch open, warm mug in hand. Low gunmetal clouds stifled a blood-orange sunrise. A couple hundred feet away, a harbor seal popped up. Doe-eyed with chin tucked, she looked to the left and right, then slipped back under. Something was pressing my thoughts into dark corners. The ritual of making coffee and glimpses of the bear and seal had only delayed the caving inward.

What is wrong with me? I wondered. Is it the shorter days? He's recovering. Glen seems happy. The breeze cooled salty tracks rolling down my cheeks. We were anchored within the country's largest national forest, surrounded by snow-flecked mountains and the ocean—a place I loved. Why couldn't I shake the bleak mood?

Amber-green stands of western hemlock rimmed the cove, except for one wide clearing. Several aluminum powerboats were tied to a dock that led back over the rocky intertidal zone and angled up to a huge log cabin. Smoke curled from its chimney. A dozen red-roofed cottages and buildings dotted the beachfront property.

Through binoculars, I read Pybus Point Lodge. My mind spun images: cheerful grandparents rocking in cushioned chairs behind picture windows; children running in and out of an oven-warmed kitchen while rhubarb pies baked; uncles, brothers, and sisters geared up for a day of fishing and wildlife viewing. Envy caught me up short. I imagined a multigenerational family sharing Alaska's wilderness with clients. My body ached to belong within the cozy interior of their main cabin. That was the life I want with Jim and Glen.

A gull's sharp call, *Ah-ow, Ahh-ow, Ah-oww!* scattered the

fantasy. Managing a business out here would have its stressors, too, I reasoned. I liked living in Juneau with friends nearby, teaching at the university, and studying marine mammals in Glacier Bay. The many weeks I'd spent camping next to Johns Hopkins Glacier—training students to observe harbor seals, collect population monitoring data, and maintain a field camp—were a source of deep satisfaction. If I can't get a raise, I'll find something else. But the idea of filling out applications, waiting and hoping for an interview, and leaving a job I still enjoyed filled me with dread.

I heard Jim stir. I did not want him to enter my space—not yet.

He came into the galley below and squeezed my calf. "Hey, hon. Thanks for the coffee. How're you?"

I remained with head poked out the hatch like a prairie dog on alert. "I'm good," I said, words measured to mask the truth. I inhaled deeply, wanting to flush out the gray within. At home lately, he'd been the one with morning mood issues. I stared toward the forest. A bald eagle soared over choppy waves. Water slapped the hull.

"You okay?" He rubbed my leg. Without seeing my face he'd detected what I was hiding.

"Yeah, I'm fine."

"Come talk to me."

His intentions were good, but I wanted to be alone, to not reveal. I lingered, then backed down the ladder, turned, and reached around him. He held me. Just right. I pressed my face against his shoulder while a grief I did not understand churned and spread inside.

I tightened my grip, blinking back tears that came anyway.

"You sure you're okay?"

"I'm okay. A little off."

"What's up?"

I stepped back. "I don't know." Fingertips pressed against my eyes, I made a decision. "I'm going to make cinnamon rolls."

He gazed at me, hands on my arms. "We're doing all right, you know."

I turned away. His concern threatened to release the crying gate. In the galley, I lifted the insulated cooler lid. The ball of dough I'd reserved from the night's dinner rolls was cool and dense. I dusted the counter with flour. The fold-press-turn-fold rhythm of kneading seemed to also massage the knot in my core. I'd started making bread in high school. One semester in college, I made six loaves for a fund-raising dinner. At home in Juneau, I rarely baked. It saddened me to realize I'd made cinnamon rolls for my son only twice in nine years.

Jim gathered charts to plan the day. He paused. "L-let me know if you want to talk."

I nodded.

Soon the dough warmed and softened beneath my palms.

Glen emerged. "Hey, good morning." His voice was scratchy with sleep. He wrapped his arms around himself and shivered deliberately, staring at me with raised eyebrows—his *Can we cuddle?* signal.

"Give me a second." I covered the smooth mound with a cloth, brushed my hands against each other over the sink, and moved to the settee. Back against a cushion, I untied my robe. While I held it open like bat wings, he climbed onto my lap. His Sponge Bob pajamas were already too small. As he nestled in. I wrapped my fleece flaps around him.

Later, while Jim worked on the engine, I finished the second kneading. When I started rolling the dough into an oblong, Glen looked up from his book. "Can I add the cinnamon?"

I showed him how to drizzle and smooth the dough with melted butter. "Don't put any on this edge, though."

"Why?"

"That's where we'll seal the roll. It needs to be sticky."

I handed him the bowl with a gritty brown sugar, cinnamon, and raisin mixture.

He scattered the crumble across the soft, buttery dough, then spooned up the last bits. "Can I have this?"

"Yes, you may."

He crunched the sweet topping, eyes twinkling.

I rolled the dough into a long cylinder and helped him cut a dozen one-inch spirals. We arranged them on a greased pan. He swung the squeaky oven door wide and slid the pan into the warmed oven to rise.

As I watched, I realized the looming angst had receded. We've been through a lot, I thought—together. We're a good team. What was I so scared of? The morning's bleak mood was vaporizing before I could fully grasp what it meant or where it wanted to drag me. We'd survived the worst. Cherish these moments, I thought. Changing jobs might not be so bad as long as I had Jim and Glen, my wingmen, by my side.

"We've got to repair the mast light," Jim announced after lunch. Glen and I had settled in around the table, laptops open. "I'll need a hand from both of you to go up."

"Aww," Glen pouted. "I wanted to play *Minecraft*. Can't you fix it in Juneau?"

"No. That anchor light has to work so other boats don't run into us in the dark."

We finished our tea and joined Jim on deck. He stepped into the bosun's chair—a sling-like chair made of webbing—and adjusted the crotch and waist straps. "The socket's got to be replaced. I have all the tools I think I'll need. But, Glen, if I forgot something, you'll be the gofer. Beth, you're in charge of the main halyard. Glen, you'll run the safety line." Clipped to the halyard, he climbed the first eight of fifty-five feet of the main mast without help, then eased his weight into the chair attached to my line. "Up now."

I cranked and he rose. Wherever there were handholds, he pulled himself up, providing intermittent bursts of easier hoisting.

At the first spreader forty feet up, he paused. "Glen, take another wrap. If something goes wrong with the main, you're in charge of braking my fall."

We craned our necks to watch. Jim stood on the spreader. One arm around the mast, he tugged to loosen a strap around his thigh. "Damn. Why can't they make these more comfortable," he muttered. "Okay. Up again." I turned the winch until he was at the top, fifty-five feet up. Four months ago to the day, I thought, and he was being medevacked to Seattle. Even though we'd replaced lights like this before, seeing him up there, watching the mast sway across the gray sky, triggered an on-and-off queasy distrust, like being on a rickety Ferris wheel.

Forty-five minutes later, Glen eased his dad down while I controlled the safety.

"I-I'm sorry," Jim said from ten feet above us. "That took much longer than I thought. Getting that cover off was a bear, and the connector was corroded."

As Glen played out the line, his father's legs dangled above the deck like a marionette's. Jim stretched a foot down to stand as Glen released the line. Instead, Jim lurched down as his leg buckled under him.

Glen threw his weight onto the line, preventing a full fall. "Dad! Why'd you do that?"

"Whoa. S-sorry about that. My-my knee's gone numb."

The next morning, when our alarm went off, Jim didn't stir—unusual for a departure day. The wind whistled through the shrouds. Finally, I slipped out to the galley. With a nine-hour run to Taku Cove ahead, we'd agreed on an early start.

"Hey, hon." I squeezed his shoulder with my free hand. "Here's your coffee."

He rubbed his face with both hands and moaned. "Geez. Wh-what time is it?"

"Seven-thirty."

He took a sip. "Man. I feel like I'm coming down with the flu."

"I hope not." I pressed my palm to his forehead. "Feels normal. I'll do engine checks. Take your time."

After breakfast, while working at the chart table, wearing shorts as usual, Jim rubbed his left knee. "Something's not right. Can you look at this knee?"

I knelt beside him. "Swing the other one out so I can compare. Hmm. It's a bit puffy." I put a hand on each kneecap. "Feels warm, too. When'd you first notice this?"

"Up working on the mast light yesterday. It started to throb."

"Did you bang it or something?"

"No. I don't think so. Let's bring the dory on board, stow gear, and get underway. It's probably nothing."

He took the helm as we plunged north through three-foot seas. An hour later he called me over. "I-I'm not feeling well," he said. "Something's off. Do you mind if I go lie down?"

Seated in the cockpit, he slowly tugged off yellow foul weather gear.

"That knee looks worse." I leaned toward him. "Does it hurt if I press here?"

"Ee-yow!" He jerked away.

"Put some pillows under it. I'll try to reach Valley Medical. We're awfully far from the downtown cell tower, though."

Jim descended the stairs, using a step-down-pause, step-down-pause pace, to keep the sore knee straight.

"Hey, Glen," I called into the main cabin. "Can you take the helm?"

After several unsuccessful attempts to get through to the doctor's office, I poked my head up into the cockpit. "How're you doing, sweetie?"

"Okay." Glen stood on the bench peering over the dodger, hands on the three-foot diameter helm. "It's kind of rough, though."

I scanned the water ahead and checked the chart plotter. "Your heading's good. Remember to check the engine temperature and watch out for logs and deadheads."

"What's a deadhead?"

"Big logs that have gotten waterlogged at one end. They bob vertically with only a few inches showing. They're hard to see, especially when it's white-capping like this. But if you come down on one, with all that mass, they can jab a hole right through the hull."

"Oh yeah. Now I remember."

"I saw one earlier today," I said.

He stretched taller on tiptoes, searching ahead. "What's up with Dad's knee?"

"We're not quite sure yet. I'm trying to reach his doctor."

An hour later, I returned to the aft cabin with a flashlight and thermometer. I patted his arm. "Sorry to wake you, hon, but I finally got through. I talked to a nurse. She thought it could be irritation from all the kneeling work you did at the dock, but the redness and warmth suggest it could be something more serious. How's it feel now?"

He bent the leg. As soon as he touched the area, he clenched his jaw. "Same."

"If it's septic bursitis, they'd want to treat it right away."

"What exactly is that?"

"Sometimes bacteria can get into the joint lining, the bursa. She told me to look for a cut or puncture wound. Maybe a spider bite."

"I didn't see anything."

"Let me check." I clicked on the flashlight and crawled onto the bed. "Whoa. It is more swollen." I scanned the puffy surface, noticing a life's-worth of scars, but no new injury. I had him turn onto his side. "Nothing on the back either." I scrunched in next to him and traced my fingers through his hair. "She said if the swelling or tenderness gets worse, or if you develop a fever, to bring you in right away. When she learned we were out on our boat, she told me to get back as soon as possible."

I took his temperature: one degree above normal.

Jim slept while I motored up Stephens Passage through gusting rain. Midafternoon, Glen opened two cans of chicken noodle soup, heated it on the stove, then carefully delivered a mug and crackers down the companionway to Jim, and one up to me. By five o'clock, Jim was groggy and feverish. Taku Harbor was three hours away, enough time to anchor there before sunset, as planned. Pounding into a headwind all the way back to Juneau would take six or seven hours.

The day felt like a bad dream. I'd been running the engine harder than normal, barely gaining a half knot. If I were the one injured, Jim would get us home without stopping. Each time I tried to play out how I could bring us in after dark, my mind argued for anchoring up. I didn't have the skill or confidence to run our boat alone at night. The seas were already rough. I didn't want Glen at the bow scanning for deadheads in the dark. Hitting a log could sink our boat. But infections like this, I thought, can get out of control fast, and he's still recovering from the stroke.

I tuned the VHF to the Coast Guard's weather update, hoping for a calmer evening forecast. Instead, the revised prediction was for thirty-five-knot gales, fifteen knots less the next day. No matter how I replayed it, my scale kept tipping away from a midnight run. Finally, I consulted with Jim.

Bedclothes twisted across his overheated body, he opened his eyes. "Where are we?" He seemed confused.

"Stephens Passage, south of Taku." I gave him an Advil and explained my concerns about running after dark, then shared the nurse's message that if bacteria get into a joint, they can multiply unchecked.

"W-why's that?"

"There are no blood vessels inside the synovial sac. The joint fluid is a perfect place for bacteria to hide from the immune system and multiply. If the infection's not treated, it could permanently damage cartilage and bone."

He stared at the ceiling, working his jaw.

"She said if it goes untreated too long, there's a risk of septic shock." I didn't tell him she'd said without antibiotics that could be fatal. He would know.

"How long?"

"She didn't say, but getting it treated after two to three days from the onset was pushing it." After hanging up, I'd worried over this detail, wishing I'd asked the nurse when to start the countdown. Would it be from two days earlier, when he'd first noticed soreness while changing the anchor light? Or the next morning when he told me about the swelling? I'd tried to call back but couldn't get through.

He squinted, thinking. "No. You-you've made the right choice. Take us into Taku for the night. Tomorrow, we'll get an early start."

Saturday morning, Jim slept while Glen helped me pull the anchor. As we motored out of Taku Harbor, the conifer ridgeline glowed with the day's first muted light. Thankfully, the wind in Stephens Passage had died to ten knots.

Midmorning, as we approached Juneau, Glen took the helm while I tied fenders along the hull and prepared mooring lines.

Ten minutes out, I woke Jim to come up and take the helm for maneuvering into the tight slip. He moved slowly from bunk to cockpit, left leg held stiff as if it were in a brace.

At last, with the boat hastily secured, we disembarked for the urgent care clinic. I ran ahead to get the car while Glen walked up the ramp beside his hobbling father.

When the nurse called us in, we left Glen in the lobby.

In the exam room, Jim lay on his back, face tense as the doctor touched and probed. "What do you think it is?" he asked.

"With this swelling, fever, and redness, I'd say it's fairly advanced septic bursitis." The doctor leaned in for a closer look. "Also known as housemaid's knee."

Jim and I glanced at each other as if he'd misspoken.

"It's common when someone spends a lot of time on their knees. You may have picked up a small splinter while kneeling on that dock. Then, restricting circulation to that leg when you were up in that climbing harness probably helped the infection take hold."

When the man pressed on Jim's kneecap he jolted and winced.

"Why'd you wait so long to come in?" the doctor asked me.

"We were out boating."

He looked at me like I was negligent. "Before the X-rays, I'll draw off some fluid to get the pressure down." He pulled out a sterile packet with a long-needled syringe. "The lab will figure out what kind of bacteria are having a field day in there. Meanwhile, we'll inject the knee with vancomycin and start an antibiotic IV. These infections can get out of hand fast—as you've experienced."

He told me if Jim's temperature went above a hundred and one or if the swelling increased, to take him straight to the ER.

"Tomorrow, come back for another IV as soon as our doors open. On Monday, first thing, contact your regular doctor. Until then, keep the leg elevated."

"Are you saying I can't walk around?" Lying there in cargo shorts, Jim looked like someone on vacation in Hawaii.

"Yes, sir. You're on bed rest for at least a week. Maybe two."

"No friggin' way," Jim blurted, making a fist. After a moment he said, "I-I'm sorry."

"I am too," the doctor said, "but you have to keep your knee up. If you rush this, you'll permanently damage the joint."

32

OFF THE MAP

Saturday afternoon, I plumped pillows under Jim's leg and delivered an egg burrito, a mug of tea, and several *Newsweek* and *Foreign Affairs* magazines. On Sunday morning, I took Jim to the clinic for another IV, brought him home, and then took Glen shopping for clothes, shoes, and school supplies.

Monday morning, I woke our nine-year-old. He dressed quickly, excited about his first day back at school. He cracked our bedroom door, peeked in, then returned to the kitchen. "He's awake. Can I take it?"

Mug cupped between hands, he walked carefully down the hall with his father's coffee. I loved hearing their soft banter.

At seven thirty, Glen and I drove through light rain to Auke Bay Elementary School. Holding hands beneath an umbrella, we approached the entry, festooned with colored-paper cutouts of chubby bears, soaring eagles, and Tlingit-stylized ravens. Midway across the parking lot, he let go of my hand. Whoa, I thought. He's never done that.

"I can go from here," he said above the throb of children arriving and teachers pumping umbrellas dry. "You don't have to come in."

Since the spring, he'd grown two inches. I fingered his bangs to the side. "Okay."

"There's Jonah." Turning away, he waved tall and called, "Hey, Jonah!"

Before I could say goodbye, he dashed off, orange backpack swinging side to side. I shrank into my eight-year-old self, left in the parking lot at a six-week summer camp. The angst was as sharp as the day my parents drove away in their Chrysler station wagon, unaware I'd run from my cabin at the far side of the camp for a final goodbye, missing them by seconds, my shouts and waving arms obscured by the rancorous gravel cloud their tires kicked back.

"Have a great day," I called out as the two boys bumped together, whooping and hugging. Embarrassed at my reluctance to leave, I turned to go.

"You too!" Glen shouted back, arm raised high. I pivoted in time to catch his smile aimed at me before he slid back into the throng of fifth graders. An ache of love, sadness, and gratitude swept in. My son. My friend.

I drove on to the university, wipers swiping cold drizzle, thinking how much Glen had shored me up through Jim's stroke and every day since.

During lunch, I picked Jim up to take him to his doctor's office for the first follow-up evaluation of his knee.

When I entered the bedroom, his first words were, "You're late."

"We'll still make it on time," I snapped.

He leaned hard on the stairway rail, using it to ease the weight on the infected leg.

"Do you want to lean on my shoulder?"

"No."

Trailing him down the stairs, I wanted to defend myself, let him know I'd had an impromptu meeting with a student and needed to stop for gas on the way home. Instead, I made a face he couldn't see, then wished I hadn't. In the car, he asked about my day in a normal tone, signaling the end of the spat. Later, I dropped him at home, relieved to return to my office and guilty for the thought.

That first week back it rained every day except one. Autumn in southeastern Alaska had arrived. Our Mendenhall Valley neighborhood felt encapsulated, a continent away from the deep fjords, warm springs, and wide ocean swells we'd so recently explored. We were trapped in an up-and-down cycle: connected and loving one moment, cool and distant the next. My husband had many attributes, but cheery gratitude while dependent on others to care for him was not one. Yes, I understood how hard this was, but I needed crumbs of appreciation, a thank-you here and there.

The next day, Glen and I stopped at the public library on the way home to check out movies and audiobooks for Jim.

I set the videos and books on his nightstand and sat on the mattress edge. "How're you feeling?" His forehead was warm but not hot.

"Crappy."

"In what way?"

"Like a bad case of the flu but without congestion." Once again, he'd barely said hello.

As I was getting an Advil and thermometer for him from the bathroom, my thoughts heated up. Can't he say one nice thing?

When I returned, he thanked me for the library materials. "S-sorry, I'm so off," he said as if he'd viewed my thoughts on a big-screen TV. "Come here." He signaled me over to the side of the bed. "I hate that I can't help out. You're already doing too much. Lie on top of me." He patted his chest.

For several minutes we held each other, mending.

On Friday, I dropped Jim off at the hospital entrance, parked, and made my way to the clinic. From across the waiting room, I saw him before he noticed me. He sat in an orange plastic chair, uncharacteristically slumped. His shirt hung loose, muscle tone diminished by twelve days of bed rest. I watched him lean over to draw a notebook from his pack. Sunlight slanting through a window revealed his dejection: four months of post-stroke physical therapy, prescribed exercises, his regime of hiking, weightlifting, and yoga stretches all eroded by days of immobility. The stark absence of his gung-ho "I'm fighting this!" stance stopped me like I was a lassoed calf.

My love for him swelled. Our trials, my frustrations with his cranky-patient moods and gruffness—what I perceived as anger toward me—were swept aside by a yearning to honor and build on all we'd worked for, shared, and survived: adventures, setbacks, and successes; love for our son. All those days stuck in a bed—again—had left him close to an emotional flatline.

In that glimpse, I saw our clashes, his gruff moods in a new light, as unintended consequences of the same fire that had fueled his burning resolve to regain what the stroke had stolen.

This damn infection could take him down, I thought. If he stops fighting, we will be adrift. I vowed to be a stronger partner in his fight. Blinking back tears, I walked to him, lifted his chin, and kissed him on the lips. I looked into his eyes and kissed him again.

That night in bed, we lay on our backs, edge to edge. I wrapped my hand around his index and second fingers, searching for words to reassure. It would not help to offer hollow promises. "I'm so impressed with you. I know this is hard."

I heard him swallow, felt emotion well and twist.

"You'll make it. We can do this."

"G-give me a moment."

The fish tank burbled as I waited.

"I remember the instant I jumped in the water—in Taku Harbor—I knew I'd screwed up. That disorientation scared the shit out of me, but this knee's shaken me up more. It felt so good to clean the boat, scrub the benches, fix the mast light. Then some ridiculous infection takes me down? If this screwed-up knee makes it so I can't walk—to get so far beyond the stroke—then have this?" He hit his left thigh.

I squeezed his hand.

"You know what else really pisses me off?"

"What?"

"That I had three great weeks out on the boat, with you, Glen, Brendan, and Corwin. All those positive experiences wiped off the map. Forgotten."

I pulled his hand onto my chest. "Oh, honey. They're not forgotten." They were not simply words, but he was right. We'd had no time to savor all we'd done—all he'd accomplished. Fourteen weeks after a stroke almost took him from us, and he'd led a three-week expedition around Admiralty Island.

"Th-those weeks out on the water together were damn magical."

I squeezed his hand. "We will remember them."

Slices of cherry pie on paper plates sat in front of us at a picnic table. Jim's hand shot to his brow. Surrounded by other parents, we were attending a welcome-back potluck dinner at Glen's middle school. Jim winced, pressing his palm onto his eye to subdue the pain.

I leaned in, hand around his waist. "How often does that happen now?"

"Ten, twelve times a day."

He hadn't let me know it was that frequent and I wasn't home during the day to notice. The morning after his follow-up exam, two weeks since we'd gotten him home from Taku Harbor, he'd powered up and down through a set of pull-ups using the doorframe chin-up bar. He'd worked in the garden, and we'd taken two arm-in-arm strolls around the block, the first since the knee infection.

Watching him massage his temple as the kids stood on risers singing, I worried he wasn't giving enough attention to our son. While he'd been in the hospital, their connection had grown stronger. Glen had motivated and helped Jim. Since we'd returned home, our son was naturally focused on friends and school, and the two of them were much less involved. I understood Jim's frustrations, but his morning gruffness was hard to take, especially for our cheerful, energetic nine-year-old. I worried this phase might lead to problems when Glen became a teenager.

I stretched tall on the hard bench to watch the children perform. Each student wore an animal mask they'd created. I searched for Glen's white, button-down shirt and brown squirrel mask with red whiskers he'd cut out of construction paper and glued on.

Jim watched the program, heel of his hand against his eye.

My husband's parenting style had never been conventional. He wasn't a sports dad. I'd been the one to enroll Glen in swimming, soccer, and gymnastics. He was caring and engaged, but his affection came in different packages than mine. Mine was out loud and physical—spontaneous hugs and snuggling, kisses on the head. Jim's was reserved and thoughtful.

I recalled when Glen was ten months old, he started pulling himself up on chairs and windowsills, bowed legs shaky but primed to walk. One night, Jim observed our son maneuvering around the coffee table. He'd take three steps, then drop to the floor on a padded diaper, pull himself back up onto bowed legs and try again. Jim got on his knees and measured Glen's height, the distance from the floor to an elbow. He would not tell me what he was doing.

The next Saturday he returned from our local hardware store. I met him in the garage, Glen on my hip. He popped the trunk open to show me a jumble of various lengths of half-inch PVC tubing and a bag full of fittings. "What's all that for?"

"A project," he announced, grinning. "A surprise." I couldn't imagine what plumbing issue needed so much tending or expanding. I returned to folding laundry as he transferred clanking tubes onto the workbench.

Sunday morning Jim emerged from the garage carrying a trapezoidal-parallelogram-ish creation.

"What is that?" I asked.

One eyebrow rose. "A carpet sled for Glen."

In the living room, Jim carried our baby boy to the walker-on-skis contraption, stood him in front of it and placed his hands on the handlebars. Glen wobbled, then leaned forward. The sled swooped ahead, and he plopped face down.

Startled, Glen looked up at his father, who scooped him back into place. This time, Jim guided, bent over from behind, large rough hands on top of tiny ones. Every few feet Jim paused to shorten one section, lengthen another. Each time he assisted, the structure worked better. On the fifth try, the resistance-to-glide ratio was tuned, and our carpet became the PVC sled's snowfield. We watched as our skinny-legged infant, at first wobbly and erratic, graduated from a crawler to a zoomer.

Glen's teacher introduced the next song, bringing me back from the fond memory. Jim stabbed a large bite of cherry pie. When I'd told him about the school potluck, he hadn't been keen about attending. Evening events like this were hard on him. But he'd agreed and showered, and helped us get out the door on time. He ate his pie, eyes on his son. I pressed my leg against his.

"Hey, Bill," Jim said. "We sure appreciate that grab bar." Bill Brown and Lesley had arrived with purple garden potatoes and king salmon to celebrate Bill and Jim's September birthdays. We'd last seen Lesley in the hospital when she'd arrived with guacamole and brie. I'd made a blueberry cheesecake and wore a teal blouse the color of Jim's eyes. Bill poured glasses of wine as we prepared food around the counter. Jim, looking younger and more relaxed than even before the stroke, prodded them with questions about what they were reading and thinking.

Beyond Jim, above the kitchen sink, taped to a cupboard, was a piece of paper with two phone numbers I'd drawn in bold, four-inch letters—Bill's and mine. Jill Bolte Taylor's harrowing account as a brain scientist at home alone when she experienced a stroke had inspired me to create the sign. In her book, *My Stroke of Insight*, she describes her forty-five minute struggle to simply remember her work number and dial for help after a blood vessel in her brain ruptured. Published by Viking Books three weeks after Jim's stroke, her book was a gift to us from friends Sarah, Pete, and Annie. Taylor's dramatic first-hand account had educated and inspired us.

I'd stopped noticing the five-month-old sign, but in that moment, seeing it taped in full view, a chill ran up my spine. What if Jim's vertebral artery had failed after I'd left for work?

Later, Glen lit the candles, and I carried the flickering cake as we sang for the two friends.

"Okay, Bill," Jim said. "Let's blow these puppies out."

Bill shook his head. "No. You've earned a wish more than anyone."

Jim stared at the ceiling, inhaled, and blew out fifty-seven flames.

"What'd you wish for?" Glen asked.

He squinted at his son. "You know the rule. If I tell, it won't come true."

Glen and I exchanged glances.

I'd have bet big money his wish was to walk like a normal person.

❜ ❜ ❜

One weekday afternoon, a month after our trip around Admiralty Island, I leaned against the kitchen sink, washing bowls and pans I'd used to make lasagna, one of Jim's favorites. Autumn was, for me, Juneau's toughest season, when gray skies prevail and rain gauges spill over. Out the window, chickadees flitted branch to branch in the slim stand of trees between our house and the neighbor's.

The downstairs door swooshed open and closed. I heard Jim's boots drop, and the familiar asymmetric padding of his feet climbing stairs.

"You're home early," he said. "What're you doing?"

"Making you dinner."

"Oh?" He entered the kitchen.

I greeted him over my shoulder.

"What's the occasion?"

"No occasion. Just you."

From behind, he slid his hands around me, tentative at first, then firm across my abdomen. He nibbled my neck—found the spot.

"Let me finish these," I said, rinsing a bowl.

"Why?" He asked, while turning me around.

Quivering beneath his touch, I inhaled his scent: cedar, earth, salt.

"How much time do we have?" he whispered.

"Forty minutes."

33

TRAINING WHEELS

"Hey, hon, can you come home early, by four thirty?" It was the first Friday in October.

I scanned my desk. "Oh . . . I can't."

"It's important. I need to show you and Glen something."

I hesitated.

"Come on," he said. "You worked late last night. It's Friday."

"Well . . . okay."

"And don't leave at four thirty. Allow time to pick up Glen. Be here *at* four thirty."

On the way home, Glen asked what I thought his dad wanted to show us.

"I don't know. He sounded excited, though. Maybe he built something."

Jim stood in the driveway as we pulled in. "Yay! You're home." He leaned in through my rolled-down window for a kiss. There was a glint of excitement or mischief in his eyes I hadn't seen in a long while. He was wearing roller-blading knee pads. His bike was propped against a garage post.

Before the stroke, Jim had ridden his bike to work most days in all months, despite Juneau's soggy autumns and snowy winters. In winter, he added a bright light and reflective vest to his commuting attire. With the first snow, he replaced regular with studded tires.

When he was in his twenties and living in Anchorage, before studded tires were available, Jim and his friend Roger invented their own. One by one, they inserted sheet metal screws into regular tires from the inside out. Next, they laid a narrow strip of rubber inside, behind the screw heads, to protect the inflated tube. With their homemade prickly wheels, they were undoubtedly the first two people to ride a loaded tandem bicycle in midwinter from Anchorage to Seward, pedaling around Turnagain Arm and over Hatcher Pass, churning steadily sixty miles a day for two days across crusted snow and ice—for fun.

As we climbed out of the car, Jim urged us to get our bikes. "We're going to the park."

I looked at Glen and back at Jim. "I don't think you're ready to ride."

"Just come with me. We'll walk there. I want to show you something at the park. It's okay–don't worry."

We strapped on helmets, pulled on gloves, and wheeled our bikes out of the garage. It was a rare, blue-sky afternoon. Beyond the residential street, glacier meltwater gurgled down the Mendenhall River through the Tongass Forest and out to the ocean. Our bodies cast long shadows as Jim and I walked and Glen rode up the familiar street, zipping ahead and back, ahead and back, like a herding border collie. Five months earlier, an ambulance had carried Jim, strapped to a stretcher, down this same street.

We crossed Mendenhall Avenue and bumped our wheels over the curb onto the sidewalk, Jim in the lead. "This way." He directed us through a gap in the chain-link fence and onto the baseball diamond. "Before I show you, I have to tell you how the day started. I-I woke up. You were both gone. First thing, I knew I had to ride my bike."

"But you haven't ridden since your stroke," Glen said. "Why today?"

"I don't know. I just had to do it. No choice. I had to get on my bike. Today. I put on my helmet, walked the bike down the driveway, checked for traffic. The grass was covered with frost. Then I pushed off and started pedaling."

"What was it like?" I asked.

"Strange. Something I've done so much, you'd think I'd never lose the feel. I was pedaling and balancing—"

"That must have been fun," Glen said.

"Well. Actually, it-it wasn't. I had to concentrate in a way I can't explain. The focus to ride almost hurt. It was exhausting. I only made it ten yards."

"Then what?" Glen asked.

"That's when I discovered something important. You know how our street curves? I could not turn. I-I drove my friggin' bike right into the curb!" His eyes crinkled and glimmered, like he was laughing at himself, but also like he might cry. "Just like that, I crashed into the damn curb. A grown man, and I fell onto the ground. I tried again, but I couldn't help it. I steered into the curb again."

"Oh, honey," I said. "Are you okay?"

"Physically? Yeah." He shook his head. "I left the bike, walked back up the driveway into the garage, dug out my Rollerblade pads—knee, elbow, wrist. Strapped those suckers on, got my bike, and walked up the road, like we did. I came here."

He swung his right leg over the crossbar and planted his foot on the pedal. Weight on his left leg, he surveyed the empty field, contemplating what to do next. "All afternoon, I rode here. In clockwise circles. Each-each time I fell, I got up and rode again. I still can't turn the damn handlebars to the left, but I want to show you." He adjusted his helmet strap, rose onto his right leg, and began pedaling.

"Good job, Dad!" Our son watched, parent–child roles reversed as Jim steered in huge, wobbly circles.

I stared in disbelief. Still struggling to walk normally and here he was riding a bicycle. Part of me wanted to rush onto the field to help, steady the wavering, or run alongside the rear wheel as a safety net like we'd done when Glen was learning.

"Watch what happens when I try to go to the left." He spoke as he might in describing an experiment. Then it dawned on me: he was.

His arms shook as he fought to make the bike obey—this man who had ridden across the United States. His front wheel traced a jerky *S* in the tan layer of dirt.

"No matter what I do," he said, "I can't make it go straight or turn left."

We watched him struggle to counteract his brain's insistence on curving to the right. He almost toppled but caught himself.

"See what I mean?" He stopped and planted a foot. "I look like a total dork, but I can ride." A mischievous smile bloomed on his face. He waved his arm taking in the entire ball field. "I can ride here."

"I'm impressed."

"Way to go," Glen said.

"You two go ahead. I'll practice."

Glen and I rode in circles around Jim in the same direction, then the opposite. Soon Glen veered away, cutting across the field to a well-worn path up a sloped berm. I followed as our son gained speed on the dirt trail, careening up, down, and around a ridge. Ahead of me, he flew over a one-foot drop-off. Airborne a split second, he landed on the edge of the field. He looped around to repeat the course, lifting his hand for a quick wave as he passed me going in the opposite direction.

After racing with Glen, I returned to the baseball field where Jim pedaled fast in high gear tracing big clockwise loops, like a drunk man but focused. As I watched, something inside shifted. Thank God, I thought. He wants this so badly he's willing to get out here and battle his way around this big flat slab of dirt.

Watching him, I thought of how many people along the way had made it possible for Jim to get this far. Where would he be right now if David Job hadn't urged me to insist on the medevac jet? What if he hadn't taken the time to spell out what I needed to do in that next hour? So many people had helped. Gratitude pressed up into my throat.

After a few minutes, I turned back toward the kids' hotrod trail. Like Glen, I stood up to pedal, body remembering to tilt the frame side to side, opposite each downward pump. As I gained speed, I felt weightless and giddy. That twelve-year-old tomboy ghost had returned. I was racing down Blue Ridge Drive in Evansville, Indiana, intent on beating my faster friend, Lisa. The air swooshed by as I caught up to our son and rode the up-and-down trail one more time with abandon.

Amber light cast deep shadows as the three of us pedaled home in autumn's cooling breath.

That night, after we'd made love, Jim and I held each other in the darkness. "Today was hard," he said. "When I woke up, I knew I had to get on my bike. But there was no anticipated joy. I didn't want Glen to know that part. It was more like, how do I get out of this cesspool? I'm trapped in this body. Can't drive." He paused. "I knew I didn't want you or Glen around. The first time I crashed, I was like, *Fuck you, body!*"

His outburst startled me.

"Pissed off, I got back on. Rode ten more yards. Fell off again. *Fuck you! I'm done.* I was so angry. Somehow, I got through that—finally realized I had to go somewhere where I didn't have to turn."

I draped my leg over his.

"It took every single fucking neuron to ride my bike."

A month passed before Jim could steer to the left. Even after overcoming that hurdle, Glen and I worried about him when he pedaled off to buy groceries or do other errands for us. In those bleak, late fall days when his recovery rate was slowing, progress came in small packets. But there was no stopping him. Riding was his salvation.

Glen rolled the dice and slid his piece forward. "Saint Charles Place. I'll buy it."

Midweek, after dinner, Glen had invited me to play Monopoly. Jim was already in bed. We hadn't played in months. As we took turns, moving the shoe and the little dog around the green board rimmed with properties, Free-Parking square, and the Go-to-Jail hazard swept me back to my childhood. On my next turn, I landed on Atlantic Avenue.

I hesitated, thinking I might hold out for a more lucrative monopoly. "Buy it," he advised. "You don't have any properties."

"Well, okay."

While he took his turn, already ahead and beaming with unabashed glee, my mind shifted to family finances. The week before, our checking account had bottomed out. I'd scrambled to find funds to transfer, but not before bouncing a check. I hadn't let that happen in a decade. For years, Jim and I had each squirreled the maximum possible into retirement accounts which were taking a hit as the pumped-up housing bubble burst. I didn't want to tap those funds, but we were draining our liquid assets. If we didn't have health insurance, the stroke could have wiped us out. The medevac flight alone had cost $26,000—thankfully covered.

"Your turn," Glen repeated, tapping my shin.

"Oh, sorry." I jiggled the cubes in cupped-together hands, then let them spill. I tapped the silver shoe forward seven spaces. "Community Chest."

Glen read the yellow card, "Pay hospital one hundred dollars."

"Dang!" I counted out the payment. The game's instructions reminded me of a letter I needed to write to the Virginia Mason neurologist. His confirmation of Jim's five-week hospital stay was required for partial reimbursement of our living expenses. Thirty-four days in a hotel added up to more than five grand.

"Hey." Glen wobbled my foot. "Pay attention. I can tell you're somewhere else. I just bought Park Place."

His comment brought me back into the room. That's the kind of thing Jim would say to me, I thought. And Glen's right. We're home together, safe. I'll sort out our finances another time. My son wants to play a game with me: be present.

"Just wait." I focused on him and rattled the dice extra hard. "I'm about to roll a six and buy Boardwalk before you can."

The cold, wet fall blurred on like previous years, except we carried the weight of the gray skies like personal burdens. From September through October, it rained forty-five days.

Twice a week, I drove Jim to therapy sessions. At home, he stretched into triangle poses, legs far apart, torso bent to one side, opposite arm reaching high. For a man who had never tried yoga, he bit at the balance-challenging exercises like a hungry fish grabs bait. While I worked at the university, and Glen attended school, Jim cooked every weeknight dinner and kept the laundry baskets empty. One evening, I came home to find him outside cleaning the six floor-to-ceiling living room windows with a long-handled squeegee and rags. He'd snaked the garden hose up one leg of the west-facing deck so he could spray the outsides.

"We've got this great view and less and less sun," he said. "We need to let it all in."

Another evening, after a soggy blanket of snow dropped on Juneau, I returned as he was unpacking groceries. I reached around his shoulders and squeezed hard. "How're you doing, wonderful man?"

"A bit tired, but good. Better now."

"You went to Fred Meyer's?" I asked, noticing an emptied bag.

"Yeah."

"How'd you get there?"

"Took the bus—there. Walked up our street through the slush. Caught the Mendenhall Loop route which was late. Waited forty minutes for a transfer. Ridiculous how bad the connections are."

"Why didn't you go to Safeway?"

"I wanted to get coffee downtown first—for a change of scenery. I figured I'd stop at Fred's on the way back." He opened the refrigerator and put away a gallon of milk, vegetables, and yogurt. "But the café was dead—on a workday, downtown in the capital, no less. At Fred's I loaded my pack and a couple of bags with groceries. The next connection was thirty minutes away. I was like, damn, I might as well walk home."

"That's more than three miles." I shook my head.

"All the waiting would've taken longer. So I walked."

I pictured him, high-volume hunting backpack loaded to the top. Extra bags, bulging with produce, swinging at each side as he marched across the parking lot and along the edge of Glacier Highway, cars and trucks speeding by, spattering slush.

"You should've called me." I set a two-pound bag of coffee beans in the cupboard. "The roads are a mess."

"No. You were at work." He pulled the last items out of the pack. "From inside our warm cars, we zip around whenever and wherever we want—barely noticing the buses coming and going. I had no idea how limited scheduling could ruin your day. There are people riding buses who have no choice. I'm stuck doing this for a few months and here I am pissing and moaning. People who rely on public transportation every day—every season—deserve better."

His outburst caught me off guard. I reached for his hand. Another part of who my husband used to be had returned.

34

THE BASICS

I tugged off boots, pulled off my wool coat, and ran upstairs from the garage. "Hey, sweetheart," I called. "I'm home." The aroma of garlic and rosemary and an erratic sizzle from the oven told me Jim was roasting a chicken. I was looking forward to celebrating a manuscript I'd finished and delivered to Brendan for his review. It was a Friday, the third week in October, and Glen was spending the night at Tenzing's.

No answer.

The table was set, a bottle of wine on the counter. I went to our bedroom. He was lying on his back, arm bent over forehead. He rarely napped late in the day. I crawled in next to him and nuzzled in.

"Mmm . . . you're home." He wrapped his arms around me.

"You okay?"

"A bit worn out." He rubbed his face then told me he went to hike the wetlands for the first time. "Being out there, the smells, hearing the geese—" He shut his eyes. "I wanted to see what it was like to hike a flat trail without poles. It was good. On the way back, I waited for a gap in traffic to cross the highway. A car was coming. There was plenty of time. I-I started to run. It didn't make sense, but suddenly the car was barreling down on me. I could not run, could not skirt it. It was like a bad dream. My legs would not move any faster. He was suddenly there. The highway was wet. Driver slammed on his brakes—"

"Oh, honey."

"What freaked me out was realizing how far off I still am from making my body do what it used to do. My legs were like two-by-fours."

While making dinner one evening, I heard Jim huffing. Concerned, I hurried to our bedroom. There, I found him perched on his bike, pedaling hard—rear wheel in a training stand Bob Tamone had loaned us. Earbuds in, he was listening to the news. He gave a quick wave and wiped the back of his hand across his sweaty forehead.

I passed him a hand towel, then stood and watched. With the bicycle cranked up to a low-pitched hum he seemed more like a man training for the Olympics, not a stroke survivor.

One morning that winter, I woke yearning for something missing in our relationship, kidnapped by the stroke. During the night, I'd dreamed about my college boyfriend. The first nights we slept together, we'd kissed and explored, but I wasn't ready for a full sexual relationship. Embracing beneath a wool blanket and two worn quilts on a mattress in an attic bedroom, his southern-dialect tales made me laugh and quiver with joy. I loved falling asleep in his arms, his skin warm against mine. Vivid stories and jokes shared like that taught me to categorize unbridled laughter with orgasm, both as sources of intimate bonding.

Years later, I married a serious and good man. My husband told engaging stories from decades of research in Alaska on brown and black bears, red foxes, and walruses. Glen and I savored his stories about Jerry and the other six African geese he raised as a teenager from fuzzy goslings into eighteen-pound adults. Our favorite was when Jim secured each pet goose in its own cardboard long necks snaking out of cutout holes. He loaded them into back seat of the car for a free-range weekend campout at the family farm. The image of skinny, wild-haired Jim driving his mother's Buick sedan down a congested DC highway, windows open with seven geese honking, always held our attention.

A trustworthy, creative, and adventurous man—an agile lover—humor buttressed our connections, but my husband never made me laugh like that boyfriend had: body recoiling, gasping, begging for reprieve, bare feet thrashing until the quilts broke free.

The stroke had dialed Jim's humor two notches backward. During the early months of his recovery, I'd had no expectations for normality. But that morning, after seven months, I woke from the dream, arms around bent knees, craving laughter like a redwood in a drought craves fog.

My knee brushed against Jim's as I set a glass of merlot on the windowsill next to his armchair. "How was your meeting with Ginny today?" I nestled into the couch across from him, legs tucked under. The Jarlsberg quiche I'd made for dinner was baking. Ginny, an invertebrate zoology professor, was a colleague and friend of ours.

"Good. She invited me to be part of a research proposal she's going to submit."

"How nice." I was relieved when Ginny, a driven academic, had contacted him. After retiring early, he had planned to become an independent researcher. But that was before the stroke.

"We met at the Thai restaurant near campus. I hadn't ridden that section of Egan—"

"You rode on these icy streets?" I leaned forward, upset. "It's winter. I thought she picked you up."

"I've switched to studded tires."

"Honey." I scowled. "Even normal people aren't riding bikes in this weather." My cheeks burned as the word "normal" emerged.

"I-I'm extra careful." He dismissed my concern with a hand flick. "Before the meeting, I stopped by Auke Bay to check on the boat. Everything looked good. Being out on the dock—the ocean smell, steam wafting off the harbor, gulls squawking—made me want to be out on the water."

"Mmm. I know what you mean." The image of a weekend getaway helped bury my lingering concerns. "What would you work on?"

"Some aspect of crab larvae transport and settlement, how oceanography influences Dungeness populations. We discussed ideas around those questions. It went well." He set his glass down. "But I was surprised at how the conversation made me feel."

"What do you mean?"

"She had no idea what a big deal it was for me to ride my bike there." He raised an eyebrow. "She was like, 'It's so great you rode here. You'll be back in the saddle in no time flat.'"

"That's encouraging."

"Maybe. But riding is still hard. I keep thinking I'll get over that hump—enjoy it again. Keeping the goddamn bike on the shoulder takes so much focus. I still can't look back to check for traffic without veering into the road."

"Honey, that's dangerous."

"That's why I added that wide-angle mirror. To cross a street, I stop, get off, and walk. While Ginny and I were talking, riding the damn bike those two miles was on my mind." He shook his head. "If we get the grant, it'd be months before we'd start. Maybe I'll be interested in research again by then."

It was hard to hear Jim express these feelings. For as long as I'd known him, he'd loved thinking about research, working out complicated logistics, collecting data in remote locations, living in field camps or with his team crowded on a research vessel, puzzling over the significance of observations and data.

"It'd be good if you had the option." I refolded my legs. As I listened, I realized the prospect of his meeting with Ginny had fanned the flames of my smoldering desire for him to return to work. He didn't know how much I worried about our income, how much I wanted him to have a job—work that inspired him. I struggled to imagine our lives together if he didn't regain his enthusiasm for being a scientist. So much of who we were, his curiosity and passion for solving problems, was wrapped in that package.

"I-I can't predict how I'll feel," he said. "And I don't want to let her down." He rocked his chair. "For months, my main goal's been to walk again. Back in Seattle, I faced it: I spent my whole life wanting to be a scientist, but if I had to give up doing research to walk, that's what I'd choose." He grimaced. "No question."

35

THE DEAN

Glowing digits clicked from 4:44 to 4:45 a.m. In one week, I'd meet with the dean. I felt good about most of my teaching and research record but couldn't stop fretting about how the review might go. In two hours the alarm would squawk. I thought about getting up to work but instead, inhaled to the count of four, exhaled to seven, trying to quiet my thoughts. It didn't work.

I debated whether to rouse Jim or pull the pillow over my head and claw back to sleep. In the kitchen, the aquarium aerator gurgled. I imagined Glen's two crawdads, scuttling to opposite corners across turquoise pebbles. I slipped out of bed, pulled our door shut, and climbed back in. Facing his warm back, I watched his torso rise and fall. A few nights before, his fitful dreaming and muttering had driven me to our son's trundle bed. There, I'd lain awake, the fear of not falling back to sleep preventing sleep.

I pressed palms together and slid cool hands between my thighs to warm them. I encircled his waist and cupped my body against his back and thighs. He murmured sleepily then inhaled sharply.

My office phone rang. To the left, a new edition of *The Biology of Marine Mammals* lay open. On the other side of the desk was of references. On my computer screen was a draft of the syllabus. Outside, large white flakes drifted to the ground.

"Hey. How's it going?" Jim asked.

"Okay."

"What time will you be home?" His voice still sounded like rocks sliding down a shovel. Despite exercises to coax it back to life, his left vocal cord remained paralyzed.

nice!

How could it be five o'clock already? Preparing for the new semester and finishing a job application had consumed the day. My student Suzie Teerlink had stopped by to tell me she'd been accepted into a graduate program. We reminisced, laughing about the time we set longlines in Taku Inlet to catch sleeper sharks. Hoping for one, seven sharks took our bait. Visiting with her made my day.

"How about six fifteen?"

"That works. I've got dinner going. Glen's doing great."

"Want me to pick up anything?"

"We're good. I shopped this morning."

I refocused on the computer monitor. I should have set a timer.

It was seven when I drove into the garage. I left my briefcase in the passenger seat. Being late *and* bringing work into our bedroom would be like setting off a bomb. As the wide door rumbled shut, I hung my coat on a hook, sat on the step, and unlaced ankle-high boots. I rubbed my thighs.

Inside, the aroma of garlic and basil beckoned.

At the top of the stairs, I entered the living room, connected to the kitchen by a wide counter. "Sorry, I'm late." I held back a string of excuses. He'd heard them all.

Ten years earlier, when we were shopping for a house, I'd fallen in love with the great room layout—a high-ceilinged space that encouraged interactions with family and friends during meal preparation. Before that, Jim and I had lived on our sailboat for seven years. By then I was ready—beyond ready—to put down roots on land again, have a home office, a yard, and a washer and dryer. On the afternoon the deal closed, I picked up the keys and drove alone to our new home in the Mendenhall Valley. Four months pregnant, I walked around the empty living room, admiring every square foot. Tall windows on three walls let light pour in. I raised both arms and did three cartwheels across the carpet, happily aware of my extra ballast.

A decade had slid by fast.

When I entered the living room, Glen was surrounded by wooden blocks.

"Hi, sweetheart." I knelt, pulled him close, and kissed the top of his head.

He hugged me back and said, "Watch this." My son never made me feel guilty about being late. He lowered a cube onto a tower next to a row of vertical blocks.

I glanced up at Jim. "How was your day?"

"Hmm . . . okay. Nothing too exciting. Same routine: did chores, took a long walk, made dinner, except that—"

"Mom, watch now," Glen said.

While I watched, I heard Jim open the refrigerator.

"Glass of wine?" he asked.

"That'd be nice."

"Here goes," Glen tapped a block that clacked into another, tracing a banging path across the floor until his tower shuddered and tumbled over.

"All right!" I clapped, then stood and went to the kitchen.

Ca-lang, ca-lang, ca-lang! Mango banged her cage door for my attention. I went to her and caressed her bowed head.

Jim poured chardonnay into a stemmed glass. "How about a kiss for your husband?"

We embraced and I held him tight, but my mind buzzed. Did

I send the email to Brendan, confirming his lecture? Would the new lab supplies arrive in time? As we separated, Jim scowled, sensing my distraction.

I took a sip of wine, hoping to calm my mind. The table was set with cloth napkins beside our plates.

He stirred a large pot of his special spaghetti with meatballs, and said, "I'll freeze half for another dinner." It was January, snow on the ground and he was wearing shorts and a Hawaiian shirt.

He poked a fork into a steaming pot and lifted strands of linguine. "Let me know if it's done."

"Not quite. Close, though. Everything smells great." Oh, how fortunate I am to have a husband who likes to cook, I thought. And he shops for us. What was I doing? I waited for our eyes to meet. "Thank you for making dinner."

He cleared his throat and asked why I was so late. "You said you'd be home at six fifteen."

"I'm sorry. We've got a new text, so I have to update assignments, lectures, and labs. I lost track of time. I worked on the Pew Foundation application. And Suzie dropped by—she's been accepted to the fisheries PhD program. It was wonderful to see her." I got excited telling him about her plans, but my shift from contrition to enthusiasm about visiting with my student was not bringing him along. I stopped talking and sliced the bread he'd set out. "How was your day?"

He took his time grating a block of cheese. "Better than most. While I exercised, I listened to a podcast I want you to hear. Bill Moyers interviewed this woman, a professor from Harvard, about her book *The Third Chapter: Passion, Risk, and Adventure in the 25 Years After 50.*" He flashed a sour look that turned sad. "I was hoping you'd be on time."

Over dinner, I asked about the Moyers podcast.

The author, Sara Lawrence-Lightfoot, interviewed twenty-five people who had reinvented themselves by taking up new, more rewarding careers, many as volunteers. "What she has to say is inspiring—important for both of us."

After Glen left, Jim asked what I'd learned about the job with the Pew Foundation.

"I like their mission, but the more I learn, the less interested I am. And it doesn't pay as well as the university."

"But you don't get overtime at UAS," he challenged. "If you count your hours, your pay is not that great."

I held back a defensive response. We'd had this conversation before.

While he ate, I cleared the table. Before the stroke, he usually finished first. I sat back down and leaned forward, gazing at him, folded hands under my chin, elbows on the table.

He squinted back at me as if to ask what I was thinking. When he finished, I stood and walked around the table to his side. "Scoot your chair back a bit." I lifted my left leg over him and eased down onto his lap, chest-to-chest. I slid my arms under his, around his back and squeezed. "Thank you," I said. "Thank you for everything."

He pressed his nose into my ear. The heat of his breath flowed onto my neck. I inhaled his scent: sweat and maleness, a hint of shampoo and oregano.

Glen entered the room and came to us. "Can I get in?"

"Sure," I tilted away from Jim to create a space.

He lifted a foot to the edge of the seat and used our arms as handholds. When he was younger this was a common after-dinner ritual. He climbed up and eased onto Jim's thighs, sideways with legs tucked in. I snuggled my arms around the two of them, cheek on Jim's neck. Mango rang her bell three times.

"Hey," Glen said. "She wants to be in the basket."

When she stopped banging, Glen became quiet. His narrow chest rose and fell and Jim's breathing was warm and steady. I closed my eyes and locked onto the moment.

⁊ ⁊ ⁊

The next morning, I showered, toweled my hair, pulled on my best khakis, navy top, and favorite jacket. It was the morning of my meeting with Dr. Pengrove, the Dean of Arts and Sciences, and I hadn't slept well. I'd worried he might not have found time to review my portfolio, even though he'd had it two months. Or worse, what if he rejected my promotion request after careful review?

In the kitchen Jim pulled me close. "Don't worry. Your record speaks for itself."

"I'm not so sure about that."

He held me at arm's length. "Okay. I'll say this as directly as I can. Number one, your research is solid. Number two, you're a gifted teacher. Remember, we taught together that whole summer when we first met. I've heard you give presentations and seminars. You connect with your audience. And number three, I've hired or done field work with five of your students. They all say the same thing."

I shook my head—close to tears.

"Just listen." He recaptured my gaze. "They all say you're one of the best teachers they've ever had."

I stared at his collar, blinking.

"You've put your heart and soul into that job." He wrapped his arms around me again. "You'll do fine. And so what if they don't give you the promotion? You are not stuck there."

The dean's secretary invited me to take a seat. "He's expecting you."

I tried to shake off the tension, wishing I could have slipped right in to get it over with. I stared out the window at the serene view of Auke Lake surrounded by mountains. To quiet my nerves, I imagined hiking the conifer-rimmed lake trail. Compared to Juneau's rainy autumns, I loved our winters when snowfall brightened the landscape. Hiking trails and frozen lakes were transformed into cross-country skiing runways. Best of all, Eaglecrest, the community-owned mountain ski area, opened for downhill and backcountry skiing. That year, though, because of Jim's situation, we'd spent much less time enjoying winter's glory. *I need to get Glen up the mountain for some skiing,* I thought.

"Beth," she said a second time. "He's ready."

I tapped on the large door, heart rate revved back up.

"Come in."

Dr. Pengrove stood up behind his desk and reached out to shake my hand. "Hello, Beth. Let's sit over here." He gestured to a round table flanked by floor-to-ceiling bookshelves.

"The lake's gorgeous today," I said, pretending to be at ease.

"Having this view is certainly a bonus of this office." He slid a stack of papers out of the way and set my binder on the table. "Let's see, you've been a tripartite, term faculty at UAS now for seventeen years. I've reviewed your performance portfolio in the three areas: teaching, research, and service." He acknowledged that my teaching evaluations were favorable and that he and the administration appreciated my work on the Research Experiences for Undergraduates program.

He glanced at his notes. "You've published an okay amount." He thumbed the notebook open to a tab. "Has this manuscript on sea lion predation on harbor seals been accepted?"

"Yes, in the *Marine Mammal Science* journal."

"Good." He wrote something down then scanned another section he'd flagged.

"Let's talk about your service component."

This was my weakest part.

"You advise students, but I don't see as much involvement with university committees as we'd like. That's something to improve."

My cheeks burned as I scrawled a note.

"On the other hand, you've been a member of this Alaska Scientific Review Group for thirteen years and the chair now for two. Tell me about that."

I explained how our team of scientists reviewed the National Marine Fisheries Service's population assessments of Alaska's marine mammals from whales to walruses and polar bears. "Our job is to make sure the federal agency is monitoring the status and conserving those populations as required by the Marine Mammal Protection Act."

"As the chair, I noticed you've written several strong letters to the head of the Fisheries Service in DC, calling them out for not doing their job." He had read my file.

"That's right. Although I signed them, those letters were very much a team effort."

"That sounds like important public service."

He flipped back a few pages. "Hmm. Interesting. So, let me get this right. You've taught and done research at UAS for seventeen years. You and Dr. Kelly started the undergraduate research program a decade ago, which supports underrepresented minority students and brings in about a hundred grand a year. You attend faculty meetings, cover about half your annual salary from grants, and you've developed a close working relationship with Glacier Bay National Park. And don't some of your former students now work there?"

I nodded.

"And you haven't gotten a promotion in seventeen years?" He'd been dean at another university for many years before taking the position in Juneau a year earlier.

"I've received cost-of-living adjustments, which I appreciate. After nine years as a visiting assistant professor they dropped 'visiting' from my title."

"Oh," He looked up at the ceiling. "Really?" He shook his head.

"But I've never requested a promotion," I continued, "until now." I fidgeted with my notes. "I should've done that."

"Well." He strummed his thumb up through the edge of my portfolio. "That's not the issue." He rubbed his jaw, gazed out at the lake then back at me. "I have to say, that you've never received a promotion in all those years is an abomination."

I sat back in my chair, hands tucked under my thighs.

"I've discussed your request with the provost. She's reviewed your file and agrees we should promote you to associate professor. The best we can do with your salary, though, is a ten percent raise."

I swallowed hard, blinking to contain a tidal wave of relief.

Part Three:
WHITE SNOW, DEEP WATER

"Being deeply loved by someone gives you strength, while loving someone deeply gives you courage."

~ Lao Tzu

36

VITAL NUTRIENTS

"What's your plan today?" I asked Jim as I lowered my cereal bowl into the dishwasher and picked up my briefcase.

"The usual: exercise, maybe go for a walk, work on the crab proposal, buy groceries." He sat across from me on a kitchen barstool nursing a cup of coffee.

"I can shop after work," I said. It was mid-December. Mounds of gray snow and melting slurry lined the streets.

"No thanks." He lifted his cup but didn't take a sip. "I-I'm going to drive."

"Wait. You haven't driven yet since—" I set my briefcase down without finishing my sentence. "Have you?"

"No. But I'm going to today."

I twisted my wedding ring. "Did your doctor say you're ready?"

"Not-not exactly. Zenkel said I'd be able to drive again, and it would take a while."

"But you haven't seen him in—what?—seven months. Why today?"

"Riding in this slush has been awful. The store's not far. I'll start slow."

"Can you wait until I'm home? I'd be glad to go with you."

"No. I'll take the back loop—"

"I'll pick Glen up," I interjected, concerned he might want to.

He flashed a hurt scowl. "You know I won't drive with Glen until I'm ready."

He was the most safety conscious person I knew, but I had to ask.

After work, when Glen and I came home, he dashed to our office to call a friend, and I went straight upstairs where I found Jim in the kitchen. "How was driving?"

"Okay." Chef's knife in hand, he sliced an onion in half with a swift *thwack*.

"What was it like?"

"I avoided traffic and drove super slow. People behind me must have thought I was some granny." He raised an eyebrow. He pressed his thumb against a garlic bulb, flicked a half-dozen papery cloves onto a second cutting board, then slid them to me to peel and slice.

"Once I'm more comfortable, I want to drive to the trailhead downtown. Hike up Mount Juneau. It felt strange, for sure. Not anything like the day Annika drove me to the Air and Space Museum, though." He scraped the chopped mound of onions and peppers into a hot skillet.

"You've made a lot of progress since then."

"I suppose. Today reminded me of returning to a big city after months of field research on an island in the Bering Sea— no driving for half a year. After that isolation, driving in traffic takes so much concentration. And you experience it for what it is: a bunch of two-ton chunks of metal flying along on wheels. In the Bering Sea, working on walruses, there were all kinds of obvious threats we faced—freezing to death, drowning, breaking a leg. We minimized those risks, because the threats were always in our face. In contrast, we get into a car day after day, and count on the behavior of strangers. We're numb to the fact that it's more dangerous than almost anything else we do."

❜ ❜ ❜

On a cold Friday in February, I phoned Jim from my office late in the day. "Hey, hon, I need an extra hour to finish the sea-lion-predation-on-seals manuscript. I'm super close to submitting it to the journal. If I do, I'll take the whole weekend off." My coauthor and I had worked on the paper for months.

Jim thanked me for the update.

After a final review, I uploaded our paper to the journal's website and pressed submit. I shut down my computer, and locked up my office.

At home, Jim had dinner ingredients prepped, but he'd waited until the garage door rumbled open to set the salmon steaks on the grill. I found him on the deck beneath a clear star-studded sky in a pocket of the grill's heat. Salmon sizzled above briquettes glowing orange. From behind, I slid my arms around him, eager to chase away the lonely chill I'd felt since closing my office door in the dim, vacated building.

"Hey, my man." I pressed my cheek against his shoulder blade. "King salmon, no less."

"Of course. Congratulations on your paper."

"I wish it hadn't taken so long."

"Doesn't matter. It's a good paper. And it's accepted." He'd critiqued an earlier draft of it for us.

I held him tighter. My lifeline. My rock. I listened to the undulating shush of meltwater trickling downriver from the glacier to the ocean, the crunch of a car's tires rolling over snow. Our time together could be cut short at any moment, I thought.

After we'd eaten, I read a bedtime story to Glen while Jim cleaned up. When I emerged from our son's room, Jim turned out the lights, took my hand, and led me to the couch. There, we stretched out head to foot. As we massaged each other's feet, we reviewed the week, savoring my milestone.

Later, we made our way down the hall to the bedroom, undressing each other as we took turns walking backward.

"Coffee?" Jim's voice jostled me from a vague dream.

I pulled off my sleep mask, sat up, and took the steaming mug he offered.

"So kind. What time is it?"

"Eight ten."

"What?" My eyes grew wide.

"It's Saturday, honey." He sat in the bedside chair.

"Oh, right."

"Glen and I are making breakfast, French toast and sausage. I have something I want to show you first, though. A surprise."

In the kitchen, Glen stood on a chair at the stove, wearing his blue robe, spatula in hand. "Hey, Mom. I'm cooking the French toast."

"It smells great, sweetie." I wrapped my arms around him and held him longer than usual.

I sat on the living room couch across from the kitchen, fleece robe wrapped tight, legs folded while Jim positioned his laptop on the coffee table.

"I found this TED talk," Jim said, "by a writer who recently published a book called *Eat, Pray, Love.* Elizabeth something. It's about the year she spent in Italy, India, and Indonesia, rediscovering herself after a divorce."

Jim still could not read for more than a few minutes. Instead, he listened to podcasts and audiobooks, consuming books three and four to my one.

"I've been watching TED talks first thing most mornings," he said. "It makes my whole day better." He pressed the space bar. "This one seemed important for you."

I reached out and squeezed his forearm.

An attractive woman walked on stage, blond hair pulled back

in haphazard, short pigtails like she'd dropped by the auditorium after a workout. From her first words, "I am a writer . . . writing books is my great lifelong love and fascination," I was entranced by Elizabeth Gilbert.

She explained what had happened since her book skyrocketed to the best-seller list in the United States and abroad. Friends and strangers expressed concern: how could she go on, knowing she'd completed her finest work? She was, after all, only forty. Wasn't she petrified she'd never be able to write another book as success-ful as *Eat, Pray, Love?* She might even be doomed to madness or worse, like other creative geniuses.

She urged listeners to not let the fear of how their work might be judged get in their way. "Why do we believe creativity and suffering have to be linked?" she asked.

I leaned toward the screen as if I might absorb vital nutrients from her sentences. Elizabeth Gilbert's presentation spoke to me as though she'd witnessed my life—my fear of failure and drive to keep us whole: be the perfect academician, mother, bread-winner, and spouse—in that approximate order. I was struck by a vision of myself sitting at a vinyl card table at an old folks home thrusting cell phone images of my publications onto other survivors of academia. "Oh, here's another one. Isn't that graph beautiful?"

Since Jim's stroke, I'd been driven by a raw fear of not being able to make our family secure again. Earning more money had seemed the logical response. But were there unexplored better alternatives?

The presentation ended and Jim spoke. "I want you to be free to think about what's next. You're not stuck in your job. You have other creative abilities. You love to draw and write. I want you to think about new opportunities."

He had spent months forced to rebuild and redefine him-self. Now he was encouraging me to slow down and reevaluate as well—recenter around a creative passion—as Elizabeth Gilbert urged. If you let fear and anxiety control you, she'd said, you risk losing access to your full creative self. "Don't be afraid. Don't be daunted. Just do your job. Show up for your piece of it. If your job is to dance, do your dance."

When she said those words, tears rolled down my cheeks.

Did I want my career at the university to be my only dance? To define me? *Yes* had been my enthusiastic answer for two decades. Teaching, field research, and advising students engaged and fulfilled me. But my work also limited quality time with Jim and Glen. And I hadn't picked up a sketch pad in years. I couldn't remember the last time I'd had a relaxed morning like this one. But if I let go of my job, who would I be?

One weekend that winter, I had an urge to ask Jim an important question. I found him in the garage varnishing the teak floorboards from our boat. "Can we talk for a moment?" I asked. "Upstairs."

We sat on either side of the dining table. "My question is about an interaction we had in the hospital, while you were in rehab that first time. Glen was visiting Chuck and Fawn, and I asked you about the morning of the stroke."

He drummed his fingers on the table. Although attentive, he acted trapped, like a person in a dentist's chair. He did not like revisiting those weeks.

"You told me you'd come to our bedroom with coffee for me, wanting to make love. We were sitting side by side on your hospital bed. I said it was good I didn't want to make love that morning because I would then believe our actions caused your stroke. That's when we discovered our views were so different. You got upset—said if we *had* made love, the stroke would not have occurred."

He shifted in his seat, massaging his forehead.

"Did we ever follow up on that disagreement?"

He cocked his head in thought. "Mmm . . . no."

"How do you view the disagreement now?"

"Well." He swallowed. A shadow darkened his face. "I-I still think my version is true."

"What?" I crossed my arms, sat back. "Even though the doctors told us your stroke was caused by all the scraping and painting the day before?"

He squared his shoulders. "What're you talking about?"

"Don't you remember? Both doctors, Neilsen and Cortez, said it was most likely the rigorous scraping and painting with your head tilted back while you worked on the skylight, and maybe the choking fit the night before, that set your artery up for the final trigger. It was not simply from being on the ladder that morning."

He blinked several times. "This is the first time I've heard this."

"You were there when they told us."

He scowled. "I might have been in the room, but I don't remember that conversation." He shook his head. "I thought I craned my neck back to do the final touch up, and just like that young woman who was getting her hair permed—Boom!—I got the stroke."

My mind swirled.

He rested his forehead in both hands. I couldn't see his face but felt the weight of this news. It had never occurred to me that, in those first heavily medicated days, he might not have absorbed all of the doctors' bedside explanations.

"I see now why you and I disagreed about that morning." He shifted his gaze to his hands folded on the table. We sat in silence as he thought. "There is something you need to know. Even if I'd had the stroke while we were making love, it would *not* have been your fault."

"But that is what I'd believe."

He drew himself up and leaned in. Composure regained, his eyes held mine. "I am telling you not to take that on. I hope I die doing something I love."

I reached for his hand.

His gaze did not waver. "If I had died making love to you, that is what I'd want. If it ever happens, I want you to find comfort in that. Not guilt."

37

BLUE WATER

Eleven months after the stroke, on March 15, a foot of snow blanketed Juneau. Ravens strutted and hopped across the stiff top layer. Spruce limbs swayed beneath the weight of captured drifts. Glen and Tenzing rolled snowballs across our front yard into sloppy, chest-high cylinders, making the most of the late winter hurrah. Their squeals of laughter made me smile as they played king of the mountain on the seven-foot hill Jim had produced with the snowblower while clearing the driveway.

Indoors, that Sunday had not played out so well. Jim had asked me to take the whole day off. I insisted on paying bills and calling my sister first. Family sledding at the glacier was, consequently, shaved by a couple of hours and ended too soon in dwindling light.

After dinner, still steamy from my transgression—I assumed—Jim angled another plate beneath running water, "I-I want to talk to you about something important." He spoke deliberately. "About leaving." Our son was beyond earshot.

My heart sped up. "What do you mean?"

"Leaving Juneau."

"What?" I crossed my arms.

He turned to face me, wiping hands on shorts. "The boat is paid off. If we sell the house, you could retire early. I've mapped out the finances. We can put the land up for sale, or hang on to it. We only need to sell the house and we can take off—go cruising."

"Cruising?"

"Yes. Leave. Take off on the boat. Head south."

"We're not ready."

"*IJsselmeer's* a blue-water cruiser, designed to cross most oceans."

Before the stroke, we'd had similar conversations about taking a year off work to sail to the tropics. The dance went something like this: Jim expressed a desire to explore south along the coast, then head west to the South Pacific. I agreed in theory, but resisted in fact. Each time, I offered the same yes-but-in-five-years reply. I wanted more time to make a difference in my teaching and research. We needed more money in the bank. Conversations like these usually ended in a prickly stalemate. Why was he bringing this up again, now?

"One of the most profound pieces of advice I've gotten," he said, "is from that summer when your nephew came with us on that two-week trip. We were in Taku Harbor. There was one other sailboat anchored out. Do you remember?"

"Umm. . . no."

He continued, focused. "During our first morning, the husband got into their dinghy, rowed over, knocked on our hull. 'Hi. I'm Craig.' He reached up to shake our hands." Jim mimed Craig's greeting.

"Now I remember. His wife was a lawyer and a professional cellist. He was also a musician. They both played in the . . . was it the Portland Philharmonic?"

"That's the couple. They were seventy-plus and starting their second expedition. He was a retired electrical engineer. In their fifties, they'd headed south out of Oregon's Columbia River— same sailboat—and traveled for three years to Mexico, then across to the South Pacific. He's the one who told us they would never have had the confidence to start an expedition in their seventies if they hadn't done one in their fifties."

I set down the pan I'd been drying and leaned against the counter, listening.

"Craig thought the two boys were ours." Jim shifted his weight to the other foot. "I told him Jeff was our nephew. Craig and his wife were admiring our boat and wondered if we were planning on cruising. I said we were thinking about it but didn't have a specific plan."

I circled my shoulders, releasing tension as the story pulled me back to the day.

"Here's what I'll never forget," Jim said. "Craig told me if we were serious about cruising, we should leave before our son was twelve. Otherwise, we'd have a hard time getting him to come with us."

I bit a cuticle. "Oh, really?"

"He rowed over specifically to share that advice."

Jim leaned against a cabinet. "Their biggest regret was they didn't go cruising when their two boys were younger."

I had been inspired by Craig and his wife. When we were out on *Ijsselmeer*, we always met fascinating people. I'd admired the couple but didn't think we could do what they'd done. Their boat was perfect. He was an electrical engineer, and his wife knew a lot more than I did about sailing. And neither of them was recovering from a stroke.

"We could do it." Jim stared at his feet, responding as if he'd heard my thoughts.

I shook my head, certain we were not ready. "I don't want to leave. I like teaching at UAS and doing research in Glacier Bay. Plus, I can't stop working this early. We need my income. And I just got a promotion." I couldn't fathom such a big change. The idea that I would purposely cut the security tether to my career and our one salary after the stroke struck me as absurd. And how could we leave our friends? Our neighborhood? We lived across the street from a spectacular national forest. In minutes we could ride bikes to a glacial lake. Glen could run down the street to visit his two best friends. Why would we sell a house that worked so well for us—where we hosted lively dinner parties? Where my students dropped by? That month, one had pushed a stroller up our driveway to introduce me to her first child.

He lowered the last plate noisily into the rack and shut the dishwasher. He crossed his arms and leaned against the counter, letting a minute slog by before responding. "I've spent a year being an old person in Juneau." The muscles in his jaw tensed. "Buying groceries, making dinners, doing laundry, riding the bus. I've worked hard at physical therapy. From the perspective of a disabled househusband, Juneau is not a supportive place. I don't want to be stuck here another year."

His shoulders drooped. "I feel bad saying that. I love Alaska. You know that." Growing up in Virginia, he'd scissored pictures of Alaskan wildlife and mountains out of magazines—*National Geographic, Audubon, The Weekly Reader*. In third grade, he wrote his first report on the frontier state, as enamored as if it were another planet. From that day on he'd dreamed of living in Alaska.

"I can't do another gloomy winter here. Not like this—with you working all the time. Gone. You're gone all the time." His gravelly voice got loud. "Why? So we can pay for this big empty house you're never in." He waved an arm toward the large room with high ceilings and tall windows, condemning with one exasperated arc the home I loved.

I stepped back, away from him. His words made my chest hurt.

"I-I want to talk about an alternative. I've done the calculations." He was worked up. "If we sell the house you can retire early."

My brain screamed: Do not agree to this. Too soon—not even a year since the stroke.

"We could sail to Mexico—"

"I'm nowhere near good enough to do that."

"You are. Imagine being where the ocean's warm and clear. We can swim anytime we want. Think about all we've done. We brought *IJsselmeer* from Seattle to Alaska in the winter. Cruising to Mexico, we can sail offshore after Seattle in deep water, away from hazards."

I folded my arms tight across my waist. I was far from ready to go cruising. How would I rescue him if he fell overboard in rough seas?

"Hell," he said. "We lived on *IJsselmeer* seven years in Alaska, explored all over Glacier Bay, did that outer coast trip to Lituya Bay, navigated into and out of Ford's Terror."

As he spoke, the story of two Alaskan couples—bringing a new boat north, back to Juneau from Seattle—flooded my thoughts. They were traveling up the Inside Passage between Vancouver Island and the west coast of Canada. Someone from the Juneau boating circuit had told me what happened. All four were competent sailors. My imagination filled in the details.

They were in big seas, and it was dark when their sailboat lurched and Husband One lost his balance. He toppled overboard into frigid seas. Someone screamed into the wind, *Man overboard!* In seconds, a football field separated them. The wife commanded the helm as her friends struggled to drop huge sails. She powered up, turning the pounding vessel around. She maneuvered in close to her husband bobbing low in the ocean.

Husband Two leaned out, got the boat hook under the man's life jacket, and guided him back to the stern. The boat pitched up and over wave after wave. Only minutes in the water, but his lips were already blue, eyes wild, body sedated by the cold. Large hands responded like sloth claws. He could not grasp the line they tossed to him.

His wife urged, begged him to climb the lowered ladder.

The couple and frantic wife—three adults—could not rescue the man, their friend. Her husband. He drowned. Right there.

The night folded in around them as an Aleutian low pressure built. No choice, surviving sailors left his body behind.

Unaware of the imagined nightmare filmstrip playing in my mind, Jim continued. "We can live on the boat. It's paid for. Take off and explore like we've talked about. We've saved enough to be okay."

I met his gaze but said nothing.

"I made a spreadsheet. I can show you."

My mind substituted *IJsselmeer* pounding under full sail, her main and jib sails both launched, huge fabric parabolas fueled by a storm's unrelenting wind. A new version of the scene erupted in full-screen Technicolor. This time, Jim bobbed in the water, image shrinking by the second. Glen was at the helm. No taller than the wheel, he stood on the bench, skinny legs spread wide, all his weight against the helm, fist revving the throttle. I was fighting the goddamned fifty-foot-tall mainsail, jammed in its track. I reached high and grabbed a fold of stiff Dacron with both hands and yanked. It did not budge. I shouted to our son. *Don't lose Jim. Turn upwind. Now!* The sail *thwapped* hard. I could not pull it down. To turn the boat we had to de-power the sails. *Turn.* I yelled at Glen. *Get Jim!* A gust yanked my feet off the deck.

"If we wait," I heard Jim say.

Shivering, I forced my mind back into the kitchen.

"Glen will be too old. Later, he won't want to go."

I pressed my fingertips onto my eyes. "It's too soon."

"What is it?" he asked. "We can do it."

I shook my head, eyes on my feet, arms tight around my waist. "I'm not . . ." I couldn't finish my sentence.

"You underestimate yourself—us. There's no one else I'd choose to do a trip like that with. You are good out there. We've been through a lot."

Fighting tears, I said, "I'm going to bed. I can't talk about this."

Lying on my side, facing the nightstand, I cataloged all the reasons we could not leave—should not leave—Juneau. I have to convince him to put this idea off for now, I thought, still rattled by the imagined storms. The clock's amber light illuminated a family photo with Glen in the middle. We were all smiling, even Jim, who had marginally tolerated the posing.

The fear that had engulfed me eased. An alternate fork in the *What if?* road between the stroke and the present emerged. I could be alone in our bed, languishing inert beneath the melancholy of regret, staring at a mother–son portrait. We came too close to that abyss.

I imagined my counselor Pat speaking to me. *Why is your husband's proposal so threatening? What really scares you?*

It's obvious: I'm afraid of losing him.

Pat's voice again: *That's understandable. Can you be more specific?*

I shut my eyes, trying to obliterate the vision of the Alaskan husband bobbing in the ocean. But then, the vision of Jim thrashing at our stern, out of reach, breaking free of my grasp—kicking to his own death—took over.

I'm afraid of not being able to save him if he goes overboard.

And how long have you two owned your sailboat?

Sixteen years.

Has he ever fallen overboard?

No.

Come close?

No.

Have you two dealt with difficult situations? Extreme weather?

Yes. Yes.

I took several slow breaths, remembering Dianne's advice

for calming myself. If I clung to my routine of working too many hours, coming home distracted, losing sleep over work and finances, too tired to make love, while he toiled at two jobs— recovering from the stroke and being a househusband—I'd be gambling with losing ourselves as a couple and a family. A cloistered homebound life would erode who Jim was, dismantle him piece by piece, prevent our son from experiencing his father in his full glory, a man who climbed mountains in winter and rode his bike across the country, a man who excelled at preparing for complex expeditions—like having a ball of parachute cord to save himself from being lost in the Bering Sea on a runaway iceberg.

I looked back at the family photo, dried my cheeks with the sheet, and rolled over to face Jim. I married a man who lives for calculated adventure, discovery, and exploration, solving problems others choose not to tackle. I could be staring at an empty mattress, cool to my touch.

Maybe he wasn't the perfect mate, but I had friends who were still searching for that mythical creature. And I had my share of shortcomings he accommodated. Wasn't it, in fact, the successes and upheavals—moving to Alaska, renting the woodstove-heated cabin our first year together, losing a house to a fire, draining our savings to buy *IJsselmeer*, choosing to have a child later in life—the challenges as much as the joys and successes that had shaped us and made us a stronger team? Life with Jim had coaxed me beyond the narrow dreams I'd conjured from my Midwestern upbringing. Despite his downshifted moods the year before and since the stroke, he was still the ethical, unconventional, and driven man I'd fallen in love with beneath a tent on Thacher Island off Massachusetts.

My response to the stroke had been to recoil, guard the status quo as if that were our only salvation. But maybe I was wrong. Through active resistance or inaction, I held the power to deny him the opportunity to explore the world with his family—expand our horizons. Did I want to look back with regret, wishing I'd said yes this time?

My mission had been to earn more money, make us financially secure, ensure a rich childhood and a good education for our son. I loved our life in Alaska. Our son had great friends and freedom to be outdoors. What would living on board be like for him? I'd always thought we were safer at home in Juneau than out on the boat. But were we? Jim's stroke had been triggered by working on the house.

As I fell asleep, one question echoed: What is the right thing to do?

38

FACING STORMS

After vacuuming our guest bedroom, I raised the shades to watch Glen and his friend Claire on the trampoline. In our backyard, patches of crusty snow persisted in the shade of towering spruce and hemlock. We'd met Claire's family one summer during a trip to Taku Harbor. Her parents also owned a sailboat. Eight-year-old Claire had worn miniature Xtratuf rubber boots and orange rain bibs over a powder-blue T-shirt. Sprawled on her belly on the floating wooden dock, she'd peered over the edge at sea anemones and mussels. She and Glen hit it off instantly. They'd jigged for fish, made grass-blade whistles, poked sticks into the mucky intertidal flats, and hammed it up in an old-style bathtub abandoned on the beach.

The two friends bounced together, hair rising and flattening at goofy angles. They ricocheted apart and crumpled onto the mat convulsing with laughter. I put a hand on the windowsill, hungry for what they shared.

When I returned to cleaning the room, a bookshelf with my journals on it caught my attention. I sat down on the carpet, legs in a V, back against the wall. I opened one across my lap and began reading my blue-ink handwriting from an April entry one year before Jim's stroke.

Saturday morning:

Jim's stomping around because I deflected his invitation to linger in bed. It was Easter morning. For him, sex is a way to heal our relationship. For me, once we're disconnected, I stop feeling attracted to him. I need time and space to sort out what's not working. Lately, it seems like most of our troubles are triggered by work pressure. The polarity in our responses to adversity makes us volatile.

After Glen and I dyed eggs, Jim suggested we go for a hike—an oblique apology for his morning gruffness which I appreciated. But why does he have to inject his dark mood into our weekends in the first place? We have so little free time. I wake up feeling good and love spending time with our son. The three days Jim was in Anchorage, Glen and I had playful, easy mornings.

When he returned, I had a salmon dinner ready. That night we made love. The next morning he woke up cranky—got mad at me for stirring too much of the oil layer into the new jar of peanut butter. What's that about? The contrast with how our home feels when he's here, compared to gone, shoves itself in my face. What am I doing with someone who's become this irritable? I get it that he's stressed about his job, but I'm not sure I can do this much longer.

Yet when he's gone, I miss him. After two nights alone, I crave his steady guidance. When he holds me at night, believing in me, I feel whole.

Small issues are tripping us up. Why can't I solve this? He's good for me.

Like him, I'm angry about his situation at work. Being told they can no longer use terms like "climate change" or rine reserve" infuriates his scientific ethic. Mine, too. And not being allowed to present his team's research at the expenses-paid National Geographic workshop in DC was illogical if not spiteful. I think he should transfer to another division led by someone with integrity like his previous boss. I support how he's sticking around long enough to be eligible for insurance and to get his team set up in other positions but hate how his work stress spills onto our family.

Is it my role to hold things together while I wait for him to find a less stressful job? At what point would it be healthier for our son if we lived apart? We could still be good parents.

I'd scratched out the last two sentences.

How could I forget our relationship had reached such a low? Two years earlier, I'd contemplated moving out. Within the walls of our home—and the straitjackets of each other's unmet needs— we'd edged close to divorce. Back then, I announced my need for time alone by reserving a National Forest cabin for a weekend, though I never followed through.

It took me weeks to make the call, but I had enlisted the help of a marriage counselor. We were having issues but not the capital D variety. We'd been faithful. There was no physical abuse.

On the next page were responses to questions my counselor Pat asked me during our second session back then.

- I want time apart because I'm afraid we'll do long-term damage.
- Jim's grown to hate my job because it takes so much of my time and emotional energy.
- I've taken on new responsibilities so I'll be able to provide more for the family when he leaves his job.

Back then, after my third session, I asked Jim to see Pat with me. He agreed.

We leaned apart at opposite ends of a loveseat. His anger occupied Pat's office like a fourth person.

"She's not available," he told her. "Even when she's home."

"His work frustration invades like a dark aura," I countered, rubbing a palm against my thigh. "No wonder I want to go to my office. No one there makes me feel bad like he does."

The following week, I returned alone for a session as planned.

"What about your husband makes you grateful?" Pat asked.

I sank into the sofa. This was not the question I expected.

What had I been drawn to? I stared at a potted philodendron. "I was attracted to his creativity and problem-solving, strength, and adventurousness. But especially his integrity. After that, I fell hard for him sexually." I pressed fingertips against my lips, suppressing an urge to cry. "He's a good lover. Lately, with having to pare down his research team, he's been moody . . . but he still looks out for me—sets me up to do well."

I remembered the drive to Bellingham from California eighteen years earlier during our move to Alaska. We'd snuggled shoulder-to-shoulder as he steered his rattling Chevy truck filled with our stuff, towing the new dory. "I'm grateful he asked me to move to Alaska with him."

She waited, pen in hand as I squirmed. "Anything else?"

"Being parents together. I handle the day-to-day pretty well, but he's better at planning—taking the longer view. He motivates us to get outdoors, go boating." I struggled to articulate a separate notion rising like acrid smoke on a horizon.

Pat had a magician's way of tapping into deeper layers, coaxing me to recognize my contributions to our faltering marriage.

"He protects me from unhealthy behaviors."

She waited, then said softly, "Like what?"

Hands under my thighs, arms stiff, I stared at her shoes. "Workaholism."

"Try understanding Jim's situation," she said. "How he feels about the energy you put into your job." She wrote something, before asking, "What is it you need and aren't getting?"

I tugged another tissue from the box and blew my nose. What was it? The question hit as if she'd asked me to calculate the square root of pi. I didn't know what I wanted. There I was, sitting on the proverbial couch, complaining. My vague intention was to make both our lives better—to preserve our family. Our son's future would be better if we remained a team, not in title only, but in reality.

"I want to feel appreciated—loved," I said. "I know I'm not doing everything right, but I am a good mother. I believe in my work. When I'm teaching I feel like I'm fulfilling something bigger than myself. And since Glen was born, I have reduced my hours. Our son is my priority. I want Jim to appreciate those things. He has no idea how much less I work since we've been together." I hooked a hand behind my neck and stared at the rug.

"Take your time," she said.

"What I want is . . . for him to be happy again."

"What if Jim—I'm deliberately being dramatic here," Pat said, "had terminal cancer. Would you treat him differently?"

The answer came without thought—tightness in my chest. "Very differently."

"How do you mean?"

"When you cast our situation like that, it makes me—" I rubbed my shoulder. "Realize how much I love him."

"Can you describe the conflict between what you each want?"

I twisted a fresh tissue into a pointed spiral. "I crave more time alone, and he wants me to care more about him than my job."

She slid her glasses down her nose. "Do those sound like fatal flaws?"

, , ,

The impact of my counselor's hypothetical scenario—posed remarkably one year to the week before Jim's stroke—had dissipated. At the time, I could not imagine my vibrant, tough husband having a serious health issue.

In my journal, the truth stared back. Since that Tuesday morning in April, we'd quietly railed at how our lives had been disrupted by the stroke. Indeed, they had, but now a clearer perspective emerged. Almost losing him had snapped me to my senses—eliminated reasons to move out like a winter storm strips leaves from a birch.

I had resented Jim's decision to retire early from his secure position as a federal research scientist, even though I supported his rationale and helped him through much of that god-awful year dismantling his productive research team. His employees were like family to us. When his mood grew too dark, I sank into despair but sought professional counseling, and we worked through those difficult months.

Without the stroke, though, would I have left Jim? Hard to say, but if we'd stayed together without the upheaval, I could have become one of those people who doesn't leave because of inertia—limping along, sniping in their heads about what bothers them, and complaining to friends. I'd been edging away from Jim, barely making time to evaluate, let alone nurture, our relationship. I'd promised myself I'd never stay with someone because I was afraid of being alone.

In Ann Patchett's memoir, *This is the Story of a Happy Marriage*, she wrestles with her failing first marriage. A friend asks if her husband makes her a better person. Is she "smarter, kinder, more generous, more compassionate. . . ?" Twenty-five-year-old Patchett answers, "It's so much more complicated than that." Her friend counters, "It's not more complicated. . . .

That's all there is: Does he make you better, and do you make him better?"

Yes was my resounding answer to Ann Patchett's friend. My husband helped me be a better and braver person, and I supported most of his ambitious goals. Yes, we had hot disagreements and sometimes blew up at each other. But we circled back, once our molten views cooled. We even worked out a compromise with the peanut butter oil: pour off half. This man brings me coffee in bed, cooks our dinners, runs a safe boat, prioritizes my well-being, and tunes up my bike. I'd shared my greatest joys and deepest fears with him, expressed anger and been heard, revealed dark insecurities without driving him away.

My Midwestern mother had graduated from college, married, and raised seven children with my father. Instead of following that path, I broke up with a college boyfriend I was tempted to marry, loaded a U-Haul truck and set out on my own for a job at a zoo in Oklahoma. Four years later, I enrolled in a graduate program in California. Yet, I assumed I'd eventually hunker down, have a career and children, and root in like my mother had. In contrast, from an early age, Jim had pursued adventure and decided to not have children. Despite those distinct visions, we fell hard for each other and built a strong relationship and a family.

In his novel, *The Course of Love*, philosopher Alain de Botton asserts that "compatibility is an achievement of love; it shouldn't be its precondition." From the beginning, Jim coaxed me beyond my comfort zones—moving to Alaska, applying for the university position, asking for a promotion, living seven years on a sailboat in Alaska. As with catching the hundred-and-fifty-pound halibut, throughout our lives, he'd set me up to accomplish things that exceeded my imagination.

My husband had the integrity and drive to lean in face-to-face within the boxer's pumped-up circle, whether it was to stand against scientific censorship, defend a native woman in Costa Rica from wealthy adolescents, or fight to make his legs walk again. Discovering we faced some of the same issues as we had two years earlier was troubling, but what struck and reassured me was I no longer thought about leaving him. Instead of renting a log cabin for a weekend, that morning in the downstairs bedroom, I was wrestling with whether to sell our beloved home and leave a satisfying job to accept his proposed sailing expedition.

One night, lying in bed, Jim told me surviving the stroke made it clear he wanted to accumulate experiences, not things. If I held tight to the status quo, choosing safety and familiarity as instinct dictated, experiences with each other and our growing son would be constrained. Jim and I were fundamentally good for, and to, each other. Hardships and losses along the way had deepened our bonds. We had a sixteen-year track record of meeting challenges on *Ijsselmeer*, beginning with her month-long expedition from Seattle up the Inside Passage to Glacier Bay in the winter to venturing into the Gulf of Alaska and navigating Lituya Bay's shallow entrance, known as "The Chopper," and countless fishing and hunting trips in Glacier Bay and Icy Strait. And the three of us had navigated the rocky, unknown terrain of Jim's recovery fight.

What if we did sail *IJsselmeer* to Mexico? The thought made me sit taller.

I closed my journal and listened to the trampoline's springs squeal and relax, again and again as Glen and Claire played outside.

Why had it taken me so long to understand there were other homes I could enjoy and jobs I'd find fulfilling, but only one of him—my adventurous lover and best friend? The stroke had stretched and strained us as a couple, simultaneously increasing our compatibility like it was an elastic container within which we existed.

Shoulder to shoulder with Jim and our son, gliding across deep waters in fair winds or facing the next storm together was where I wanted to be.

EPILOGUE

Two years and two months after the life-altering morning when a mundane skylight repair threw our lives off track—on the longest day of summer—Jim, eleven-year-old Glen, and I cast off *IJsselmeer's* dock lines. The three-year expedition sailing south from Juneau, Alaska, along the North American coast, and around the Baja Peninsula into Mexico's magnificent Sea of Cortez would again stretch and test us as a couple and a family.

Jim maintained and improved our boat and grew stronger, shedding most stroke symptoms. I managed Glen's homeschooling, wrote and posted stories at our sailing blog, and kept one toe in my research world. In La Paz, Mexico I joined the Sea of Cortez Writing Group, my first sharing and critiquing experience. Although I didn't recognize it at the time, that's when I began this memoir.

During offshore passages, *IJsselmeer* became our universe, connecting us with nature, sailing, self-sufficiency, and each other in ways we'd never before experienced. We also faced harrowing challenges at sea, overcoming them as a tight team with Glen as essential crew. A few close calls triggered me to temporarily lose faith in our cruising goals. Glen learned to surf and snorkel, and soon spoke Spanish better than either of us. He made friends with sons and daughters of other boating families, but after three years, our mobile lifestyle conflicted with his, and my, social needs for a stable community. Sailing *IJsselmeer* from

Alaska to Mexico was the ultimate physical therapy for Jim, and the expedition made us more resilient as individuals, a couple, and a family—hard-earned outcomes I hope to never underplay or forget.

WORKS CITED

Bolte Taylor, Jill. 2008. *My Stroke of Insight: A Brain Scientist's Personal Journey.* Viking Penguin. 183 pages.

de Botton, Alain. 2016. *The Course of Love: A Novel.* Simon and Schuster, New York, N.Y. 225 pages.

Doidge, Norman. 2007. *The Brain that Changes Itself: Stories of Personal Triumph from the Frontiers of Brain Science.* Penguin Books. 427 pages.

Gilbert, Elizabeth. 2006. *Eat, Pray, Love.* New York, NY: Viking Press. 368 pages.

Lawrence-Lightfoot, Sara. 2009. *The Third Chapter: Passion, Risk, and Adventure in the 25 Years After 50.* Farrar, Straus and Giroux. 272 pages.

Mathews, Elizabeth A. and Milo D. Adkison. The role of predation by Steller sea lions in a large population decline of harbor seals. *Marine Mammal Science.* 26(4): 803–836.

Motyka, Roman J., Shad O'Neel, Cathy L. Connor, and Keith A. Echelmeyer. 2002. Twentieth century thinning of Mendenhall Glacier, Alaska, and its relationship to climate, lake calving, and glacier run-off. *Global and Planetary Change*, 35: 93-112.

Patchett, Ann. 2013. *This is the Story of a Happy Marriage.* HarperCollins Publishers, New York, NY. 308 pages. (Quoted passages from p. 249.)

ACKNOWLEDGMENTS

Several authors encouraged me at crucial moments on the long journey to writing *Deep Waters*. Dan O'Neill's "You could write a book" comment, over coffee one morning in Alaska months after my husband's stroke, was a seed which quietly rooted and grew. His confidence in me meant more than he could possibly know. Sarah Mansfield Taber's early advice to keep learning and revising to "produce the best book I could" helped me persevere. Author and mentor Sarah Rabkin and poet Craig Atkinson encouraged me right when I needed a boost.

Memoir-writing teacher Steve Boga taught me the power of incorporating dialogue into my stories, the value of reading scenes in front of classmates every week, and how to get the most out of sometimes harsh feedback. I thank Katie Watts for her astute purple-pen edits which taught me more than any grammar manual.

I'm indebted to Skye Blaine for believing in my writing, introducing me to Scriviner software, and inviting me to join a women's critique group with Laura McHale Holland, Marie Judson, and Patrice Garrett, accomplished writers who made it safe for me to tell the hardest, most personal stories.

I thank peers in two critique groups who provided constructive comments on evolving versions of my chapters: Kate Frick Sheridan, Dez Beck, Skye Blaine, the late Karen Guggenheim, Faith Bugely, Gay Bishop, John Postma, Sue Steenvoorde-Mathis,

Isabelle Felder Gillis, Bill Amatneek, Janet Ciel, Mary Binger, Vera Steinfels, Sheridith Maresh, Nancy Jo McLaughlin, and the late Jeremy Mitchell. In her class at the Santa Rosa Junior College, Skye Blaine added breadth to my knowledge of the craft of writing memoir. I thank classmates Phina Borgeson, Julia Dreyer Brigden, Linda L. Stamps, Sue Foster, Barbara Gude, Jeanette Koshar, Sandy Koshari, Jude Marks, Nicole Ours, Jan Pane, Margreet Fledderus, Cheryl Perry, Kit Carson, and Steve Rowland for their camaraderie and critiques. Without my community of fellow writers' instructive responses and feedback, my chapters could not have coalesced into a book. I thank each person who told me when a word or sentence confused them, or a scene was too long or convoluted, or too scientific.

Andromeda Romano-Lax, my developmental editor and writing coach, provided crucial guidance and insights on how to improve my book's pacing and story arc, and helped me to better understand the themes that were buried in an earlier draft. So much of writing is in solitude, but in working with Andromeda, I gained an astute partner and mentor.

I thank gifted poet, author, and editor Laura McHale Holland for her sensitive and thoughtful review, and GIS expert Sanjay Pyare for jumping in as my essential map-making collaborator.

A number of people generously provided feedback on beta versions of the manuscript and to them I'm indebted: Dr. Rachel Friedman, Kate Frick Sheridan, Fawn Bauer-Young, Lara Dzinich, Dr. Debbie Goldman, Seattle's TBD Book Club (Janey Fadely, Susan Wagner, Catherine Brandenburg High, and Deby Rourke), Phina Borgeson, Boudewijn Boom, Jennifer Andeman, Marv Jensen, Robin Mathews Cox, Susan Bennett, and Rusty Yerxa.

I'm grateful to She Writes Press publisher Brooke Warner for her wisdom and leadership, and to project manager Samantha Strom, art director Julie Metz, managing editor Krissa Lagos, and interior layout designer Katherine Lloyd. I'm in awe of Georgia

Feldman who designed my book cover. I thank the entire team at She Writes Press for their scrutiny and expertise in shepherding *Deep Waters* through the publication process. I thank Caitlin Hamilton Summie, my publicist, for her belief in my story and her passion and expertise in shepherding *Deep Waters* forward. Without the immediate help and advice of Dianne Bigge, Kim Courrette, and David Job, friends who happened to be working at the hospital in Juneau the morning of Jim's stroke, I'm convinced my husband's recovery would not have been so successful. My gratitude to each of you is unmeasurable.

While writing this book, I experienced fresh waves of profound appreciation for others, as well, who helped us during the initial ordeal and beyond, especially Brendan P. Kelly; Chuck Young, Fawn Bauer-Young, and Kiana and Forrest Young; Janey, Brian, and Sara Fadely; Nan Leiter and Ina Oppliger; Bill S. Brown; the late Mike Sharp; Randy, Sally, and Skyler King; Lesley DeKrey; Sudie Hargis; Rusty Yerxa and Janene Driscoll; and Peter Thomas and Sarah Taber; Bob and Tenzing Briggs; Sherry, Bob, and Mali Tamone; Alex Andrews, Ellen Naughter, and Tristan Walker-Andrews; the late Beth Bishop; Gretchen Bishop; Tom and Susan Shirley; Julie Nielsen; Jennifer Mondragon; Jim deLa Bruere; Ginny Eckert; Brooke Gunstrom; and Matt Heavener and Carrie Talus.

My husband's three sisters, Adelle, Eileen, and Sheila, and their spouses and children, and my father and six siblings—Robin, Kitsy, Carol, Nora, Jim, and Tom, their spouses and my nieces and nephews—supported us with their love, phone calls, and correspondence.

My mother, Bettie Macon Mathews, loved reading to her seven children. Every year, to our delight, my siblings and I received a book along with a foil-wrapped chocolate bunny in our Easter baskets. Her nightstand always had books and *New Yorker* magazines stacked on it. My mother devoured women's literature and introduced me to important authors: Alice Munro, Margaret Atwood, Toni Morison, and Nadine Gordimer. I'm saddened I cannot share *Deep Waters* with her so she could see her influence.

To everyone who connected with us at the CaringBridge website, your concern and uplifting notes—which filled seventy-three pages—shored us up throughout Jim's ordeal.

I offer lifelong gratitude to the doctors, nurses, physical therapists, and staff at Bartlett Regional Hospital in Alaska and the Virginia Mason Medical Center in Seattle. Your expertise and personal attention to Jim's unusual and urgent circumstances played pivotal roles in his recovery.

Our Yulupa Cohousing community in Santa Rosa provided a nurturing environment during my five-year writing stage. I offer special thanks to neighbors Linda Proulx, Barbara Moulton, Jim Riedy, Susan Friedman, Susan Bennett, Marie Piazza, Robin Seeley, and Suzanne Sackett.

I thank our wise son for being there with me from moment one onward, for sustaining me through the rockiest segments of his father's crisis and recovery, encouraging me as a budding writer, and for his ability to make me laugh when I most needed that release.

My deepest gratitude goes to my husband for fighting so hard to recover from the stroke. He also trusted me to write about our rejuvenating adventures and intimate moments as well as our struggles and unflattering moments. Without his support, I could not have revealed the full breadth of our family's journey, and there would not be a book worth sharing.

ABOUT THE AUTHOR

Beth Mathews grew up with six siblings in the Midwest, studied Animal Science at Purdue University, worked at the Tulsa Zoo, and earned a master's degree in marine biology at the University of California, Santa Cruz. Mathews was a professor at the University of Alaska Southeast for twenty years where she taught courses and did research on marine mammals. Her research has been published in *Marine Mammal Science* and other journals. Beth lives with her husband and their schipperke on an island in Puget Sound, Washington. They still own *IJsselmeer* (renamed *Resilience*) and connect best when sailing.

How Readers Can Help Debut Authors

This is Beth's first book. If you're inclined, please consider posting a brief review of *Deep Waters* at Amazon.com, Goodreads.com, or your favorite online book review site. For debut authors like Beth, book ratings and reviews greatly improve the chances of reaching readers who might benefit from their stories. Beth invites you to visit her online at elizabethannmathews.com.

SELECTED TITLES FROM SHE WRITES PRESS

She Writes Press is an independent publishing company founded to serve women writers everywhere. Visit us at www.shewritespress.com.

But My Brain Had Other Ideas: A Memoir of Recovery from Brain Injury by Deb Brandon. $16.95, 978-1-63152-246-8. When Deb Brandon discovered that cavernous angiomas—tangles of malformed blood vessels in her brain—were what was behind her the terrifying symptoms she'd been experiencing, she underwent one brain surgery. And then another. And then another. And that was just the beginning.

Room 23: Surviving a Brain Hemorrhage by Kavita Basi. $16.95, 978-1-63152-489-9. Kavita Basi had a seemingly perfect world—a nice job, excellent holidays, strong family bonds—until she was diagnosed with subarachnoid hemorrhage, a serious illness with a 50 percent mortality rate, and everything changed.

Headstrong: Surviving a Traumatic Brain Injury by JoAnne Silver Jones. $16.95, 978-1-63152-612-1. After a sudden assault by a stranger left JoAnne Jones with severe traumatic brain injury (TBI), fractured hands, and PTSD, she learned—with the help of a community that gave her the foundations of hope—to live with TBI in a society bursting with violence.

Not a Perfect Fit: Stories from Jane's World by Jane A. Schmidt. $16.95, 978-1-63152-206-2. Jane Schmidt documents her challenges living off grid, moving from the city to the country, living with a variety of animals as her only companions, dating, family trips, outdoor adventures, and midlife in essays full of honesty and humor.

48 Peaks: Hiking and Healing in the White Mountains by Cheryl Suchors. 978-1-63152-473-8. At forty-eight years old, Cheryl Suchors vows to summit the highest forty-eight peaks in New Hampshire's challenging White Mountains—and discovers, in the years that follow, that in order to feel truly successful, she will have to do much more than tick off peaks.

Excess Baggage: One Family's Around-the-World Search for Balance by Tracey Carisch. $16.95, 978-1-63152-411-0. When frazzled working mom Carisch finds herself staggering through a turbulent midlife crisis, she and husband launch their family out of the rat race and into an around-the-globe expedition—a remarkable journey that gives them a new understanding of the world and their place in it.